DUAL RELATIONSHIPS IN COUNSELING

BARBARA HERLIHY, PhD
University of Houston–Clear Lake

and

GERALD COREY, EdD
California State University, Fullerton

American Association for
Counseling and Development
5999 Stevenson Ave., Alexandria, VA 22304

American Counseling Association
5999 Stevenson Avenue
Alexandria, VA 22304

Cover design by Sarah Jane Valdez

Library of Congress Cataloging-in-Publication Data

Herlihy, Barbara.
  Dual relationships in counseling / Barbara Herlihy and Gerald Corey.
  p. cm.
  Includes bibliographical references.
  ISBN 1-55620-090-0
  1. Counselor and client. 2. Counselors—Professional ethics.
I. Corey, Gerald. II. Title.
BF637.C6H425 1992
158′.3—dc20

                                                        91-32929
                                                        CIP

Printed in the United States of America

*To our colleagues who wrestle with
the issues explored in this book*

CONTENTS

ABOUT THE AUTHORS

 **Barbara Herlihy** is associate professor of counselor education at the University of Houston–Clear Lake. She also maintains a limited private practice in counseling. She received her doctorate in counseling psychology from Northwestern University and has completed 2 years of postgraduate training in Gestalt therapy. She is a Licensed Professional Counselor in Texas and a National Certified Counselor. She is co-chair (with Madelyn Healy) of the ACES Ethics Interest Network and served on the AACD Special Task Force on Impaired Counselors. She has served as chair of the AACD Ethics Committee (1987–1989) and as a member of the Professional Standards and Ethics Committee of the Association for Specialists in Group Work. She received (with Larry Golden) the 1990 Professional Writing Award of the Texas Association for Counseling and Development.

Dr. Herlihy has authored or coauthored numerous articles on ethical and legal issues in counseling. Much of her writing has focused on confidentiality and privileged communication in the helping professions. Her recent book, with coauthor Larry Golden, is the fourth edition of the AACD *Ethical Standards Casebook* (1990).

Dr. Herlihy regularly teaches courses in professional ethics and group counseling, and she supervises counselor interns. She consults with school districts, professional groups, and a victim/offender restitution program. In her leisure time she likes to travel, play racquetball, or curl up with a good novel.

 **Gerald Corey** holds a joint appointment as professor of human services and counseling at California State University, Fullerton, and served as the coordinator of the Human Services Program from 1983 to 1991. He is a licensed counseling psychologist, and he received his doctorate in counseling from the University of Southern California. He is a diplomate in counseling psychology, American Board of Professional Psychology; is a National Certified Counselor; and is registered as a National Health Service Provider in Psychology. He is a fellow of the American Psychological Association (Counseling Psychology) and of the Association for Specialists in Group Work. He has served as a member of the Professional Standards and Ethics Committee of the Association for Specialists in Group Work. He was given the Outstanding Professor Award for 1991 by California State University, Fullerton.

Dr. Corey has authored or coauthored numerous articles and has 10 books in print in the field of counseling. Among these books are *Theory and Practice of Counseling and Psychotherapy* (4th ed., 1991), *Theory and Practice of Group Counseling* (3rd ed., 1990), and, with Marianne Corey and Patrick Callanan, *Issues and Ethics in the Helping Professions* (3rd ed., 1988).

Dr. Corey has a special interest in teaching courses in ethical and professional issues, group counseling, and theories and techniques of counseling. In his leisure time, he likes to travel, hike in the mountains, and bicycle ride.

GUEST CONTRIBUTORS

Our guest contributors have enriched this book immensely. By sharing their thoughts and opinions, they have provided a diversity of viewpoints and have raised issues that are well worth considering. Following is a list of these individuals, their institutional affiliations, and the chapters in which their contributions appear:

L. DiAnne Borders, associate professor of counselor education, University of North Carolina at Greensboro (chapter 5, Supervision)

A. Michael Dougherty, professor and head, Department of Human Services, Western Carolina University, Cullowhee, North Carolina; and former elementary and junior high school counselor (chapter 8, School Counseling, and chapter 11, Consultation)

Holly Forester-Miller, associate professor of counseling, University of West Virginia College of Graduate Studies (chapter 4, Preparation of Group Counselors)

George M. Gazda, research professor, associate dean for research, and acting head for the Division of Counseling, Educational Psychology, and Instructional Technology, University of Georgia; and clinical professor, Department of Psychiatry, Medical College of Georgia (chapter 4, Preparation of Group Counselors, and chapter 10, Group Counseling)

Larry Golden, associate professor of counseling, University of Texas at San Antonio (chapter 6, Private Practice)

Karen Strohm Kitchener, professor and training director, Counseling Psychology Division, University of Denver (chapter 6, Private Practice)

Arthur P. Lloyd, professor of counselor education, Idaho State University, Pocatello (chapter 3, Counselor Education)

Susan L. Naas, graduate student in counseling, University of Houston–Clear Lake (chapter 3, Counselor Education)

Sue Spooner, associate professor of college student personnel administration, University of Northern Colorado, Greeley (chapter 7, College Personnel Work)

Holly A. Stadler, professor of education and medicine, University of Missouri–Kansas City (chapter 3, Counselor Education)

Rex Stockton, professor of counseling and educational psychology, Indiana University (chapter 5, Supervision)

George T. Williams, associate professor of counseling, California State University, Fullerton (chapter 4, Preparation of Group Counselors)

Mary Ellen Young, assistant professor of physical medicine and rehabilitation, Baylor College of Medicine; and adjunct professor, University of Houston–Clear Lake (chapter 9, Rehabilitation Counseling)

ACKNOWLEDGEMENTS

We thank the following reviewers, who carefully read the manuscript and offered valuable suggestions for improvement: Debra Borys of the California School of Professional Psychology, Jeffrey Kottler of The Citadel, Sharon E. Robinson of Arizona State University, and Jim Witgil of Ohio State University. We want to acknowledge others who read parts of the manuscript and gave us helpful feedback: Marianne Schneider Corey, consultant, Idyllwild, California; Jorja Manos Prover, University of Southern California; Patrick Callanan, private practice, Santa Ana, California; George Williams, California State University, Fullerton; and Amy Manfrini, California State University, Fullerton.

Student reviewers were Susan L. Naas, who assisted with research and reacted to the chapters in their early stages, and Lynn Henning and Glennda Gilmour, two graduate assistants from California State University, Fullerton.

Marlene Lewis assisted with word processing and resolved countless technical questions.

Finally, we want to express our appreciation to the AACD staff members who worked closely with us throughout this endeavor. In particular, Elaine Pirrone, acquisitions and development editor, has been an enthusiastic source of support and assistance. The careful work of Lucy Blanton, copyeditor, greatly improved the book's clarity and format.

PREFACE

As helping professionals, we enter into a dual relationship whenever we have another, significantly different relationship with one of our clients, students, or supervisees. When we play dual roles, the potential exists for a conflict of interest and for exploiting those who seek our help. Our profession has become increasingly concerned about dual relationships as an ethical issue. Throughout the 1980s, sexual dual relationships received a great deal of attention in both the professional literature and the popular press. Today, there is clear agreement that sexual dual relationships are unethical, and prohibitions against them have been codified into ethical standards and law.

Lately, nonsexual dual relationships have been getting more attention. Articles on the topic have been appearing more frequently in our professional journals. Recent revisions of the ethical standards of some professional associations have dealt more extensively with dual relationship issues. There has also been an increase in legislative and governing board activity. For example, in California the Board of Behavioral Science Examiners and the Board of Psychology are developing regulatory language that attempts to address effectively the issue of nonsexual dual relationships in psychotherapy. The enforcement programs of both boards are faced with many consumer complaints and disciplinary cases that involve harm to clients as a result of a variety of dual relationships.

Nonsexual dual relationships can be complex. The issues are pervasive and affect counselors and human development specialists in all work settings and in relationships with individual clients, students, or supervisees; in relationships with families; in relationships with groups; and in supervision or consultation activities. Just a few examples of problematic or potentially problematic situations are bartering with a client for goods or services, counseling a friend, providing therapy to a student or supervisee, conducting experiential groups as part of a group counseling class, becoming involved in a discipline matter with a student client, and managing the case budget for a client in rehabilitation counseling.

When conscientious professionals look for guidance regarding dual relationships, they may find conflicting advice. The AACD *Ethical Standards* (1988) state that "dual relationships with clients that might impair the member's objectivity and professional judgment **must** be avoided. . ." (emphasis ours). Yet, many writers have asserted that not all dual relationships can be avoided nor are they necessarily harmful.

Considerable disagreement exists around some dual relationship issues. We (Barbara Herlihy and Gerald Corey) have seen this disagreement in our own recent experiences. During the summer of 1990, Gerald Corey proposed to the faculty in his university's human services program that a policy statement be created on the subject of faculty seeing students as clients. His proposal stirred up quite a bit of controversy and evolved into a lengthy, two-part position paper reflecting a diversity of viewpoints. At much the same time, Barbara Herlihy was asked to consult with the staff of her university's counseling center to help develop a policy on referring students to counselors in private practice. The first question raised was whether it is ever appropriate for college counselors to refer clients to themselves when they also have a private practice. This generated a host of related questions and led to a series of extended discussions. As each of us began to talk with friends and colleagues around the country, it became apparent to us that interest in dual relationships is widespread and that there is a broad spectrum of opinion surrounding many issues. This impression was reinforced during the 1991 AACD Convention in Reno, when the topic of dual relationships received a great deal of attention and a number of issues were heatedly debated.

We hope that this book will be useful to others who share our interest in dual relationships and who struggle, as we do, to find a clear personal stance on the issues involved. We intend it to be a resource that reflects the current thinking of our profession on the topic. We also want it to represent the diversity of opinion that exists. To that end, we have asked several guest contributors to present their positions on various specific topics.

We have organized the book so that part I presents a general introduction and overview of dual relationships. In chapter 1, we define the issues and areas of concern. In chapter 2, we focus on sexual dual relationships, reviewing and discussing the considerable body of existing literature and raising questions about some "gray areas." The remainder of the book focuses primarily on nonsexual dual relationships. In part II (chapters 3, 4, and 5), we examine issues in the preparation and supervision of counselor trainees. Part III (chapters 6 through 11) focuses on how dual relationships affect practitioners in various settings and aspects of their work. We discuss issues that confront counselors in private practice, college personnel workers, school counselors, rehabilitation counselors, group counselors, and consultants. At the end, in part IV (chapter 12), we identify key themes, ask questions to encourage integration and reflection, and offer a decision-making model. We make no claim to having discovered answers to complex and difficult questions. Rather, it is our aim to raise issues, present a range of viewpoints on these issues, and discuss our own positions. We hope that you will use this material as a springboard for further reflection and discussion. We invite you to think about the issues that are raised, apply them to your own situation, and discuss them with colleagues.

This work focuses on a specialized topic in counselor preparation and counseling practice. Because dual relationships are becoming a topic of increased discussion, this book can be used as a supplement to any of the textbooks that are used for courses in ethical and professional issues. We also expect that counselor educators will find this book useful for getting a current view of the potential problems and promises that are associated with dual relationships. The book can also be used in practicum, fieldwork, and internship seminars. Finally, we hope the book will be useful to practitioners who struggle with dual relationship issues in their work.

We anticipate that dual relationships—especially nonsexual dual relationships—will continue to be discussed and debated well into the 1990s. As with any complex ethical issue, complete agreement may never be reached nor would it necessarily be desirable. However, as conscientious professionals, we must strive to clarify our own stance and develop our own guidelines for practice, within the limits of ethical codes, current knowledge, and divergent opinions.

PART I:
INTRODUCTION

CHAPTER 1

DUAL RELATIONSHIPS
IN PERSPECTIVE

Dual relationships occur when professionals assume two roles simultaneously or sequentially with a person seeking help. This may mean two professional roles, such as counselor and teacher, or combining a professional and a nonprofessional role, such as counselor and friend or counselor and lover. Dual relationship issues, both sexual and nonsexual, affect virtually all counselors and human development specialists regardless of their work setting or clientele.

We assume that you, the reader of this book, have struggled with some complex and difficult dual relationship issues in your work as a helping professional. We hope that as you read the book, you will take time to reflect and consider how the material applies to you and your situation. Questions that may be useful to ask at the outset include the following:

- What are some of the dual relationship struggles you have faced in the past or are now facing?
- How have you dealt, or how are you coping now, with these issues?
- What information do you hope to find in this book that will help you resolve your questions and concerns about the issues you confront in your work?

Over the past decade, much has been written about the harm that can be done when helping professionals enter into sexual relationships with their clients. The dangers of sexual dual relationships between counselor and client, supervisor and supervisee, and faculty member and student have been well documented. Chapter 2 will examine sexual dual relationships in detail.

In this chapter, we focus on nonsexual dual relationships. We look at general issues that arise in all settings. These questions guide our discussion:

- What guidance do our codes of ethics offer about dual relationships?
- What makes dual relationships so problematic for practitioners?
- What factors create the potential for harm?
- What are the risks inherent in dual relationships, for all parties directly or indirectly involved?
- What are some possible benefits in dual relationships?
- What safeguards can be built in to minimize risks?

ETHICAL STANDARDS

Most professional codes of ethics address the issue of dual relationships, as the following excerpts of standards from ethical codes for counselors, psychologists, and social workers that speak to nonsexual dual relationships illustrate:

- When the member has other relationships, particularly of an administrative, and/or evaluative nature with an individual seeking counseling services, the member must not serve as the counselor but should refer the individual to another professional. Only in instances where such an alternative is unavailable and where the individual's condition warrants counseling intervention should the member enter into and/or maintain a counseling relationship. Dual relationships with clients that might impair the member's objectivity and professional judgment (e.g., as with close friends or relatives) must be avoided and/or the counseling relationship terminated through referral to another competent professional. (American Association for Counseling and Development [AACD], 1988)
- Psychologists are continually cognizant of their own needs and of their potentially influential position vis-à-vis persons such as clients, students, and subordinates. They avoid exploiting the trust and dependency of such persons. Psychologists make

every effort to avoid dual relationships that could impair their professional judgment or increase the risk of exploitation. Examples of such dual relationships include, but are not limited to, research with and treatment of employees, students, supervisees, close friends, or relatives. (American Psychological Association [APA], 1989)

• Clinical social workers use care to prevent the intrusion of their own personal needs into relationships with clients. They recognize that the private and personal nature of the therapeutic relationship may unrealistically intensify clients' feelings toward them, thus increasing their obligation to maintain professional objectivity. Therefore, specifically:

   Clinical social workers avoid entering treatment relationships in which their professional judgment will be compromised by prior association with or knowledge of a client. Examples might include treatment of one's family members, close friends, associates, employees, or others whose welfare could be jeopardized by such a dual relationship. . . .

   Clinical social workers do not initiate, and should avoid when possible, personal relationships or dual roles with current clients, or with any former clients whose feelings toward them may still be derived from or influenced by the former professional relationship. (National Federation of Societies for Clinical Social Work [NFSCSW], 1985)

As we noted in the preface, nonsexual dual relationships are receiving increased attention. One example of this increased scrutiny is a set of proposed draft regulations regarding dual relationships that would impact the work of helping professionals in California. These draft regulations were the subject of a joint hearing of the Board of Behavioral Science Examiners and the Board of Psychology held in December 1990. The proposed draft, which made a comprehensive attempt to address the issues involved in dual relationships, includes these statements:

(a) Psychologists, psychological assistants, registered psychologists, and psychological interns shall avoid dual relationships which could impair their professional judgment or increase the risk of exploitation and/or harm to the patient. Involvement in such dual relationships is prohibited and constitutes unprofessional conduct and grounds for disciplinary action.

(b) A dual relationship exists when a psychologist, psychological assistant, registered psychologist, or psychological intern has a relationship which is in addition to, or outside of, the primary relationship of providing professional psychological services. In addition to personal, social, and business relationships, dual relationships include secondary financial relationships.

(c) When a psychologist, psychological assistant, registered psychologist, or psychological intern reasonably should know that a dual relationship is developing, the provider shall determine whether the dual relationship can be prevented and the primary professional relationship protected. At a minimum, this shall include consultation by the provider with another psychologist for the specific purpose of objectively assessing the situation.

(d) When the psychologist, psychological assistant, registered psychologist, or psychological intern reasonably should know that a prohibited dual relationship cannot be prevented, appropriate steps shall be taken to terminate all relationships to ensure that the professional relationship has been adequately resolved to best protect the interests of the patient. (Board of Behavioral Science Examiners, 1989)

As can be seen, these proposed regulations address dual relationships quite extensively. Dual relationships include personal, social, business, and secondary financial relationships. Practitioners are expected to "reasonably know" that a dual relationship is developing and to consult with a colleague to see whether it can be prevented. If it cannot be prevented then the relationship should be terminated.

During the hearing held to discuss these proposed regulations, differing reactions were voiced. One attendee suggested that avoidance of *all* dual relationships should be encouraged, whereas others were concerned that written regulations might end up prohibiting innocent conduct. A middle-ground suggestion was that "instead of trying to ban every conceivable dual relationship that might cause harm. . . the boards try to ban specific conduct that is clearly improper and upon which there is consensus" (Leslie, 1991, p. 18).

A second example of increased attention to nonsexual dual relationships can be found in the draft of proposed revisions to the American Psychological Association (APA) code of ethics. This draft contained a section on "potentially harmful dual relationships":

(a) Psychologists who have a professional relationship with a patient, client, student, supervisee, research subject, or organization refrain from becoming involved in another concurrent personal, professional, financial, or other relationship with such party if it is reasonably foreseeable that doing so might interfere with their effectively rendering professional psychological services or might harm or exploit that party.

(b) Likewise, whenever feasible, psychologists refrain from taking on professional obligations in which preexisting relationships would create such risks.

(c) Minimal or remote relationships are unlikely to violate this standard.

(d) When a psychologist knows or should know that a potentially harmful dual relationship has arisen, the psychologist promptly attempts to resolve it with due regard for the best interest of the affected person and with maximum feasible compliance with the Ethics Code. ("Draft," 1991)

At this time, we do not know whether regulations like those proposed in California and by the APA represent the wave of the future, or whether it will eventually be decided that it is best left to professionals' judgment to distinguish between harmful nonsexual dual relationships and those that are benign. In the absence of specific guidance, we are left with many areas of uncertainty.

Although ethical codes generally prohibit or warn against entering into dual relationships, most practitioners agree that not all dual relationships can be avoided. Recent attention to nonsexual dual relationships in our profession has highlighted this dilemma and has left conscientious practitioners wondering how they are supposed to avoid the unavoidable.

WHAT MAKES DUAL RELATIONSHIPS SO PROBLEMATIC?

Dual relationships are rarely a clear-cut matter. Often, judgment calls and the careful application of ethical codes to specific situations are needed. Dual relationships are fraught with complexities and ambiguities. They can be problematic along a number of dimensions: (1) they are pervasive, (2) they can be difficult to recognize, (3) they are sometimes unavoidable, (4) they can be very harmful but are not always harmful, and (5) they are the subject of conflicting advice from expert sources.

Dual relationships are pervasive. Dual role relationship issues exist throughout our profession. A broad array of issues present themselves—for example, bartering with a client for goods or services, counseling a friend or social acquaintance, the counselor educator's dual role as educator and therapeutic agent with students, or the propriety of dating a former client. Dual relationship issues confront counselors and human development specialists in diverse roles, including counselor educator, supervisor, private practitioner, school counselor, college student personnel specialist, and rehabilitation counselor. They affect the dyadic relationship between counselor and client, and they also emerge in complex ways when relationships are tripartite (as in client/supervisee/supervisor or client/consultee/consultant) or involve families or group work. No professional remains untouched by the potential difficulties inherent in dual relationships. In later chapters, we will focus on concerns that are specific to various settings and formats.

Dual relationships can be difficult to recognize. Pope and Vasquez (1991) have noted that dual relationships are relatively easy to define but much more difficult for us to recognize in our daily practice. Dual relationships can evolve in some extremely subtle ways. This is particularly true when they are sequential rather than simultaneous. Yet, "the mere fact that the two roles are apparently sequential rather than clearly concurrent does not, in and of itself, mean that the two relationships do not constitute a dual relationship" (Pope & Vasquez, 1991, p. 112). A host of questions present themselves here: Can a former client eventually become a friend? How does the relationship between a supervisor and supervisee evolve into a collegial relationship once the formal supervision is completed? What kinds of posttherapy relationships are ever acceptable?

Dual relationships are sometimes unavoidable. Several writers (Keith-Spiegel & Koocher, 1985; Kitchener, 1988; Kitchener & Harding, 1990) have pointed out that not all dual role relationships can be avoided. Relationships that involve some blending of roles may be inevitable. For example, counselor educators serve as teachers, as therapeutic agents for student growth and self-awareness, as supervisors, and as evaluators, either sequentially or simultaneously. There is always the possibility that this role blending can present ethical dilemmas involving conflicts of interest or impaired judgment. One of the major difficulties in dealing with dual relationship issues is the lack of clear-cut boundaries between roles. Where exactly is the boundary between a counseling relationship and a friendship? How does a counselor educator remain sensitive to the need to promote student self-understanding without crossing the boundary and counseling the student? How can a supervisor work effectively without addressing the supervisee's personal concerns that may be impeding the supervisee's performance? It seems as though it requires superhuman wisdom to know exactly the point at which the line is crossed in every instance, and to know it in time to avoid it.

Dual relationships are not always harmful. There can be some positive aspects to the combining of roles, however. In fact, we would argue that a wide range of outcomes to dual relationships is possible, from harmful to helpful. Some dual relationships are clearly exploitative and do serious harm to the helpee (and to the professional involved). Others are benign; that is, no harm is done. Still others, we think, can be facilitative and serve a positive purpose. To take three examples:

- A high school counselor enters into a sexual relationship with a 15-year-old student client. All professionals will agree that this relationship is exploitative in the extreme. The roles of counselor and lover are never compatible, and the seriousness of the violation is greatly compounded by the fact that the client is a minor child.

- A couple invite their marriage and family counselor to attend a social occasion. The couple plan to renew their wedding vows and host a reception after the ceremony. The counselor attends the ceremony, briefly appears at the reception to offer her best wishes to the couple, and leaves. The couple are pleased that the counselor came, especially because they credit the counseling process with helping to strengthen the marriage, and apparently no harm has been done. In this case the counselor's blending of a social role with her professional role could be argued to be benign.

- An agreement to collaborate on a manuscript is made between a graduate student and a professor who sits on the student's dissertation committee. The writing relationship is productive, the manuscript is accepted for publication, and both the student and professor are pleased with the outcome of their endeavor. The outcome of this mixing of collegial and supervisory roles seems to be beneficial.

We should note that our opinions here—that some dual relationships are beneficial and that they are not always avoidable—are not universally shared. According to Pope and Vasquez (1991), for instance, claiming that a dual relationship is beneficial for the client can be a strategy for justifying inappropriate behavior. They reminded us that there is virtually no research evidence to support the hypothesis that dual relationships are a safe and effective means to produce therapeutic change. They also warned us of the dangers in assuming that some dual relationships are unavoidable. In their view, asserting that a dual relationship is unavoidable constitutes another type of rationalization and is an attempt to evade responsibility as well as a failure to explore and create acceptable alternative approaches.

Dual relationships are the subject of conflicting advice. Finally, conscientious counselors looking for guidance regarding dual relationships will find conflicting advice. As was noted earlier in this chapter, virtually all codes of ethics prohibit or warn against dual relationships. Yet experts disagree as to how these codes should be interpreted. Some writers believe that ethical codes should be viewed as guidelines to practice rather than as rigid prescriptions, and that professional judgment must play a crucial role. The views of one of the authors of this book, Gerald Corey, tend to lean toward this end of the spectrum. He has reminded us that ethical codes are creations of humans, not divine decrees that contain universal truth. Elsewhere (Corey, Corey, & Callanan, 1988), he and his co-authors have stated that they do not wish to assert dogmatically that all dual relationships are always unethical, and they have challenged readers to reflect honestly and think critically about the issues involved. As will be seen as a consistent theme in Corey's commentaries on the position statements of various contributors in later chapters, his stance is nondogmatic and underscores the role of professional judgment and flexibility in applying ethical standards.

Others in the profession take a more "conservative" stance, arguing that ethical codes would be pointless if left to individual interpretation. Some even go so far as to suggest that leaving codes subject to interpretation invites professionals to justify whatever behaviors they are tempted to perform out of self-interest, in effect leaving the fox to guard the chicken coop. The views of Barbara Herlihy, the other author of this book, although hardly that extreme, lean more toward this end of the continuum. Although she has not advocated a rigid adherence to stated guidelines, she has suggested that when guidelines are unclear, practitioners should err on the side of caution.

To summarize what we have discussed up to this point: We have suggested that dual relationship issues are inherent in the work of all helping professionals and that no counselor remains untouched by the potential difficulties they can create. Although codes of ethics caution us to avoid dual relationships, it seems clear to us that not all dual relationships *can* be avoided. In fact, we have suggested that they are not always harmful and in some instances can even be beneficial. Except for the issue of sexual dual relationships with current clients, there is no clear agreement regarding the stance that counselors should take toward dual relationship issues.

Consider for a moment:

- What is your stance toward dual relationships? Do you agree more with a nondogmatic approach that emphasizes flexibility, or are you more "conservative"?
- How did you arrive at this stance? What do you see as its risks and benefits?

In the next sections, we examine factors that create a potential for harm, the risks involved, some possible benefits, and some safeguards for minimizing risks in dual relationships.

THE POTENTIAL FOR HARM

Whatever the outcome of a dual relationship, a potential for harm almost always exists at the time the dual relationship is entered. To illustrate, let us revisit two of the examples given earlier of relationships whose outcomes were benign and facilitative: As it turned out, no apparent harm was done when the marriage counselor attended the renewal-of-wedding-vows ceremony and reception. But what would have happened if the counselor had been approached at the reception and asked how she knew the couple? Had the counselor answered honestly, she would have breached the privacy of the professional relationship. Had she lied or given an evasive answer, harm to the clients would have been avoided, but the counselor could hardly have felt good about herself as an ethical person. In the example of the collaborative writing relationship between the graduate student and dissertation adviser, both parties were pleased with the outcome. However, despite their good intentions things could have turned out differently. Had the collaboration not proceeded smoothly, their student/adviser relationship might well have been adversely affected.

One of the major problems with dual relationships is the possibility of exploiting the client (or student or supervisee or consultee). Borys studied a variety of possible nonsexual dual relationship behaviors and concluded that they all were related to the principle, "Do not exploit" (Borys, 1988; Borys & Pope, 1989). Kitchener and Harding (1990) contended that dual relationships lie along a continuum from those that are potentially very harmful to those with little potential for harm. They concluded that dual relationships should be entered into only when the risks of harm are small and when there are strong, offsetting, ethical benefits for the consumer.

How does one assess the potential for harm? Kitchener and Harding (1990) have identified three factors that counselors should consider: (1) incompatibility of expectations, (2) divergence of responsibilities, and (3) the power and prestige of the professional. First, the greater the incompatibility of expectations in a dual role, the greater the risk of harm. For example, John, a supervisor, is also providing personal counseling to Suzanne, his supervisee. Although Suzanne understands that evaluation is part of the supervisory relationship, she places high value on the confidentiality of the counseling relationship. John is aware that her personal concerns are impeding her performance as a counselor. In his supervisory role, he is expected to serve not only Suzanne's interests but also those of the public that she will eventually serve and of the agency in which she is employed. When he shares his evaluations with her employer and notes his reservations about her performance (even without revealing the specific nature of her personal concerns), Suzanne feels hurt and betrayed.

Second, as the responsibilities associated with dual roles diverge, the potential for divided loyalties and loss of objectivity increases. When counselors also have personal, political, or business relationships with their clients, their self-interest may be involved and may compromise the client's best interest. For example, Lynn is a counselor in private practice who has entered into a counseling relationship with Paula, even though she and Paula are partners in a small, part-time mail-order business. In the counseling relationship, Paula reveals that she is considering returning to college, which would mean that she would have to give up her role in the business. Lynn is faced with divided loyalties because she does not want the business to fold but she does not have the time to take it over. As this example illustrates, it is difficult to put the client's needs first when the counselor is also invested in meeting his or her own needs.

The third factor has to do with influence, power, and prestige. Some writers believe that clients, by virtue of their need for help, are in a dependent, less powerful, and more vulnerable position. For example, Dr. Wilcox is a counselor educator who is also counseling Jack, a graduate student in the program. When a faculty committee meets to assess Jack's progress, Jack is given probationary status because his work is marginal. Although Dr. Wilcox assures Jack that he revealed nothing about Jack's personal problems during the committee meeting, Jack's trust is destroyed. He is fearful of revealing his personal concerns in counseling with Dr. Wilcox because he knows that Dr. Wilcox will be involved in determining whether he will be allowed to continue his graduate studies at the end of his probationary period. He would like to switch to another counselor, but he is afraid of offending Dr. Wilcox. Counselors and counselor educators must be sensitive to the power and authority associated with their roles. They must resist using their power to manipulate clients. Kitchener and Harding (1990) insisted that because of the power differential it is the professional's responsibility to ensure that the consumer is not harmed.

Pope and Vasquez (1991) identified several major problems with dual relationships. Two of them—the potential for conflicts of interest and the power differential—have already been discussed. Another problem is that dual relationships distort the professional nature of the therapeutic relationship, which needs to rest on a reliable set of boundaries on which both therapist and client can depend. Yet another problem is that dual relationships affect the cognitive processes that benefit clients during therapy and help them maintain these benefits after termination. A further problem is that if a therapist were invited or compelled to give testimony regarding a client, the objectivity and integrity of the testimony would be suspect if a dual relationship existed.

RISKS IN DUAL RELATIONSHIPS

In this section, we examine how the potential for harm can translate into risks to all parties involved in a dual relationship and how these risks can extend to others not directly involved in the relationship.

Risks to consumers. Of primary concern is the risk of harm to the consumer of counseling services. A client who comes to feel exploited by a dual relationship is bound to feel confused, hurt, and betrayed. This erosion of trust may have lasting consequences. The client may be reluctant to seek help from other professionals in the future. Other consequences may be similar to those involved in a patient-therapist sex syndrome (Pope, 1988) even when the dual relationship is nonsexual. Clients may develop ambivalent, conflicting feelings of anger and fear of separation. They may be angry about being exploited but feel trapped in a dependence on the continuing counseling relationship. Some clients, not clearly understanding the complex dynamics of a dual relationship, may feel guilty. They may be left wondering, "What did I do wrong?" Suppressed anger is a potential outcome when the power differential is a factor. Students or supervisees, in particular, may be aware of the inappropriateness of the dual relationship, yet feel that the risks are unacceptably high in confronting a professional who is also their professor or supervisor. Finally, consumers can be left with a sense of isolation, a feeling that "no one can help me." Any of these feelings, left unresolved, could lead to eventual depression, despair, and helplessness—the antitheses of desired counseling outcomes.

Our first concern is the potential harm to the consumer. However, we need to be aware that dual relationships also involve risks to the professional, to other helpees or potential helpees, and ultimately to the profession.

Risks to the professional. Risks to the professional who becomes involved in a dual relationship, aside from damage to the clinical relationship, include loss of professional credibility, violations of ethical standards, revocation of license or certification, and risk of malpractice litigation. Factors that increase the risks include role conflicts, the potential for impaired professional judgment, exploitation of clients, injury to clients, lack of mention of dual relationships in clinical notes, specific legal or ethical prohibitions, and failure to seek consultation and/or supervision when the practitioner proceeds with a dual relationship. When a dual relationship is sexual, in some states the professional also risks the possibility of a felony conviction (Vasquez & Kitchener, 1988).

The consequences just described assume that the dual relationship has come to light and has been dealt with by the ethics committee of a professional association, licensure or certification board, or the court system. Many dual relationships, however, go undetected or unreported. These relationships also have an effect on the professionals involved, causing them to question their competence and diminishing their sense of moral selfhood. Repeated violations of any ethical standard lead professionals down a slippery slope

(Bok, 1979) along which further violations become easier to perform and which ends in counselor impairment.

Effects on other consumers. Dual relationships can create a ripple effect so that they may impact even those who are not directly involved in the relationship. Other clients or potential clients can be affected. This is particularly true in college counseling centers, schools, hospitals, counselor education programs, or any other relatively closed system in which other clients have opportunities to be aware of a dual relationship. Other clients might well resent that one client has been singled out for a special relationship. When a power differential is also involved, as in counselor education programs or supervisory relationships, the resentment may be coupled with a reluctance to question the dual relationship openly for fear of reprisal. Even independent private practitioners can be subject to the ripple effect. Former clients are typically a major source of referrals. A client who has been involved in a dual relationship and who leaves that relationship feeling confused, hurt, or betrayed is not likely to recommend the counselor to friends, relatives, or colleagues.

Effects on other professionals. Fellow professionals who are aware of a dual relationship are placed in a difficult position. Confronting a colleague is always uncomfortable, but it is equally uncomfortable to condone the behavior through silence or inaction. This creates a distressing dilemma that can undermine the morale of any agency, center, hospital, or other system in which it occurs. Paraprofessionals or others who work in the system and who are less familiar with professional codes of ethics may be misled and develop an unfortunate impression regarding the standards of the profession.

Effects on the profession and society. As Stadler (1986) has noted, the counseling profession itself is damaged by the unethical conduct of its members. She stated that the "profession is diminished in its own eyes and in the eyes of others when its members do not take their ethical responsibilities seriously. The ensuing loss of morale, prestige, and credibility can produce any number of unwanted results and significantly alter the viability of the profession" (p. 138). As members of the counseling profession, we have an obligation both to avoid causing harm in dual relationships and to act to prevent others from causing harm. If we fail to assume these responsibilities, our professional credibility is eroded, regulatory agencies will intervene, potential clients will be reluctant to seek counseling assistance, and fewer competent and ethical individuals will enter counselor training programs. Conscientious professionals need to remain aware not only of the potential for harm to consumers but also of the ripple effect that extends the potential for harm.

POSSIBLE BENEFITS

Earlier we stated that we do not think that all dual relationships are necessarily harmful. In fact, we do see some possible benefits that could result from certain kinds of dual relationships. Because both of us are counselor educators, we are most attuned to the potential benefits that some blending of roles might have in relationships between educators and students.

Mentoring relationships with students (which are discussed in more detail in chapter 3) are often cited as an example of a type of dual relationship that our profession encourages and supports. Many counselor educators consciously attempt to teach their courses in ways that have a therapeutic impact—challenging students' values, asking them to take personal risks, and expecting them to involve themselves in their coursework in personal as well as academic ways. If we believe that the process of becoming a counselor is one of personal as well as professional growth, it is difficult to see how we could do otherwise than to teach in this manner. One benefit here is that we can model behavior to our students. If we do indeed combine some roles, and do so with respect for the students and in a way that students gain from this combining of roles, then we are teaching them a valuable lesson. Perhaps the key is that we ask no more of students than we, ourselves, are willing to do. This means that we need to be willing to be challenged, to take risks, and to involve ourselves in the teaching/learning process with more than just our intellects.

In chapter 4, one of us (Corey) describes how he teaches a group counseling course. He admits to combining multiple roles, functioning as teacher, supervisor, facilitator of group process, model-setting participant, consultant, and group counselor. He discusses some of the ways that this combining of roles has real benefit for the students, both academically and personally.

However, as we have stated previously, a *potential* for harm always exists in dual relationships. Dual relationships must be entered with caution. There are, however, some steps that can be taken to minimize the risks, and we now focus on these.

SAFEGUARDS TO MINIMIZE RISK

Whenever we as professionals are operating in more than one role, and when there is potential for negative consequences, it is our responsibility to develop safeguards and measures to reduce (if not eliminate) the potential for harm. These include the following:

- *Informed consent.* It is important that consumers have options, and they have a right to be fully informed about any potential risks. For instance, before students sign up for Corey's group counseling class, they are screened and prepared for the course, and they are not required to take that particular class.

- *Ongoing discussion.* Practitioners who are involved in dual relationships will do well to keep in mind that despite informed consent and discussion of potential risks at the outset, unforeseen problems and conflicts can still arise. This may necessitate that discussion and clarification be an ongoing process.

- *Consultation.* Consultation with other professionals can be useful in getting an objective perspective and identifying unforeseen difficulties. We encourage periodic consultation as a routine practice for professionals who are engaged in dual role relationships. We also want to emphasize the importance of consulting with colleagues who hold divergent views, not just those who tend to support our own perspectives.

- *Supervision.* When dual relationships are particularly problematic, or when the risk for harm is high, it will be prudent for the practitioner to work under supervision.

- *Documentation.* As more a legal than an ethical precaution, professionals will be wise to document any dual relationships in their clinical case notes.

Again, in pausing to reflect, what are your perspectives on these issues? In your own work, where is there potential for conflicts of interest? What criteria do you use—or might you develop—to assess the potential for harm when you are faced with the possibility of a dual relationship? What steps might you take to minimize the risk?

CONCLUSIONS

In this introductory chapter, we have examined what some existing and proposed codes of ethics advise with respect to dual relationships. We have seen that a number of factors make dual relationships problematic. Factors that create a potential for harm, and the risks to parties directly and not directly involved in dual relationships, have been identified. Finally, we have suggested some possible benefits in dual relationships and some strategies for reducing risks. We think that some dual relationship issues can be extraordinarily subtle and complex. In the last analysis, we agree with a statement made by Larry Golden, a guest contributor, in chapter 6. He suggests that when counselors find themselves in the uncharted waters of dual relationships, they must be guided by an internal compass.

An internal compass becomes a necessity for ethically conscientious counselors when they face issues for which there are no clear answers. Dual relationships can certainly comprise one such set of issues.

The diversity of viewpoints about dual relationships will become increasingly apparent to you in later chapters as you compare and contrast the opinions reflected in the literature, in the position statements of guest contributors, and in our commentaries. It is our hope that, as you read about these views, you will apply what you are reading to your own experiences and your own ethical concerns about dual relationships. We welcome your comments and reactions and would like to receive brief examples of struggles you face, questions you raise, and solutions you develop.

CHAPTER 2

SEXUAL DUAL RELATIONSHIPS

Sexual relationships with clients are among the most serious of all ethical violations. These relationships can have devastating effects on clients. The consequences for counselors who engage in sex with their clients can be severe: They may have their licensure or certification revoked, be expelled from professional associations, be restricted in or lose their insurance coverage, be fired from their jobs, be sued in court, or be convicted of a felony (Vasquez & Kitchener, 1988). Supervisors of counselors who engage in sexual relationships with clients are also vulnerable to these consequences. According to the doctrine of "respondent superior," supervisors who are in a position of authority are responsible for acts of their trainees (Austin, Moline, & Williams, 1990).

Although this book deals primarily with issues pertaining to nonsexual dual relationships, sexual dual relationships have been much more extensively addressed in the literature. Because they are such serious violations, they deserve careful consideration. In this chapter we focus specifically on sexual dual relationships and address these questions:

- How widespread is the practice of engaging in sexual relationships with clients?
- How do professional codes of ethics address the issue?
- What are the legal sanctions against these behaviors?
- What makes sexual dual relationships so particularly harmful to clients?
- Who are the likely perpetrators?
- What are the ethics of sexual relationships with former clients?
- How can counselors deal with sexual attraction to clients?

- What is sexual harassment and what are its effects?
- What steps can our profession take to increase awareness of the problems involved in sexual dual relationships and to prevent sexual misconduct?

INCIDENCE

It is difficult to determine the actual incidence of sexual intimacies between counselors and clients. Some studies have shown that it is the most consistently violated ethical standard among psychologists (APA, 1987) and is the second most frequently claimed type of violation against licensed professional counselors (Herlihy, Healy, Cook, & Hudson, 1987). Even so, sexual misconduct is thought to be grossly underreported (Gartrell, Herman, Olarte, Feldstein, & Localio, 1987). Pope and Bouhoutsos (1986), after reviewing national surveys, estimated that sexual contact occurs between male therapists and clients in 9.4% to 12.1% of cases, and between female therapists and clients in 2% to 3% of cases. Pope and Vasquez (1991) noted an interesting trend: There is a fairly consistent decrease in the self-reported rate of sexual involvement with clients. They cautioned that this trend may reflect either a genuine decrease or increasingly less candid reporting.

Although prevalence rates are difficult to determine, it is clear that male therapists engage in sex with their clients at much higher rates than do female therapists. It is also clear that a significant number of cases involve clients who are minor children (Bajt & Pope, 1989). Later in this chapter, we describe attempts to identify therapists who are likely to engage in sexual relationships with clients and steps that can be taken toward prevention and remediation. First, however, we review the ethical and legal sanctions that apply to sexual intimacies with clients.

ETHICAL STANDARDS

Virtually all professional codes of ethics prohibit sexual intimacies with clients, as can be seen in the following excerpts of ethics codes:

- The member will avoid any type of sexual intimacies with clients. Sexual relationships with clients are unethical. (AACD, 1988)
- Sexual intimacies with clients are unethical. (APA, 1989)

- The social worker should under no circumstances engage in sexual activities with clients. (National Association of Social Workers, 1990)

- Clinical social workers do not engage in or condone sexual activities with clients. (NFSCSW, 1985)

- Sexual intimacy with clients is prohibited. Sexual intimacy with former clients for 2 years following the termination of therapy is prohibited. (American Association for Marriage and Family Therapy [AAMFT], 1991)

- The necessary intensity of the therapeutic relationship may tend to activate sexual and other needs and fantasies on the part of both patient and therapist, while weakening the objectivity necessary for control. Sexual activity with a patient is unethical. Sexual involvement with one's former patients generally exploits emotions deriving from treatment and therefore almost always is unethical. . . .

  Sexual involvement between a faculty member or supervisor and a trainee or student, in those situations in which an abuse of power can occur, often takes advantage of inequalities in the working relationship and may be unethical because: (a) any treatment of a patient being supervised may be deleteriously affected; (b) it may damage the trust relationship between teacher and student; and (c) teachers are important professional role models for their trainees and affect their trainees' future professional behavior. (American Psychiatric Association, 1989)

- Sexual relationships between analyst and patient are antithetical to treatment and unacceptable under any circumstances. Any sexual activity with a patient constitutes a violation of this principle of ethics. (American Psychoanalytic Association, 1983)

- Certified counselors do not condone or engage in sexual harassment, which is defined as deliberate or repeated comments, gestures, or physical contacts of a sexual nature. (National Board for Certified Counselors, 1989)

The draft of proposed revisions to the American Psychological Association code of ethics contains a section on "exploitative relationships (with persons other than patients or clients)":

- (a) Psychologists do not exploit, sexually or otherwise, their professional relationships with current students, supervisees, employees, research participants, or other persons over whom they have significant supervisory or other authority.

(b) Sexual relationships with current students or direct supervisees are so likely to be exploitative that they are always unethical. ("Draft," 1991)

These existing and proposed codes are explicit with respect to sexual harassment and sexual relationships with clients, students, and supervisees. However, they do not, and maybe they cannot, define some of the more subtle ways that sexuality may be a part of therapeutic relationships. For example, sexual attractions between counselors and clients do occur, and it is not the attraction per se that is problematic but rather the inappropriate acting on the attraction that can become an ethical problem. Also, most of the codes do not address the question of sexual relationships with former clients, although there is current debate on whether it is ethical or legal to become sexually involved with clients after the termination of therapy. Interestingly, the proposed revisions to the APA code do attempt to address this issue. The draft document states that psychologists do not engage in sexual intimacies with former patients or clients "except in the most unusual circumstances," and that "In no case may a psychologist engage in sexual intimacy with a former psychotherapy patient or client within 1 year after cessation or termination of professional services" ("Draft," 1991). Thus, these codes do provide some guidance, yet they do not always provide the help needed when practitioners must deal with the more subtle ramifications of this problem.

LEGAL SANCTIONS

Professional counselor licensure laws, which had been enacted in 34 states at the time of this writing, have added the force of law to ethical sanctions. An example of a standard within a state licensure law is as follows:

- A counselor shall not engage in sexual contact or intimacies with any client or with a person who has been a client within the past 2 years. A counselor shall not provide counseling services to a person with whom the counselor has had a sexual relationship. (Texas State Board of Examiners of Professional Counselors, 1990).

In addition to standards within state licensure laws, several states (including Colorado, Minnesota, and Wisconsin) have enacted laws that make therapist-client sexual activity a felony crime. Sexual intimacies are one of the major causes of malpractice suits. Austin et al. (1990) reviewed relevant court cases and concluded that few if any arguments in defense of therapists who have sex with clients are likely to succeed in court. In particular, courts have rejected claims that the client consented, determining that consent was not voluntary or informed because it was affected by transference. Further, courts are likely to find the therapist liable regardless of whether sex was part of or separate from therapy.

Losses and actions of professional liability insurance carriers are another indicator of the seriousness of sexual relationships. Pope (1986) reported that the American Psychological Association's insurance carrier lost over $7 million during a 10-year period due to sexual improprieties, which was nearly 45% of monies paid out for all claims. Most professional liability insurance policies limit payments for claims of sexual misconduct. It seems clear that sexual dual relationships carry serious consequences in both ethical and legal terms.

HARM TO CLIENTS

Kenneth S. Pope, who has produced an impressive body of research into sexual dual relationships, has provided a clear and comprehensive picture of the harm that may be done to clients by sexual relationships with their therapists. In an excellent article describing a therapist-patient sex syndrome, Pope (1988) noted that clients may have reactions similar to those of victims of rape, battering, incest, child abuse, and posttraumatic stress. Ten general aspects commonly associated with the syndrome are ambivalence, guilt, emptiness and isolation, identity/boundary/role confusion, sexual confusion, impaired ability to trust, emotional liability, suppressed rage, cognitive dysfunction, and increased suicidal risk. We believe it is worth examining each of these indicators in more depth.

Ambivalence. Clients who are sexually involved with their therapist may experience a sense of deep ambivalence, fearing separation or alienation from the therapist yet longing desperately to escape from the therapist's power and influence. Loyalty to the therapist may prevent clients from acting to protect themselves (resisting sexual advances or reporting the abuse) for fear that their action could destroy the therapist's personal or professional life. This ambivalence and misplaced loyalty help to explain why the behavior can go unreported completely or for a number of years.

Guilt. Clients may feel guilty, as though they are somehow to blame for what has happened. Their reactions may be similar to those of incest victims. They may have a sense of guilt that they did not do more to stop the sexual activity, or that they enjoyed the relationship, or that they did something to invite such a relationship with a person they deeply trusted. It should be clearly understood that even if clients behave in seductive ways, it is always the therapist's responsibility to maintain a professional distance in the relationship. Therapists can help clients to understand such behavior on their part as a manifestation of transference (Group for the Advancement of Psychiatry, 1990). The therapist, not the client, has the responsibility to evaluate the therapeutic situation and to monitor the boundaries of this relationship. Therapists who have trouble in keeping clear boundaries in the professional relationship are often guilty of poor judgment in other areas of their practice.

Emptiness and isolation. Sexual activity between a therapist and client can seriously erode the client's sense of self-worth. Clients may feel emotionally isolated, alone, and cut off from the world of "normal" human experience.

Identity/boundary/role confusion. A phenomenon often involved in a patient-therapist sexual relationship is a reversal of roles. As the therapist becomes more self-disclosing, and as meeting the therapist's needs becomes more important in the relationship, the client becomes responsible for taking care of the therapist. Clients become confused, not knowing where safe and appropriate boundaries lie, and this adds to the erosion of their sense of identity and worth.

Sexual confusion. Many clients seem to manifest a profound confusion about their sexuality. Lingering outcomes can take two forms: Some clients will be threatened by any sexual activity, and others may be trapped into compulsive or self-destructive sexual encounters.

Impaired ability to trust. Because therapy involves such a high degree of trust, violations can have lifelong consequences. When therapists abuse this trust, they are taking advantage of their clients in the most fundamental way. This is perhaps the core issue in sexual violations, and the consequences can extend far beyond the therapeutic relationship in question. Client victims are likely to mistrust other helping professionals, particularly therapists, and the damage may reverberate outward to other, less intense relationships.

Emotional liability. This can be a long-term consequence. Clients who have been sexually involved with a therapist often feel overwhelmed by their emotions, both during the relationship and afterwards. Even with subsequent therapy, victims may reexperience traumatic emotions when they become involved with a new and appropriate sexual partner. Pope (1988) cautioned counselors who work with these victims to keep these setbacks in perspective so that clients will not lose hope.

Suppressed rage. Victims may feel a justifiable, tremendous anger at the offending therapist. But this rage may be blocked from awareness or expression by feelings of ambivalence and guilt, and by manipulative behaviors of the therapist. Offending therapists may use threats and intimidation to prevent clients from reporting the behavior and can be adept at eliciting compliance, hero worship, and dependency. As is true of those clients who feel guilty, these feelings of anger need to be identified, expressed, and worked through in later therapy with another therapist (not with the offending therapist). If this anger is bottled up, it is likely to affect the clients' relationships with significant others in their lives and with any other therapists they might later have.

Cognitive dysfunction. The trauma caused by sexual involvement with a therapist can be so severe that clients may experience cognitive dysfunction. Attention and concentration may be disrupted by flashbacks, nightmares, and intrusive thoughts.

Increased suicidal risk. Finally, suicide risk is increased as some clients feel hopelessly trapped in ambivalence, isolation, and confusion. These feelings, coupled with an impaired ability to trust, may prevent victims from reaching out for help.

An excellent source to consult in order to learn more about harm to victims is *Sex in the Therapy Hour: A Case of Professional Incest* (Bates & Brodsky, 1989). This book gives a personal account of a victim's experience.

Clearly, the effects on clients can be profound and violate one of our most fundamental moral principles: to do no harm. One step toward prevention is to understand the seriousness of the harm that is done. It may also be useful to attempt to understand who the professionals are that commit these offenses.

PERPETRATORS OF SEXUAL RELATIONSHIPS WITH CLIENTS

It would be relatively easy to discover and prevent sexual victimization of clients if the perpetrators fit a single personality and behavioral profile. However, it seems that there is wide variation in the personality types of counselors who commit these offenses and in their reasons for doing so. At this point, our level of understanding yields only two clear facts: First, male therapists are far more likely to engage in sexual relationships with clients than are female therapists. Pope (1988) examined prevalence studies that were published over a 15-year period and reported that aggregate averages were 8.3% for male therapists and 1.7% for female therapists. Second, the majority of therapists who become sexually involved (about 80%) do so with more than one client (Holroyd & Brodsky, 1977). In fact, the most effective predictor of whether a client will become sexually involved with a therapist is whether the therapist has previously engaged in sex with a client (Bates & Brodsky, 1989). The client's personal history or characteristics were not found to be significant factors in predictability.

Attempts to describe "typical" perpetrators have recognized the wide range of types of professionals involved. Golden, interviewed in a *Guidepost* article (Schafer, 1990), suggested that they generally fall into one of three categories: professionals who are ignorant of the standards, those who are aware of the standards but are blinded by what dual relationships can offer romantically, and sociopaths who know the standards but willfully and repeatedly violate them.

Schoener and Gonsiorek (1988) have done much to extend our understanding by offering a comprehensive description of six categories of perpetrators: *Uninformed and naive* therapists are led into sexual relationships through ignorance. They genuinely lack knowledge of ethical standards and professional boundaries and have difficulty distinguishing between personal and professional relationships. *Healthy or neurotic* counselors are aware that sexual relationships are unethical, are typically involved in limited or isolated instances, are experiencing situational stressors, and are remorseful about their behavior. They often terminate sexual intimacy on their own and may self-report and request help. *Severely neurotic* counselors have longstanding and significant emotional problems, especially depression, feelings of inadequacy, low self-esteem, and social isolation. Typically, they begin by becoming emotionally or socially involved with a client, and professional boundaries disintegrate as intimacy grows. These counselors may feel guilt and remorse, but they are less able to terminate the inappropriate behavior and may deny, distort, or rationalize their behavior.

Other counselors with *character disorders and impulse control problems* have longstanding problems and a history of legal difficulties. They are often caught due to their multiple violations and poor judgment. When consequences are pending they show guilt and remorse, but they rarely have a true appreciation of the impact of their behavior on others. *Sociopathic or narcissistic character disordered* individuals have characteristics similar to the previous group but are more cunning and detached. They are adept at manipulating clients and colleagues into helping them avoid the consequences of their acts. Finally, *psychotic or borderline personality disordered* counselors have in common poor social judgment and impaired reality testing.

It is obvious that counselors who fall into these last three categories are poor candidates for rehabilitation. We think it is important to note here that when we categorize offenders, we can be lulled into a false sense of security that they are somehow "different" from us. We would do well to remember that we are all vulnerable. Most of us have experienced sexual attraction to a client, and each of us is capable of denying our feelings and rationalizing our behavior.

In addition to identifying six categories of offenders, Schoener and Gonsiorek (1988) have presented an excellent approach to assessment and rehabilitation for impaired practitioners. The American Association for Counseling and Development has formed a Special Task Force on Impaired Counselors. Aside from this work, very little has been done within the counseling profession to investigate impairment or to acknowledge that there is a need to look at this phenomenon (Stadler, 1990). Clearly, more work is needed in this area if we are to reduce the incidence of these violations. In the last section of this chapter, we make some recommendations regarding steps that can be taken.

SEXUAL RELATIONSHIPS WITH FORMER CLIENTS

The counseling profession has not completely resolved the question of whether sexual relationships with former clients are ever acceptable. Many of our major codes of ethics, including the AACD *Ethical Standards* (1988), are silent on this issue. There is only a limited body of research that investigates the incidence. Bouhoutsos, Holroyd, Lerman, Forer, and Greenberg (1983) reported as part of a larger study some data on clients who revealed to a therapist that they had experienced sexual intimacy with a previous therapist: 4% of these clients stated that these intimacies had begun within 3 months of terminating the previous relationship. Holroyd and Brodsky (1977) surveyed psychologists and reported that 4.4% acknowledged having had sexual intercourse with at least one former client within 3 months after termination.

More recently Borys (1988), in a landmark dissertation study, surveyed 2,400 psychologists, psychiatrists, and social workers regarding their ethical beliefs and a second group of 2,400 clinicians regarding their actual practices. Since we refer extensively to Borys' study throughout the book, an explanatory note is needed regarding her procedures. Random assignment to the two groups (ethical beliefs and actual practices) was utilized, so they are comparable for statistical purposes although it is important to remember they were not the same respondents. Borys found that 3.9% of the respondents to the actual practices survey reported that they had engaged in sexual activity with one or more clients after termination. In the ethical beliefs survey, Borys found that only 68.4% believed it was never ethical to engage in sexual activity with a client after termination, 23.2% believed it to be ethical under rare conditions, 4.8% rated it as ethical under some or most conditions, and 0.3% believed it was always ethical.

Only a few codes of ethics or state licensing boards specify a minimum length of time that must elapse between termination of a professional relationship and initiation of a sexual one. The American Association for Marriage and Family Therapists' code of ethics specifies a 2-year time limit, and the American Psychiatric Association states that sexual involvement with a former patient is "almost always unethical." Licensed counselors in Texas and in California are prohibited from having sexual relationships with clients for 2 years after counseling has terminated. In Florida, it is illegal for a therapist to have sex with a former client no matter how long it has been since the therapy ended. Woody (1988, pp. 183–184) cites the rule of the Florida Board of Psychological Examiners: "For purposes of determining the existence of sexual misconduct. . . ., the psychologist-client relationship is deemed to continue in perpetuity." Professionals are likely to be held in violation when sexual intimacy occurs with a former client regardless of whether their jurisdictions have specific prohibitions. Sell, Gottlieb, and Schoenfeld (1986) surveyed state ethics committees and licensing boards and found that psychologists who asserted that a sexual relationship had occurred only after termination were actually more likely to be found in violation than those who did not make that claim. Over a 2-year period, there were no cases in which a psychologist was absolved of charges solely because a sufficient amount of time had elapsed after termination of the professional relationship.

The study by Sell and his colleagues focused on psychologists. There is some evidence to indicate that ethics committees dealing with complaints against counselors may reason similarly. A case study presented in the *Ethical Standards Casebook* (Herlihy & Golden, 1990) describes a situation in which a counselor and client confessed to a mutual attraction, terminated the counseling relationship, and soon thereafter began a sexual relationship. In this case (which was hypothetical but based on actual cases received by the AACD Ethics Committee), the counselor was found in violation of the standard that prohibits meeting the counselor's needs at the client's expense.

It appears, then, that the fact that the counseling relationship had been terminated does not present an adequate defense against charges of an ethics violation. Sell et al. (1986) have argued that members of the profession need to know what guidelines are used to determine the propriety or impropriety of sexual relationships with former clients, and they have suggested that the ethical standards of the American Psychological Association be amended to state that sexual intimacies with clients or with former clients are unethical.

Although such a blanket prohibition would clarify the issue, it is doubtful that all counseling professionals agree with the psychoanalysts' stance that the therapeutic relationship never ends. Some might argue that there is a significant difference between the intense, long-term relationship of an analyst and analysand and other brief-term, less personal, or less intimate counseling relationships. What should be the appropriate response, for instance, to Ellen's question in the following scenario?

> Ellen served her counseling internship at her university's counseling center. One of her clients was Craig, a graduate student who was a businessman returning to college for his MBA. Craig sought counseling because he was having second thoughts about committing himself to a lifelong career in the cut-throat competitive field he was in. During five counseling sessions with Ellen, he completed a series of inventories, weighed his values, and decided to switch majors to a service-oriented field. One and a half years later, Craig and Ellen ran into each other at a social event. Craig asked her out on a date.

> Assume that Ellen approaches you for consultation. She tells you that she does not want to be unethical, yet she also wants to accept Craig's offer for a date. Because Ellen had only five sessions with him, because the focus was on career counseling, and because the counseling took place 1½ years ago, Ellen does not think that accepting a date with Craig is unethical. However, she wants to get your opinion and would like to know if she is overlooking some important issues. What might you say to Ellen?

If Ellen consults with us, we will first ask her to state what she sees as the pros and cons of each decision. We will explore with her the reasons she is seeking consultation. Although she does not think that accepting the date is unethical, she seems uncertain. Can she see potential problems in accepting, or is she hoping to receive "expert" affirmation that dating Craig is appropriate? We will certainly ask her if there is a pattern here. Has she dated other former clients? We will not flatly tell Ellen that accepting the date is wrong, although we will explore with her any possible consequences, especially if the jurisdiction in which she lives or a professional association to which she belongs imposes a time limit on social or romantic relationships with clients after termination. Our goals for the consultation are to have Ellen understand her reasons for choosing whatever course of action she may follow and be aware of and take responsibility for the possible consequences (both positive and negative) of her decision.

There is disagreement within the profession on the issue of sexual or romantic relationships with former clients. Some contend that the transferential elements of the therapeutic relationship persist forever, and therefore, romantic relationships with former clients are unethical. Others contend that there are cases in which the probability for harm is not high and that each case needs to be considered individually. For instance, we know of a number of therapists and counselor educators who have married their former clients or students. Could they be prosecuted under law in Florida, where psychologist/client relationships continue in perpetuity?

Therefore, we believe that it would benefit the counseling profession to be as clear about sequential sexual relationships with clients as it is about simultaneous ones. Whether sexual relationships with former clients are ever acceptable, and if so when and under what circumstances, needs to be a subject of continuing discussion. On the one hand, we need to remain aware of the harm that can result from sexual intimacies that occur after termination, of the aspects of the therapeutic process that continue after termination including residual transference, and of the continuing power differential. On the other hand, we need to consider the wide range of circumstances that could arise, especially the differences between long-term intense counseling relationships and brief career-oriented or other types of counseling. If a counselor does consider entering into a romantic relationship with a former client, there are some safeguards that could be followed. These include consulting with a colleague or going for a therapy session conjointly with the former client to examine mutual transferences and expectations.

> After reading about disparate points of view, what is your position on sexual involvement with former clients? Consider the following questions: Do you think that sexual relationships with former clients are ethical, regardless of the time elapsed? What specific factors might lead you to determine that such involvements are unethical? How can you determine whether or not a former client might be exploited or harmed if he or she becomes romantically involved with a former therapist? If you were a member of an ethics committee, what specific recommendation, if any, might you make regarding a guideline on this subject?

SEXUAL ATTRACTION

It may be inevitable that most counselors will at some time feel a sexual attraction to a client. Brenda, a counselor in private practice, related this anecdote:

> The client was my prototype of the physically attractive man. He was tall, lean but muscular, and very good looking. As counseling progressed, it became apparent that he was sensitive to others, had a solid sense of personal integrity, and had a great sense of humor—all qualities that I admire. I realized that I found him attractive but wasn't particularly concerned about it. After all, I

had it in awareness and certainly didn't intend to act on my feelings. Then, during one session he began to relate a lengthy story, and my attention wandered. I drifted off into a sexual fantasy about him, I don't know for how long, probably only a few seconds. I snapped back to reality, and as I refocused on his words I realized he was now talking about sex. I nearly panicked: Had I somehow telegraphed my thoughts?? I felt my face begin to redden, and compounded my discomfort by wondering if he saw me blushing and thought I was embarrassed about the subject of sex. With real effort I directed my concern away from myself and back to him and got through the rest of the session. But I was so shaken by the incident that I immediately sought consultation.

Assume you are the person to whom Brenda turns for consultation. She wonders whether she should continue counseling this man or whether she should make a referral. Brenda tells you that she does not know how to best deal with her feelings toward him and that she worries about the affect of her attraction on the counseling process. Yet she is also concerned about making a referral and wonders what she might tell him if she decided to suggest a referral to another professional. What input might you offer to Brenda? If you found yourself in a situation similar to hers, what course of action might you take?

Despite the likelihood that sexual attraction to a client is a common occurrence, there has been a lack of systematic research into the topic (Pope, 1988; Pope, Keith-Spiegel, & Tabachnick, 1986). This silence gives a misleading impression that counselors are somehow immune from this experience or that those who do encounter it are unusual, aberrant, or guilty of therapeutic error (Corey et al., 1988). Counselors who believe that their feelings are "abnormal" or "wrong" may resist getting help in dealing with them and may be left feeling overwhelmed by an attraction and increasingly tempted to act it out with the client.

The results of a study by Pope and his colleagues (1986) have made a significant contribution to countering our ignorance and denial. Although research indicated that most therapists (87%) experience attraction to some of their clients, most respondents in their study (82%) stated that they had never seriously considered acting out their feelings in a sexual relationship with a client. Although acting out seems to occur in relatively few instances, most therapists reported feeling guilty, anxious, or confused about the attraction. Nonetheless, 69% believed that their feelings of sexual attraction could be beneficial in therapy. Training implications are also raised by the study: Only 9% of respondents felt they had received adequate preparation in their graduate programs to deal with sexual attractions, and those who had received some graduate training were more likely to have sought consultation.

In light of these findings, we recommend that counselor education programs place more emphasis on the issue of sexual attraction. Prospective counselors need to be reassured that their feelings are a common manifestation of countertransference, that these feelings are natural, and that with awareness and preparedness they can still counsel effectively with clients to whom they feel attracted. The importance of consultation should also be emphasized, in both pre-service and in-service education, to help prevent sexual attraction from crossing the boundary into an inappropriate dual relationship. Training programs have a responsibility to help students identify and openly discuss their concerns about sexual feelings and sexual dilemmas pertaining to counseling practice. Ignoring the subject in training programs denies the importance of the topic and interferes with the potential effectiveness of trainees.

Recently, Rodolfa, Kitzrow, Vohra, and Wilson (1990) described their training experiences that focus on the personal, professional, ethical, and legal issues involved in sexual attraction between therapists and clients. The main goal of their training program was to encourage interns to examine and express thoughts and feelings in a way that facilitates working through some of the complex issues involved. Training involved discussion of the differences between sexual attraction and sexual acting out. They acknowledged that most therapists will encounter sexual dilemmas during their careers and suggested that programs include formal training in this area.

Pope and Vasquez (1991) have summarized nicely the issue of sexual attraction. They stated that "To feel attraction to a client is **not** unethical; to acknowledge and address the attraction promptly, carefully, and adequately is an important ethical responsibility" (p. 107). In addition to improving training programs, they suggest that consulting with colleagues, obtaining supervision, and seeking our own therapy are helpful measures.

Consider, for a moment, how this subject applies to you. Have you had to struggle with the matter of sexual attractions in counseling relationships? If so, how did you deal with your feelings and the feelings of your clients? What would you do if you found yourself attracted to a client, or a client to you? What would you like to see included in training programs about issues of sexual attraction?

SEXUAL HARASSMENT

Sexual harassment has been defined as "deliberate or repeated comments, gestures, or physical contacts of a sexual nature" (AACD, 1988). The *Ethical Principles* of the American Psychological Association use a similar definition and specify that these contacts "are unwanted by the recipient or expressed in a relationship wherein power differential is a factor" (APA, 1989). Hotelling (1991) has noted that there are problems with definitions of sexual harassment; for instance, terms such as *repeated* and *unwanted* allow for excuses and loopholes. Hotelling also noted that sexual harassment refers to a broad range of behaviors and there is controversy over exactly what behaviors fall within that range.

Just how widespread is the practice of sexual harassment? Although there are problems in interpreting prevalence studies, data indicate that 20% to 30% of college women are victims of sexual harassment and that women graduate students are more at risk than undergraduate women (Hotelling, 1991). These general findings stand in contrast to the specific findings of a recent survey of psychology faculty. Tabachnick, Keith-Spiegel, and Pope (1991) found that sexual harassment (as defined by APA) was the most rare of a variety of behaviors reported, acknowledged as even a rare occurrence by only 1% of the respondents. It may well be that faculty in psychology and counselor education programs are more sensitive to the behavior than are faculty in some other academic areas. However, Hotelling (1991) cited studies that suggest a prevalence rate of sexual harassment of women psychology students far exceeding that reported by the respondents in the study by Tabachnik et al.

Among the three factors that create a potential for harm in dual relationships (see chapter 1), the power differential is the key factor in sexual harassment. A power differential implies that the recipient does not have equal choice in the relationship. As Hotelling (1991) has so aptly stated, "controversies remain about what constitutes sexual harassment, although most agree that the power differential between harasser and victim is central to the definition, its existence, and lack of reporting" (p. 500). Howard (1991) reminded us that although there is debate about the appropriateness of consensual sexual relationships between faculty and adult students, there are those who suggest that such relationships are inherently nonconsensual because they involve an inescapable power differential.

It is clear that women experience sexual harassment much more frequently than men. Yet, sexual harassment is thought to be grossly underreported. In a recent article, Riger (1991) suggested that it is gender bias in policies and procedures that discourages women from making complaints rather than an absence of harassment or a lack of assertiveness on the part of victims. She pointed out that women perceive sexual harassment differently than men and that their orientation to dispute resolution also differs from that of men. Her suggestion that "policymakers and others need to learn to 'think like women' to define which behaviors constitute harassment and recognize that these behaviors are unacceptable" (p. 503) is well worth considering.

In addition to gender-biased institutional policies and procedures, other obstacles exist to reporting sexual harassment. According to Hotelling (1991), fear of reprisal is the foremost barrier to reporting. Riger (1991) has suggested, additionally, that some women may consider the behavior to be normative; that outcomes of grievance procedures are unlikely to provide much satisfaction because harassers are rarely or only mildly punished; and that reporting can adversely affect a complainant's academic standing and have serious emotional consequences.

We can learn a great deal about these emotional consequences of sexual harassment from a graduate student who has written about her experiences with Professor X, a charismatic professor of counseling (Anonymous, 1991). Although Professor X singled out this student for special attention, praise, encouragement, and hugs, she trustingly failed to consider that he was "coming on to her" sexually until she learned that he had had affairs with other students. After much soul-searching, she filed sexual harassment charges with the university and the ethics committees of professional associations. A lengthy process followed, filled with frustrations and disappointments for her, but in the end Professor X was found in violation and disciplined.

This student successfully resisted the professor's attempted seduction, and her complaints were successfully resolved. Nonetheless, the experience was traumatic for her, and her experiencing parallels many aspects of therapist-patient sex syndrome. Her ambivalence, confusion, guilt, anger, isolation, and cognitive dysfunction are all evident as she progresses through the experience:

> I sat for hours, staring off into space, unable to focus. I saw Professor X as two images that refused to meld. . . his well-meaning, kind, and caring persona as opposed with a lustful and menacing one. I wondered if I had inadvertently given him some signal that I was approachable sexually. (p. 503)

After she fully understood his intentions and had begun to avoid him, she experienced conflicting emotions:

> I felt an increasingly intense desire to return to the more comfortable state I'd been in before I'd learned about my professor's reputation. I also became aware of a longing for a return to his good graces. I wanted to feel good about us and to be welcomed back inside his comfortable, reassuring aura." (personal communication, April 15, 1991)

> My anger grew as the week wore on. It emanated from deep within me—I felt consumed by it, and I felt that I would not be able to stop myself from expressing it the next time I saw Professor X. I avoided having any contact with him." (p. 505)

> I felt obsessed by the experience—it drew attention away from every area of my life. To keep myself going, I read about sexual harassment and about research regarding sexual intimacy between therapists and clients. . . . These activities helped me to combat the worst aspect of this problem—the loneliness." (p. 506)

This student's experiences speak eloquently to the effects of sexual harassment on one recipient. Hotelling (1991) has summarized the effects more generally in terms of emotional, physical, and behavioral outcomes. Ambivalent feelings toward the harasser are common, and some women will blame themselves and feel responsible. Feelings of powerlessness can erode self-esteem and self-confidence both academically and personally. Anger, hurt, depression, and a generalized distrust of men may occur. Physical problems may be experienced along with decreased concentration and listlessness.

What can be done to prevent sexual harassment? Howard (1991) suggests that institutional grievance procedures need to include both formal and informal channels. Beyond the formation of clear policies and procedures, efforts must be directed both toward improving the campus climate and expanding education and training. Riger (1991) summarized the need nicely when she stated that "Organizational leaders should not assume that their job is completed when they have established a sexual harassment policy. Extensive efforts at prevention need to be mounted at the individual, situational, and organizational level" (p. 503). Howard (1991) concurred, concluding that "a truly effective program for the prevention and remedy of sexual harassment will be tied to larger efforts to improve the climate and to achieve equity for women within the organization" (p. 510).

For a fuller understanding of the issue, we recommend Riger's article (1991) and the entire special feature on sexual harassment that appeared in the July/August 1991 (Vol. 69) *Journal of Counseling and Development.*

PREVENTION AND REMEDIATION

Sexual dual relationships are one of the most harmful types of unethical behavior. Our literature helps us to understand how destructive they can be for clients, counselors, and the profession as a whole. Since violations are common—and probably occur more frequently than we realize—we need to make concerted efforts toward awareness and prevention. Steps that could be taken include consumer education, support for the victims, counselor education, and monitoring professional practice.

Consumer Education

As professionals, we are communicating well with each other about sexual dual relationships, as is evidenced by the large number of articles in our professional journals. However, it is probably more important that we communicate clearly to consumers that they have the right to services that are free from sexual exploitation. Statements of client rights should include this information and be routinely distributed. An important step in prevention is to educate the public so that they have clear expectations about the counseling process and knowledge of the boundaries of the relationship.

In addition, Hotelling (1988) has noted that many clients do not know what avenues of redress are available to them when they have been victimized. She described the ethical, administrative, and legal options that clients can use when they have had a sexual relationship with their counselor. This information needs to be routinely shared with consumers. A helpful step in this direction was preparation of a booklet entitled *Professional Therapy Never Includes Sex* by the California Department of Consumer Affairs. The booklet stresses that once sexual involvement begins, therapy for the client ends and the original concerns of the client are postponed and neglected. This booklet was specifically designed to help victims of sexual exploitation by therapists. It describes some warning signs of unprofessional behavior and presents the rights of clients.

Support for the Victims

Counselors may feel unprepared to help clients, students, or others who have had sexual relationships with their therapists. It is important to remember that clients who have been sexually exploited tend to be exceptionally vulnerable to revictimization when counselors fail to recognize their clinical needs (Pope & Vasquez, 1991). An abused client can be empowered by taking action against the offending therapist. As Hotelling (1988) has aptly stated, "The reality of what happened and its inappropriateness and destructiveness is affirmed; the burden of responsibility can be shifted to its rightful owner" (p. 233). Despite the potential for healing, it is extremely difficult for an abused client to pursue a complaint. In addition to the emotional toll that the process takes, it requires perseverance and some sophistication about the ethical complaint process and/or legal system.

Counselors who work with these clients need a high degree of preparedness. They may need to deal with their own feelings of discomfort at being involved in a complaint against a colleague. They need to know all the possible avenues of redress and the advantages and disadvantages of each, so that these can be communicated accurately to the client. And finally, they need to keep in mind that the decisions—whether to pursue a complaint, what avenue(s) to take—rest with the client.

Despite the increase in the number of complaints of sexual misconduct against therapists, women still report great reluctance in filing complaints for disciplinary action against their therapists or trainers (Gottlieb, 1990; Hotelling, 1991; Riger, 1991). These women often have ambivalent feelings about themselves, but they also encounter institutional barriers within the profession that contribute to their feelings of intimidation and deter them from following through with the complaint process. Gottlieb (1990) suggested that there is a need for an organizational structure within the profession that will reach out to these women and assist them in the complaint process.

Counselor Education

Although we will more fully discuss issues in counselor education in the next chapter, at this point we want to note some concerns specific to sexual dual relationships. We have the impression that, generally, counselor education programs are not giving much emphasis to the topic. Whether this is due in part to erotophobia (a reluctance to discuss sex), as Vasquez (1988) has suggested, or to an assumption that there is no need to belabor the obvious, it creates a serious omission in the counselor training process. Vasquez (1988) made the point that counselor education programs have a dual responsibility: to train prospective counselors and to protect the public whom they will eventually serve. Her description of training strategies to prevent counselor-client sexual contact—which include knowledge, self-awareness, program climate, and faculty behavior—is an excellent source for counselor educators who want to assess or strengthen their programs.

Bartell and Rubin (1990) contended that education can play an important role in helping trainees first to recognize sexual attraction and then to take the necessary steps to avoid acting on this attraction. They conclude that trainees need to be made aware of the prohibitions issued by the professional organizations. They suggest that the injunctions against sexual relationships be emphasized in training programs and that these statements be well publicized as a way to eliminate dangerous liaisons.

On the matter of providing trainees with education on this subject, we think this topic is ideally introduced in a beginning class in counseling, then dealt with in more depth in an ethics course, and further addressed in seminar sessions attached to the student's field work or internship experiences. Students are bound to encounter attractions as a part of their fieldwork. They can be encouraged by fieldwork instructors to bring in for discussion such personal reactions. Students can learn to deal with their own countertransference feelings by openly discussing them in the safety of a supervision session. Some students may need to consider seeking therapy for themselves as an option, in order to explore their countertransferences and sexual attraction to clients.

Before attempting to educate others, however, instructors must gain their own clarity. It seems to us that counselor educators and faculty who teach in related programs have a special obligation to be role models for what constitutes ethical behavior. Counselor educators who lack clarity will pass along their confusion to future generations of helping professionals, and counselor educators who behave in ethically questionable ways imply that those behaviors are acceptable. A recent study by Tabachnick and colleagues (1991) sheds some light on the beliefs and behaviors of psychologists who work in academic settings. Among their findings:

- On the question of dating a student, 80% reported the *belief* that this behavior was never or only rarely ethical, whereas 95% reported that they had engaged in this *behavior* never or only rarely.

- On the question of becoming sexually involved with a student, 91% reported the *belief* that this behavior was never or only rarely ethical, whereas 99% reported that they had engaged in this *behavior* never or only rarely.

- On the question of being sexually attracted to a student, 27% reported the *belief* that this behavior was never or only rarely ethical, whereas 71% reported that they had engaged in this *behavior* never or only rarely.

- On the question of becoming sexually involved with a student only after he or she has completed your course and the grade has been filed, 47% reported the *belief* that this behavior was never or only rarely ethical, whereas 96% reported that they had engaged in this *behavior* never or only rarely.

This study surveyed attitudes and behaviors regarding a wide variety of issues. The authors found it intriguing that half of the items considered "controversial" (yielding diverse judgments) concerned sexual thoughts or behaviors. Another interesting finding was that respondents reported disclosing sexual attraction to a student less frequently than they reported actually becoming sexually involved with a student. Tabachnick et al. also discussed "little boundary blurrings" that can compromise objectivity. They acknowledged that numerous social and other types of activities exist for both students and faculty on and off campus, so that "boundary blurring seems practically built into the academic system" (p. 514).

These findings suggest that the sexualization of relationships between faculty and students remains a problematic issue.

Monitoring Professional Practice

Without question, professionals have been reluctant to report their colleagues who engage in sexual relationships with clients, students, or supervisees. Tabachnick et al. (1991) found that 79% of respondents in their study of psychology faculty had ignored unethical behavior by colleagues. There may be several sources for this reluctance (Levenson, 1986). In large measure, our sense of professional identity depends on strong interpersonal bonds. We may fear being ostracized by colleagues for speaking out against "one of our own." The possibility of a defamation suit if charges prove unfounded could contribute to our hesitancy to take action. Many of us are reluctant to stand in judgment of others, particularly when we recognize our own fallibilities and when the situation is not blatantly unethical.

Consider what you might do in the following situation:

You become aware that a student intern in a counseling center has dated several of his clients. You and the student intern are in the same program and are serving as interns in the same center. Assume that you approach your colleague and inform him that you have heard from one of his former clients that they were involved in a sexual relationship. He tells you that he has no problem with this because both he and his client are consenting adults, and that because he is not a licensed professional he is not bound by a set of ethical codes. In essence, he informs you that you are interfering in his personal business. Where would you go from here?

It is difficult for professionals to take action against colleagues. However, despite our reluctance, we clearly have an ethical responsibility to take action when we have reason to believe that a colleague has or is engaging in sex with clients. In fact, to fail to do so is in itself an ethical violation. It may help to keep in mind that it is not our role to investigate, judge, or punish. These responsibilities belong to ethics committees, licensing boards, and the courts. It may also help to remember the effects that our actions can have on the clients who turn to us for help. The graduate student whose experiences we quoted earlier writes movingly about how she felt after she filed her complaints:

> Each time I communicated with. . . . a counseling official about my ethics complaints, I felt the weight of the harassment lift a little more. My concerns were taken seriously and addressed efficiently, and I was always treated with kindness and respect. In addition to easing my pain, my interactions with these counseling professionals allowed me to restore my faith in and respect for the profession. (Anonymous, 1991, p. 506)

SUMMARY AND CONCLUSIONS

Most helping professionals agree that sexual relationships with clients are one of the most serious types of all ethical violations. Virtually all professional codes of ethics prohibit sexual intimacies with clients. The effects of a sexual relationship can be profound for the client and the consequences can be severe for the counselor.

Although agreement is nearly universal that sexual relationships with current clients are unethical, there is no consensus of opinion about some other issues related to sexual relationships. For instance, there is disagreement as to whether sexual relationships with former clients are ever acceptable. Standards for some professionals have created a 2-year time period between the termination of the professional relationship and the beginning of a sexual one, whereas others have insisted that the professional relationship continues in perpetuity.

Sexual attraction to clients is not unethical, but acting on that attraction can create problems. It seems that this topic has not been fully addressed in counselor education programs and is deserving of more attention.

Of course, not all forms of unethical behavior are as blatant as sexual misconduct. And, as we suggested in chapter 1, not all dual relationships are harmful or exploitative. A wide range of issues present themselves in counselor preparation and in counseling practice in diverse settings. In part II of this book, we will focus on dual relationship issues in counselor preparation.

PART II:
ISSUES IN COUNSELOR PREPARATION

CHAPTER 3

COUNSELOR EDUCATION

Numerous dual relationship issues present themselves in counselor education. Some of them involve subtle and fairly controversial questions about where boundaries should be drawn when counselor educators play multiple roles and have multiple responsibilities with their students. In this chapter we explore dual relationship issues that commonly arise in counselor education programs and present the thoughts of three guest contributors: Holly Stadler and Arthur Lloyd offer contrasting views on counseling relationships between educators and students. Susan L. Naas presents a student perspective on the issues.

The focus questions that guide us through our discussion include the following:

- What guidance is offered by our codes of ethics? Do ethical standards conflict with each other? Are there also conflicts between ethical standards and preparation standards?

- How ethical or unethical is it for an educator to counsel a student?

- How can counselor educators avoid conflicts between their roles as educator and therapeutic agent in the classes they teach?

- How can counselor educators who also have private practices keep these roles separate? What are potential areas of conflict?

- Can some forms of dual relationships between professors and students be beneficial?

- How do students view the dual relationship issue? Do students and professors tend to agree or disagree?

- What are graduate programs doing to create policies or guide-lines regarding dual relationships?
- What is the responsibility of counselor educators in teaching students about dual relationships? How can the issues best be raised and explored, and how can students be prepared to deal with dual relationship dilemmas?

ETHICAL CODES AND PREPARATION STANDARDS

Section H (Preparation Standards) of the AACD *Ethical Standards* (1988) contains three standards that relate to the issue of dual relationships between professors and students. Standards H.12 and H.13 speak to the student's right to have personal growth experiences kept separate from graded experiences:

- Members must ensure that forms of learning focusing on self-understanding or growth are voluntary, or if required as part of the educational program, are made known to prospective students prior to entering the program. When the educational program offers a growth experience with an emphasis on self-disclosure or other relatively intimate or personal involvement, the member must have no administrative, supervisory, or evaluating authority regarding the participant.
- The member will at all times provide students with clear and equally acceptable alternatives for self-understanding or growth experiences. The member will assure students that they have a right to accept these alternatives without prejudice or penalty.

Standard H.5 addresses the counselor educator's responsibility to maintain professional standards and screen out inappropriate candidates for counseling degrees:

- Members, through continual student evaluation and appraisal, must be aware of the personal limitations of the learner that might impede future performance. The instructor must not only assist the learner in securing remedial assistance but also screen from the program those individuals who are unable to provide competent services.

Although we agree that student rights need to be protected and that faculty have a responsibility to the profession to graduate only those students who can provide competent counseling services, we also think these standards can actually compete with each other. Sometimes it is through a nongraded experiential component of a course that we become aware of personal problems or limitations of graduate students that are impeding their performance. It might be a dyadic practice session between two students, in which one is serving as the counselor and the other as the counselee, or it may occur in an experiential portion of a group counseling class. If we raise our concerns with these students in a way that leads to a negative evaluation or administrative action, we violate our ethical standard to keep such experiences nonevaluative. If we fail to raise the concerns, we may violate our responsibility to monitor the profession. This leaves counselor educators in a quandary.

Lloyd (1990) framed the issue as centering around the potential misuse of trust. He noted that counselor educators commit an ethical violation when they obtain information about a student from a counseling session, and then use that information to give a lower evaluation or deny admission or continuation in a program. He took issue with the AACD *Ethical Standards* (1988), which seem to prohibit counselor educators from even placing themselves in situations where there is an increased opportunity for misuse of trust. He stated that "This gray area (where the increased opportunity for the misuse of trust exists) may encompass much of the counselor education field. Teaching, supervision, and other faculty-directed student experiences all tend to be a combination of learning about oneself and at the same time being evaluated as a potential counselor" (pp. 85–86).

Like Lloyd, we also take exception to the wording of the AACD *Ethical Standards* (1988). We have trouble with the clause that self-understanding and growth experiences are voluntary. Sometimes such experiences are required, and in these cases we hope that a rationale is presented for them and that every attempt is made to enlist the voluntary participation of students. We do agree that personal growth aspects of a program should be made known to prospective students prior to their entrance into a program. In this way, if they do not like the total package, they are free to select another program.

We also have some difficulty with the last part of the standard (H. 12) that states that "the member must have no administrative, supervisory, or evaluating authority regarding the participant." Certainly, counselor educators wear more than one hat, and we have the challenge of knowing which hat we are wearing. We admit that there are serious potential problems in combining therapeutic roles with administrative or evaluative roles. Yet in most counselor education programs, it seems to us that there will be situations in which counselor educators are fulfilling dual or even multiple roles.

If we do not at least attempt to help students become aware of personal factors that could impede their functioning as counselors, we are neither doing them a service nor helping their future clients. As personal problems or limitations of students become evident, do we not have an ethical duty to encourage and even challenge them to face and deal with these issues, lest these issues impede the students' performance as helpers? If students who have unresolved personal issues or who hold rigid and dogmatic attitudes, values, or prejudices are allowed to graduate from our programs, can we say that we have kept the welfare of the consumer in mind? We think that programs should provide, as part of the curriculum, opportunities for students to examine their personal lives, with special emphasis on their needs, motivations, and life experiences that may impact their abilities to function effectively as practitioners. This point of view is supported by Council for Accreditation of Counseling and Related Educational Programs (CACREP) accreditation standards (1988) specifying that "Students have the opportunity to participate in workshops, seminars, or similar professional growth activities that enhance program requirements and facilitate students' personal and professional development."

CACREP standards also require students to complete a supervised practicum and internship in which students are expected to gain supervised experiences in individual and group counseling with clients. The practicum and internship require weekly individual and group supervision. The supervision sessions provide excellent opportunities for students to focus on their personal dynamics, including their strengths and weaknesses that are an integral part of their work with clients. It is hoped that these sessions encourage students to become aware of their role in the therapeutic relationship, especially of such factors as how their needs and potential countertransferences influence their counseling. Although these sessions should not be "therapy sessions," they can provide a balanced focus on both the client's dynamics and the student counselor's dynamics.

To summarize, we consider it essential that safeguards be built in to minimize the potential dangers that can result from certain types of dual relationships. As counselor educators, most of us challenge students to think about their personal lives and their values, and we also invite them to identify and explore a range of feelings. We perform multiple functions, and sometimes it is almost impossible to keep various roles neatly separated. Students have a right to know when there are potential problems. Furthermore, we think we ought to tell our students what we are doing to ensure that we are keeping their best interest and welfare in mind. We should talk about the procedures and practices we use to minimize the potential negative consequences of any dual relationships.

SHOULD A COUNSELOR EDUCATOR EVER COUNSEL A STUDENT?

This is one of the most controversial questions pertaining to dual role relationships of counselor educators. Some writers have very clear and definite positions on this matter. For instance, Stadler (1986) suggested that there are many negative repercussions from the practice of educators serving as counselors for their students. These repercussions include the following:

- *Effects on the student.* Students' autonomy may be compromised if they fear that an academic evaluation will be influenced by information divulged during counseling. Further, students who seek counseling from a faculty member are likely to assume that dual relationships are ethical and may go on to engage in those types of relationships when they enter the profession.

- *Effects on other students.* Assuming that students are aware that dual relationships in most cases violate ethical standards, they may lose respect for the counselor educator involved as well as the graduate program and a profession that appears to support unethical behavior. Further, resentment may build up with those who have not been singled out for what may appear to be a privileged relationship with a faculty person.

- *Effects on other faculty members.* Fellow counselor educators can be placed in the difficult position of having to either confront their colleague or condone this behavior.

- *Effects on the counseling profession.* Ethical violations are especially detrimental when violators are those responsible for the education of beginning professionals.

- *Effects on the counselor educator.* The faculty person who violates an ethical standard by engaging in dual relationships is also adversely effected. Dual relationships may lead to conflicts of interest that would otherwise not occur.

Although Stadler's position is clear, counselor educators in general seem to be divided over the issue of whether it is ever acceptable to counsel their students. Roberts, Murrell, Thomas, and Claxton (1982) found that 34% of counselor educators surveyed believed it was ethical for faculty members to have ongoing counseling relationships with students currently in their classes, and 56% believed it was ethical to have ongoing counseling relationships with students in their department who were not currently in their classes.

More recently, Borys (1988), in her dissertation study, obtained these findings:

- On the question of providing therapy to a current student or supervisee, 75% of the respondents to the ethics questionnaire reported the *belief* that this practice was either "never ethical" or "ethical under rare conditions," and 97% of respondents to the practice-form questionnaire reported that they engaged in this *practice* not at all or with only a few clients.

- On the question of allowing a client to enroll in one's class for a grade, 67% of respondents to the ethics questionnaire reported the *belief* that this practice was either "never ethical" or "ethical under rare conditions," and 97% of the practice-form respondents reported that they engaged in this *practice* not at all or with only a few clients.

When one of the coauthors (Corey) discussed this issue at faculty meetings at his institution, it became clear that faculty had diverse perspectives on this complex issue. He asked each faculty member to write a position statement regarding his or her stance. One of these is as follows:

> Professors should not solicit clients in their classes. If students come to me and want me to see them, I tell them about the ethical guidelines regarding dual relationships and explain the possible damage to them as a client. I refer them to counselors I know or the university counseling center.
>
> However, to say that no professor shall see any student in the department might not work. For example, a client was referred to me by a psychologist from a local hospital who got my name from a mutual colleague because I am experienced in a certain area. It just so happened that this client is also a student in our department who has never been in my classes. I told her I wouldn't

see her if she planned to take one of my classes. She chose to be my client instead. I do not see this as unethical.

Whether a student should see a professor once they've graduated to me is a clinical issue. It would be difficult to change relationships, but perhaps not impossible, depending on transference issues and student personality structure.

I personally don't think it is a good idea even to see the students' family as clients. I say things as a teacher that I would not say as a therapist.

Another faculty member took the position that it is important to maintain clear-cut boundaries:

I feel it is very important to maintain very clear-cut boundaries between instructor and student, therapist and client. I would be strongly opposed to crossing these boundaries, both ethically and therapeutically. The agendas would be different and confusing and would prompt numerous unanswered transference issues. However, I feel it is unrealistic to make a blanket statement that an instructor could not treat any students within the department, as this is beyond my control as it is for other instructors. . . .

Further, I encourage treatment for any students who require therapy and feel if they have confidence and comfort with their instructor, initiating or entering a therapeutic relationship would be appropriate, once termination from any of that instructor's courses has taken place. . . .

Obviously, there are numerous questions within the issue of counseling relationships between educators and students: whether a professor should ever counsel a current student, or counsel a student in the program or university who does not have a class with the professor, or counsel a former student. One variation that we have not yet explored is the situation in which a client later becomes a student. What if a student is first a client with a professor and then, at some later time, wants to take a class with this professor? This is a situation that may arise with some frequency in certain fields, such as substance abuse counseling in which many counselors are themselves recovering individuals. They receive counseling in the process of achieving sobriety and then go on to become counselors to others who are recovering. If their counselors are also involved in counselor education programs, there is a good chance that their paths will cross in the educational setting. Generally, in such cases we think that the best course for a student to follow is to take another professor for a class when possible. However, this alternative is not always feasible. This example shows that the matter is not always clear-cut.

⸻⸺⸻

Now that we have touched on a number of issues surrounding the question of whether counselor educators should counsel their students, we turn now to our first guest contributor.

Counseling Relationships Between Students and Educators

Holly A. Stadler

Codes of ethics can be useful action guides for the professional. However, they are not without myriad limitations (Mabe & Rollin, 1986). Although they offer guidance or proscribe certain activities, professionals may require further explanation and justification when trying to decide upon an ethically sensitive course of action. I have been asked to take a position and to uphold that position through ethical argument reflecting upon the dual relationship action guide as it relates to counselor educators counseling their students. Since I have undertaken this task elsewhere (Stadler, 1986), I will use this opportunity to draw on those earlier ideas and to expand the rationale for my contention that ". . . the dual relationship standard of ethical conduct can and should be used to set the boundaries of educational and supervisory relationships between students and counselor educators . . ." (p. 136).

I will begin my considerations by noting that some authors have established that educators think it is important to examine this type of dual relationship in counselor education. Then I will attempt to formulate an ethical justification for the prohibition of nonemergency, ongoing counseling relationships between educators and students. This justification ultimately hinges on defining the duties of counselors as opposed to those of counselor educators and the negative consequences of conflicts between those duties.

Educational Concerns. Engels, Wilborn, and Schneider (1990) have discussed the need for clarity about the types of relationships that are ethically appropriate between counselor educator and student. Such clarity is essential because ". . . counselor educators, unlike many other educators, are more often forced to confront the issue of how far to extend the boundaries of educational relationships to teach students the affective and cognitive components of counseling" (Stadler, 1986, p. 135). Although some counselor educators believe that educators may counsel students not currently in their classes (Roberts et al., 1982), others have noted problems with this practice. Patrick (1989) has identified the conflicts between the client welfare and client autonomy concerns of counselors and the screening and monitoring responsibilities of educators. Wise, Lowery, and Silverglade (1989), Keith- Spiegel and Koocher (1985), and Newman (1981) encourage referral of students or supervisees who might benefit from personal counseling.

Ethical Justification. The concerns of these authors can be framed within an ethical context because they appeal to considerations about what we ought to do or should do in human relationships. The considerations from an ethical standpoint become: What types of relationships ought counselor educators to have with students, and under what conditions should these relationships occur? With regard to the issues at hand, we can then ask: Are counseling relationships the type of relationships educators ought to have with students, and are there conditions that might confine such relationships? It might be tempting, after having framed this as an ethical dilemma, to dispatch further discussion with a simple statement of how something should be (e.g., that with certain exceptions, counselor educators should refrain from counseling students in their training programs). This is usually what codes of ethics are able to address. However, if we truly are to engage in moral reflection we must look beyond unidimensional responses and instead try to offer an argument that explains why this simple statement is a morally praiseworthy one that might be adopted as a standard policy in counselor education programs.

Duties of Counselors and Counselor Educators. Pellegrino has written extensively about professionalism in the health care arena (1983, 1984a, 1984b, 1985), and his ideas have relevance to counseling and to the position I am advocating here. He contends that professionals have special duties to their clients above and beyond duties they might have to others. These special duties are derived from the unique attributes of the interpersonal relationship between practitioners, counselors in our case, and those seeking their help. Because clients most often seek out counselors when they are in psychological need, clients find themselves, in a time of great vulnerability, dependent upon and trusting in the competence and integrity of a counselor before whom they must lay bare the most private and personal aspects of their lives if they are to be helped. They seek a "promise of help" while faced with their vulnerability. Pellegrino says that the special moral quality of the professional relationship is in the professional's declaration of willingness to help. If one chooses to profess a willingness to help and engages in relationships with clients in such circumstances, then one incurs certain obligations to any client, including those who might also be students. Among these are the obligations to make and keep the promise of help, to be trustworthy, and to act in the client's best interests. The last of these obligations is most relevant to my argument. If we look at our issue of students as clients of counselor educators, we note that student clients, like other clients, trust that their welfare is the highest priority in the counseling relationship. In the language of ethics: Except when their behavior is dangerous to others, clients trust that counselors will act in their welfare interests. Carl Rogers, among others, was of the belief that clients must trust that this is the case in order to derive benefit from counseling. Counselors work diligently to foster the conditions that lead to this trust. To encourage clients to disclose those personal and private aspects of their lives that house their pain, counselors place client welfare above other considerations. In our case, then, educator counselors like other counselors place student clients' welfare interests above other interests. However, there are other interests that educators confront that may conflict with student client interests. Later I will discuss what some of these other interests might be and the duties that attend those interests. To summarize my argument to this point: The special relationship between counselor and client, including educator counselors and student clients, undergirds the duty to act in the client's best interests that takes precedence over other duties and interests.

Let's turn to a discussion of the role of the counselor educator and the duties derived from that role: Educators in general have the responsibility to "inform and enlighten, to systematically cultivate the learning capacity within students" (Stadler, 1986). The National Education Association (1975) develops the notion of obligations to students by noting, "The educator therefore works to stimulate the spirit of inquiry, the acquisition of knowledge and understanding, and the formulation of worthy goals" (p. 1). In counselor education we meet these obligations through instructional and supervisory activities that further personal awareness, knowledge, and skills as the students develop their capacities to undertake various counselor roles and functions. Inherent in this obligation to students are activities such as monitoring and evaluating progress. In counselor education we are not only interested in students' cognitive abilities but also in their interpersonal skills. Most frequently we observe these abilities and skills in classroom and supervisory settings. Having made judgments about cognitive abilities and interpersonal skills, student remediation and termination may be obligatory components of the educator's duty.

In addition to student-related duties, educators in the professions have duties to the public and to their respective professions. The growing emphases on program accreditation and counselor credentialing are expressions of these duties in the counseling profession. So educators in the professions protect the public from the harm that might occur at the hands of unsafe practitioners. In counselor education we meet these obligations by thoughtful reflection upon the needs of a pluralistic society and the careful preparation and delivery of high-quality educational programs that address some of these societal needs.

We also screen out unfit applicants for admission, evaluate student progress and terminate students who might be harmful to clients, adhere to high standards for preparation of counselors, and support program accreditation and counselor credentialing. These measures also protect the reputation of the profession so that clients and potential clients may be encouraged to hold counselors in high regard and feel confident in seeking out their services.

Conflicting Duties. The preceding analysis leads to the conclusion that counselors and counselor educators have different duties. The duty of the counselor to act in the client's best interests is what I think most educators are drawn to when they offer or agree to requests to counsel students. I believe they downplay their role as educator in these situations when they think they can be of assistance to students in need. As educators they know that student welfare is important, but surely the preparation of competent counselors who can safely and skillfully serve the public and represent the profession well is at least of equal importance. Examining two scenarios of possible negative outcomes of educator/student counseling relationships highlights the inherent ethical inadvisability of pursuing options that involve conflicting obligations.

Consider the counselor educator who, while counseling with a student in a counselor education program, becomes aware of information that would negatively affect the student's progress, such as cheating on an exam, inappropriate sexual behavior with a client, or psychopathological manipulation. Clearly, this situation raises the issue of client interests in regard to confidentiality as well as in successfully completing his or her program of study and in receiving counseling from a counselor whose duties as an educator do not conflict with these interests. The primacy of these client interests may be called into question in a situation in which concern for public welfare is high.

In a second example, consider the student client who knows that the educator counselor may control or have input into his or her access to certain educational benefits such as graduation or letters of reference. Not being certain what might influence the educator counselor's decisions regarding these benefits, the wise and prudent student client will be circumspect in personal disclosures and would withhold certain information while a client of the educator. This kind of compromised relationship is not only therapeutically nonbeneficial but can also be harmful to the student client who could be receiving uncompromised services elsewhere. The short- and long-term effects of engaging in counseling relationships in which the full benefits cannot be obtained can have devastating effects on the psychological well-being of clients. One could argue that students are autonomous agents and ought to be free to decide about the relationships in which they engage. There is merit to this point, but this freedom does not require educator counselors to accede to student requests to involve themselves in counseling relationships of reduced benefit or potential harm.

With these issues in mind, the morally praiseworthy course of action for counselor educators who are aware of student counseling needs is to develop a list of well-regarded local counseling professionals to whom students can be referred for assistance. In this way students can receive the help they need from a counselor who is not concerned with also fulfilling duties as an educator. The potential negative outcomes for both student and educator are averted.

Gerald Corey's Commentary

Although I think that Holly Stadler makes some excellent points, I have trouble with what I consider to be some rather extreme prohibitions of any mixture of counseling and teaching roles and processes. First of all, I am generally in agreement with her stance that ongoing counseling relationships between educators and students are inappropriate and unethical. I am certainly not advocating that counselor educators get themselves into a position in which they accept current students as clients in their private practice of counseling. Doing so opens the door to many potential abuses. For instance, students can be exploited by professors for financial motives. Counselor educators could (though unethically) recruit clients from their classrooms. As a counselor educator, the professional often must make difficult decisions such as screening students for a graduate program or failing students who are not learning the material in a course. These decisions may not always be in the best interest of a given student. If this same professional is also the student's personal counselor, then real conflicts arise at times.

In my view, however, all dual relationships are not necessarily harmful. Most of us who are counselor educators teach courses that challenge our students to examine critically their values, attitudes, and life experiences. For example, in a multicultural course, students are likely to confront their own prejudices and cultural encapsulation. Learning about their own racist or sexist attitudes may be a jarring experience. A good multicultural counseling course can affect students emotionally as well as intellectually. Indeed, if they are open to questioning and open to learning about other world views, they might undergo therapy-like experiences. Thus, a counselor educator might well be helping students to challenge their beliefs, to identify and express their feelings in classroom discussions, and to change some of their dysfunctional behavior pertaining to dealing with people who are culturally different. Depending on the course we teach, we sometimes carry out therapeutic functions.

Elsewhere, Stadler (1986) said that counselor educators are sometimes forced to confront the issue of how far to extend the boundaries of educational relationships to teach students the affective and cognitive components of counseling. I agree with Stadler that there are difficulties in establishing clear boundaries between personal learning and academic learning. Perhaps the crux of the ethical dilemma

*of many dual relationships, especially in the area of counseling re-
lationships between students and educators, is in the potential for
harm to students and clients. Kitchener and Harding (1990) admitted
that there is a potential to misuse and abuse the power counselor
educators have when they also function as a student's personal
counselor on an ongoing basis. But Kitchener and Harding also spoke
about the possible benefits that might offset the potential risks. Students can benefit from a counseling relationship with one of their
former counselor educators. Once a course is over, and there is no
likelihood of having another course with a professor, is the student
free to request a therapy relationship with the former professor?
Students may well argue that they have the right to select a counselor
that they know and trust. The prior relationship as a student and
teacher may be the foundation for another professional relationship
at a later time.*

Barbara Herlihy's Commentary

*My thoughts sometimes converge with, and sometimes diverge
from, those of Holly Stadler as well as Gerald Corey. I agree with
Stadler's stance that prohibition of nonemergency, ongoing counseling relationships between educators and students is ethically justified. She does a superb job of explicating the point that counselor
educators who counsel students have conflicting duties.*

*I am reluctant to share Stadler's contention that the AACD ethical
standard on dual relationships can and should be used to set the
boundaries for the prohibition. I have trouble with its wording and
hope it will be revised. I think, rather, that the prohibition can be
justified on other grounds. First, it is justified on moral and ethical
grounds, as Stadler has argued so persuasively. Second, it seems
to me that the potential for harm is great since all three factors are
clearly present: the differences in expectations that are held about
a counseling relationship versus a student/professor relationship,
the divergence of responsibilities (or conflicting duties) between the
professor and the counselor roles, and the power differential between
professor and student. Finally, the prohibition is justifiable on practical grounds. This is one type of dual relationship that can be
avoided. Most universities that house counselor education programs
have a university counseling center to which students can be referred
for free or low-cost services. Perhaps I am fortunate in that I can
refer with complete confidence to my university's counseling center.
But even if that were not the case, there are other competent profes-*

sionals in the community. Even in a rural, isolated community it seems that there should be at least some referral sources available.

I agree with Corey's point about counseling relationships with former students. As a counselor educator who also has a private practice, I do not see this practice as problematic. Although it could be (and has been) argued that a counseling relationship never ends, the relationship between a student and professor does end when the student graduates. I think former students are free to seek counseling from any professional they know and trust, including former professors in their roles as private practitioners.

Although Corey makes a good point about multicultural and other such courses having a therapeutic impact, I think we can distinguish between the issues involved in the multiple functions performed by counselor educators in their instructional role and those issues inherent in playing the separate (and separable) roles of educator and counselor to the same student. A good multicultural course, or a well-taught experiential course, might well challenge students' beliefs and attitudes and have a therapeutic effect. In these cases, we are simply fulfilling our obligation as instructors to further student personal awareness, knowledge, and skills. The role blending that occurs within our instructional capacity is probably inevitable. However, an educator can avoid entering into an ongoing counseling relationship with a current student, and indeed ought to avoid doing so in all but emergency conditions.

Arthur Lloyd takes a view that contrasts from Stadler's on the issue of dual relationships between counselor educators and students. We turn now to his contribution.

Dual Relationship Problems in Counselor Education

Arthur P. Lloyd

During an unpleasant interval in U.S. history, individuals who held views similar to socialism were censured, black-listed, and labeled as *communists*. These individuals were denied work, slandered, and avoided simply because they held views that were unpopular at the time. The nation was "communist phobic," and this fear resulted in the misuse of power and the loss of due process rights for honest citizens. Many of these once-unpopular views, however, are now generally accepted.

The term *dual relationship* has become an emotionally charged concept in the counseling field. That which began as a reasonable caution for the helping professions—to avoid dual relationships that might impair objectivity—has now escalated to a central ethical problem to the extent that a "dual relationship phobia" seems to have developed in counselor education. The point that has been forgotten is "that dual relationships are not inherently unethical" (Haas & Malouf, 1989).

Trust and Responsibility. Trust is an essential part of the counseling process. Counselors agree that the misuse of trust violates the relationship and is unprofessional. Part of the trust relationship is the belief in the confidential nature of counseling and the belief that the counselor's first (highest) loyalty is to keep the client's conversations private. For most counselors, however, numerous other loyalties also exist. Laws, ethical standards, agency policies, and other mitigating circumstances all have some influence on the counselor's ability to honor the client's trust.

Few counselors are able to act independently in all situations with all clients. If a professional functions in an environment in which conflicting loyalties exist, however, the professional does not run away from the responsibility; the professional simply assumes responsibility for the complex, difficult situation and decides which choice needs to be made.

For example, according to the AACD *Ethical Standards* (1988), counselor educators "through continual student evaluation and appraisal, must be aware of the personal limitations of the learner that might impede future performance [and] . . . screen from the program those individuals who are unable to provide competent services." This responsibility of maintaining high standards for persons entering the profession is clear. If, however, as a function of being a mentor, adviser, or some other nonteaching role, the counselor educator receives information that indicates that the learner is not likely to become a proficient counselor, a conflict of interest has occurred.

Is that conflict of interest, though, truly harmful to the profession or to the student? Is discouraging a person from entering a profession for which he or she seems unsuited a misuse of trust, or would it rather be a misuse of trust to allow a person to continue spending his or her money and time when proficiency in developing the art of counseling seems unlikely?

Strict adherents to the AACD *Ethical Standards* (1988) will say that the counselor educator should not have allowed any other relationship with the student to occur. They will say that if the counselor educator is to be the person's teacher and evaluator, the counselor educator *must not* be the person's friend, mentor, colleague, or have any other relationship that *might* provide a conflict of interest.

This seems like a narrow interpretation. The question that should be asked is Will the multiple constituencies (institution, student, profession) be better served simply by avoiding the multiple relationships?

1. Is the profession better served by a counselor educator who makes decisions about students but does not really know the students outside the formal classroom?

2. Is the student who is relatively unknown to the counselor educator better served by progressing through a training program to enter a profession for which he or she may be ill-suited?

3. Is the student better served by being denied the opportunity to háve his or her counselor educator also as a friend or mentor, consequently enhancing his or her chances of developing as a professional?

4. Is the development of the counselor educator better served by hiding behind a "dual relationship sanction" and being denied the opportunity to be a multifaceted person with his or her students and colleagues?

Assuming Responsibility for Decisions. Counselor educators who are faced with conflicting information because of multiple roles are confronted with difficult decisions. "In fact, most ethical dilemmas do not lend themselves to simple solutions" (Corey & Corey, 1991). Whenever a judgment must be made, however, the fairness of the judgment is usually related to the amount of knowledge available and the ability of the person to evaluate the various elements fairly. At least that is the basis for some forms of counseling.

Why should counselor educators, and counselors in general, be allowed to avoid the struggle of making responsible decisions by hiding behind a prohibition concerning multidimensional relationships? Are counselor educators more likely to misuse the trust placed in them than the persons with whom the student will consult if the counselor educator denies the student the benefit of the counselor educator's wisdom?

According to existential thought, making decisions is a major part of our humanness; therefore, counselor educators should actively participate in this process. If the profession has something of value to offer, it is the ability to help in the process of making fair and just decisions. In fact, counselor educators should be placing themselves in the center of the decision-making process, not avoiding even the possibility of being confronted by conflicting information.

The dual relationship prohibition encourages counselor educators to choose ignorance about their students by denying students the opportunity through free choice to cross the boundaries established by titles, institutions, and ethical standards.

Interestingly, the ethical standards do not prohibit certain dual relationships when the consequences may be even more dramatic than simply being discouraged from pursuing training in counseling. Counselors have legal obligations concerning persons who are considering crimes, persons who are considering suicide, and persons who are involved in child abuse. The ethical standards allow these persons freedom of choice even though the counselor may eventually make a judgment to report the client to a legal officer. In the case of a student who may be judged as unsuited to the profession and may be excluded from graduate study, however, the counselor educator is prohibited from serving this student as a counselor, friend, or mentor and helping this person to make alternate choices.

Something seems very wrong with this. Counselor educators who do not want the responsibility of mediating tough decisions, and who are afraid that they might misuse the trust of the student, probably should avoid all situations where conflicting interests might exist. Some might question why these persons have entered counselor education in the first place. Their timidity, however, should not be imposed on the rest of the profession under the guise of ethical standards.

If some counselor educators are relationship-phobic, they should seek professional help. Their phobia should not be elevated to the level of an ethical standard, however, and imposed on all.

Dual Relationships Versus Demonstrating and Supervising. Dual relationship concerns, and certain other ethical standards, have negatively influenced the ability of counselor educators to provide the best training available. Students entering a counselor education program should expect that the most sophisticated teaching procedures will be used to prepare them as counselors. They should expect their professors to teach effectively and to provide each student with continuous feedback about progress and potential.

No single best model for teaching exists, but general agreement indicates that programs that include supervised experience, demonstrations, and opportunities for personal growth have merit. To deny students the opportunity to participate in training demonstrations and experiences with their instructors seems to violate the goal of providing the best preparation available. Yet individual and group counseling experiences and demonstrations have been identified as being in violation of ethical standards, if the participants are counselor educators and their students (Lloyd, 1990).

Some counselor educators may be nervous about providing live demonstrations, such as performing individual and group counseling demonstrations with their own students. These counselor educators may be hesitant to subject themselves to the close analysis of their graduate students. They may choose to use more structured, less personal ways of teaching the skills of counseling. These counselor educators should not, however, as a result of their own cautiousness be allowed to label counseling demonstrations and counseling experiences (provided by counselor educators for their students) as prima facie unethical, whether or not a misuse of trust has occurred.

The Counselor Education Environment. Counselor education is supposed to be a unique educational experience. An openness among faculty and students is supposed to exist in counselor education programs beyond that which exists in most other areas of higher education. Counselor education programs are similar to small communities in which all members have numerous opportunities for contact with each other (Haas & Malouf, 1989).

In an article concerning ethical considerations in small counseling centers, Keene (1990) stated that "on small campuses it is almost impossible for center staff not to engage in dual relationships without hiding behind one's office door." As an even smaller part of the campus and with student expectations for sharing and disclosing frequently similar to those of a counseling center, the problem of avoiding dual relationships is even more difficult in a counselor education program.

Conclusions. Counselor education is a unique part of the counseling profession. Counselor education has been given the responsibility for selecting and preparing the best counselors available. It is the laboratory for training, demonstrating, and experimenting. The survival of the counseling profession is dependent upon counselor education programs being free to provide the best procedures in existence to produce the highest quality professionals possible.

The AACD *Ethical Standards* (1988) should be rewritten to handle the unique needs of counselor education training programs. The standards should be rewritten to allow the following:

1. The acceptance of friendships and collegial relationships between counselor educators and students while still maintaining student/teacher standards
2. The encouragement of individual and group demonstrations with clients and students as an expected part of teaching (Pierce & Baldwin, 1990)
3. The use of supervision models that employ a counseling relationship between the supervisee and the supervisor (Bernard, 1979).

Gerald Corey's Commentary

I particularly like Arthur Lloyd's points that dual relationships do not necessarily impair objectivity and that they are not always inherently unethical. Although much has been written about the dangers of dual relationships, not much has been written about the potential advantages of such relationships. Lloyd raises some excellent questions that help us think through the issue of whether students are better served by avoiding all forms of multiple relationships. Indeed, counselor educators should accept the challenge of struggling with making responsible and independent ethical decisions rather than retreating to the security of a blanket prohibition against all multidimensional relationships.

I agree with Arthur Lloyd's view that counselor educators owe their students the best opportunities for training. Students can learn a great deal from the modeling of professors who are willing to take the risks involved in performing individual and group demonstrations with their own students. Certainly there are cautions that need to be exercised, and professors have a serious responsibility to avoid misusing the trust and power they possess.

If any kind of personal demonstrations are prohibited in counselor education classes on the grounds that this puts the professor and the students in a dual relationship, then I wonder what the professor does during class time. Are professors to limit their interaction with students to lecturing and discussion methods? Should this form of education be restricted to content and to the cognitive domain alone? Although the potential for abuse and exploitation is inherent when counselor educators are involved in multidimensional roles, there are consequences from a learning perspective when educators maintain a strict adherence to functioning exclusively within the role of educator.

Barbara Herlihy's Commentary

I question Arthur Lloyd's contention that counselor educators have become "dual relationship phobic." My own perception is that as awareness of issues in nonsexual dual relationships has increased, there is debate that includes some point/counterpoint, but I question whether participants in the debate have "forgotten" that dual relationships are not inherently unethical. Rather, I see counselor educators working to distinguish between those dual relationships that are facilitative to student growth and those that hold a significant potential for harming students.

Now, having suggested that Lloyd overstates his point, let me add that I agree with some of what he writes. I concur with his assertion that as counselor educators, we cannot and should not duck our responsibilities both to provide the best possible training and to discourage students from continuing in our programs when they are deficient in skills or ability. I agree that good teaching often involves live demonstrations.

However, I do not believe that a counselor educator can be friends with students. Friendship is by definition a peer relationship, and the evaluation and power differential inherent in the student-professor relationship preclude a peer relationship. I recognize that in many counselor education programs, particularly doctoral programs, social relationships between students and professors are much the norm. Issues raised during a class session are often continued over a cup of coffee after class, and I have no problem with counselor educators being available to students beyond class time and structured office hours. I do think it is unwise for counselor educators to attend parties with students on a purely social basis or to enter into dating rela-

tionships; and I think we delude ourselves when we believe we can be students' friends. Perhaps I can clarify by example: A counselor educator is very involved in athletics. She frequently attends sports events and works out in the gym with a small group of graduate students who share her interest. Other students in the program are quite convinced, despite any real evidence, that the professor gives better grades to these students who socialize with her.

I appreciate Lloyd's perspective, even while taking issue with much of it. On the one hand, I think Lloyd reminds us that we lose something important in our relationships with students if we become phobic, rigid, and overly dogmatic in our adherence to codes. On the other hand, I believe that there are—and should be—some limitations to these relationships.

***

A spectrum of viewpoints has been presented on the issue of dual relationships between counselor educators and students. Where do you stand on these issues? Do you find the diversity of opinions to be thought provoking? With what points do you agree, and with what points do you take issue?

Before moving on to other issues, we want to explore further a question that is closely related to our guest contributors' comments. That question is How can counselor educators avoid conflicts between their roles as educator and therapeutic agent in the classes they teach?

If we are teaching counseling courses, we are likely to be therapeutic agents at times; but this does not mean that we become therapists to our students. However, a course well taught often involves challenging students to examine their needs and motivations for even getting involved in a graduate program in counseling. Educators worth their salt will do their best to encourage their students to explore how their countertransference might negatively impact their work as counselors, or how their own unresolved personal problems might interfere with their work as counselors. Even though educators are not serving as therapists to their students, a good course might have much of the same impact as a therapy experience.

Role conflicts are most likely to arise in experiential courses. As Patrick (1989) has noted, experiential training has long been recognized as a necessary component of counselor education. The laboratory model usually includes the teaching of specific counseling skills with the student participating in exercises designed to promote the acquisition of these skills. Feedback and evaluation are provided to help students achieve mastery. Problems arise when the professor becomes aware of personality traits in a student that he or she believes will interfere with the student's ability to function as a counselor. Patrick suggested that informed consent is crucial: Students must know clearly and in advance whether information revealed in practice sessions will be used to evaluate their ability to be a counselor.

The issue of conflicting demands within laboratory training experiences emerges in bold relief when one considers how to best teach a group counseling course. Because this issue has generated a substantial amount of debate among counselor educators who teach group counseling courses, we devote a separate chapter (chapter 4) to issues in the preparation of group counselors.

To summarize, a key to avoiding conflicts between the roles of educator and therapeutic agent, from our perspective, is to be very clear about our primary function in our classes. Although we draw upon our knowledge and skills as therapists to help us in carrying out our tasks as counselor educators, it is essential that we keep our main purposes clearly in mind.

COUNSELOR EDUCATORS IN PRIVATE PRACTICE

How can counselor educators who also have private practices keep these roles separate? What are potential areas of conflict?

It is unethical for faculty members who have private practices to use their classes as a forum to announce, recruit, or solicit potential clients from these classes. Indeed, most of the ethical codes warn against the potential abuse involved in using our institutional affiliation to foster our financial interests in our private practice. Three examples of such codes are as follows:

- It is unethical to use one's institutional affiliation to recruit clients for one's private practice. (AACD, 1988)

- Mental health counselors are discouraged from deliberate attempts to utilize one's institutional affiliation to recruit clients for one's private practice. Mental health counselors are to refrain from offering their services in the private sector, when they are employed by an institution in which this is prohibited by stated policies reflecting conditions for employment. (American Mental Health Counselors Association [AMHCA], 1987)

- It is inappropriate to solicit members from a class (or institutional affiliation) for one's private counseling or therapeutic groups. (Association for Specialists in Group Work [ASGW], 1989)

Although blatant recruiting efforts are clear ethical violations, we also need to be careful of indirect and subtle solicitation. In this regard, in keeping with the spirit of the above codes, it is a prudent measure to have separate professional cards for one's private practice and for one's institutional (teaching) affiliation. Despite such safeguards, however, difficulties can arise in subtle ways. Consider the following example:

> Marilyn teaches one course (counseling techniques) in a graduate counseling program and is a licensed counselor in private practice. Marilyn draws from her clinical experience as she teaches students about applications of various counseling techniques, and she demonstrates brief individual counseling sessions using volunteers from the class. Her students have high regard for her and value her practical slant. Several of her students have sought her out for therapy in her private practice. Marilyn makes it a policy not to accept a student as a client, but she is willing to consider accepting students in her private practice once they finish the course. She is careful not to promote her private practice in her class. She expects to teach only this one course, so her students will not have her again as an instructor.

> Her department chairperson expresses his concern about accepting former students as clients. He tells her, "Even though I know that you are not recruiting students for your clients, it think it is very difficult for students to shift roles from student to client. Also, I think we need to be careful about the appearance of a conflict of interest. So I strongly prefer that you refer to other therapists any potential clients who have been in your class."

- What are your thoughts about this situation? Are you more inclined to defend Marilyn's position or that of the department chairperson?

- If you are a student in a counselor education program, do you see risks to yourself if you were a client in a counselor educator's private practice and at the same time were a student of that professor? What if you wanted to become a client of a former professor? Do these risks outweigh a desire you might have to seek counseling from a professor whom you know and trust?

BENEFICIAL ASPECTS OF DUAL RELATIONSHIPS

Can some forms of dual relationships between professors and students be beneficial? The mentoring relationship between professor and student stands out as one type of dual relationship that is not necessarily harmful. In fact, such relationships are often seen as good learning opportunities (Kitchener & Harding, 1990). For example, Corey has had positive experiences with mentoring. His experiences with James, his first mentee, showed him the value of such relationships. When James was enrolled in an undergraduate human services program, he asked Corey to serve as his mentor. While James was a student, he enrolled in several courses with Corey and assumed leadership in accompanying Corey to various community colleges to recruit students for the program. At various times during the relationship, Corey carried out the roles of teacher, supervisor, confidant, evaluator, and adviser to James. James is now employed at a community college where he works with minority students and is seeking admission to a graduate program. They maintain regular contact and their relationship is collegial.

Mentors become the mentee's adviser, confidant, friend, teacher, supervisor—and there are possibilities that the mentee can benefit a great deal from this special relationship. For such relationships to work as they are intended, it is essential that the professor and student talk openly before engaging in them to determine whether the benefits outweigh the risks and to establish clear guidelines for proceeding.

Some counselor educators work in small graduate programs with a limited number of faculty. In these situations it is likely that one professor might serve in a number of roles with a given student: as academic adviser, as instructor in both didactic and experiential coursework, as sponsor of a project or thesis, and as supervisor of the student's practicum or internship. There are some real advantages to the close working relationship that can develop, so long as the professor remains aware of the appropriate boundaries of the various roles and communicates them clearly to the student.

THE STUDENT PERSPECTIVE

How do students view dual relationship issues in counselor education? In raising questions for discussion in our ethics classes, we typically find that students have not given a great deal of thought to the many types of nonsexual dual relationships. Because we are interested in the student perspective and in seeing how student and professor viewpoints compare, we have collected some data. The ACES Ethics Interest Network is planning to survey the membership regarding their opinions of seven scenarios that describe a wide variety of actual or potential dual relationships. With its permission, during the spring of 1991, we distributed the scenarios to a small sample of graduate students (201) from various areas of the country and collected the reponses of 20 professors to the same scenarios.

These preliminary data serve as a beginning point for addressing our questions. Susan Naas has collated and analyzed the responses, and in her paper that follows, she describes the results and presents a student's perspective.

Dual Relationships: A Student Perspective

Susan L. Naas

In a recent survey, graduate students and counselor educators from a cross-section of universities in different regions of the United States were asked to read seven dual-relationship scenarios and to rate them on the following scale:

0: no violation

1: a minor violation, calling for a reprimand and corrective action by the AACD Ethics Committee

2: a moderately serious violation, which would lead the committee to suspend membership for a period of time and place the member on probation

3: a very serious violation, warranting permanent expulsion of the member from AACD.

The results of the responses from 201 graduate students and 20 counselor educators are summarized in Table 1.

- **Scenario 1—a professor and graduate student working on a project together.** The student is asked by his major professor to assist in research for a manuscript to be written by the professor. The student ends up doing most of the work after the professor unexpectedly becomes distracted by other duties. The professor prepares the manuscript and submits it with herself as the sole author, acknowledging the student only in a postscript. The student is left feeling exploited.

The majority of the students (48%) believed only a minor violation had occurred. Interestingly, about equal percentages of students saw no violation (24%) as saw a moderately serious violation (23%). The spread of these responses may correlate to students' professional goals: Students who want to publish may see the violation as more serious. When I discussed this scenario with fellow students, several who saw no violation stated that the student should have been honored and pleased to accept any kind of recognition from the professor. Many of those who rated the violation as moderately serious reported that the professor should have given coauthorship to the student or at the very least acknowledged him as a contributing author.

It concerns me that 80% of the counselor educators believed either no violation or only a minor violation had occurred. Without the encouragement and support of these role models, how will students who want to make a contribution through writing have an opportunity to learn from those with the experience?

- **Scenario 2—a dating relationship between a professor and a student.** In this scenario, a counseling professor is

Table 1
Scenario Ratings

Scenario	No violation (0)		Minor violation (1)		Moderately serious violation (2)		Very serious violation (3)	
	% of students	% of counselor educators	% of students	% of counselor educators	% of students	% of counselor educators	% of students	% of counselor educators
1	24	30	48	50	23	10	4	10
2	22	10	33	40	38	25	7	20
3	24	25	56	55	18	20	3	0
4	48	25	42	45	8	25	3	5
5	2	5	13	5	32	25	53	65
6	62	60	23	30	12	5	2	5
7	44	60	35	35	16	5	3	0

attracted to one of his students. They are both unmarried and in their late 30s. The professor refrains from asking the student out until the semester is over, then they become involved in a mutually agreeable relationship. The professor is also the student's adviser and will be the student's internship supervisor the next semester because he is the only professor scheduled to supervise that internship.

The majority of the students (71%) felt that either a minor or moderately serious violation had occurred, and 65% of the counselor educators agreed. Some of the students who viewed this as a nonviolation indicated that because the professor was no longer the student's classroom instructor it was appropriate for them to date. Other students noted that the professor was the student's adviser and that alone constituted a dual relationship. More counselor educators than students saw this as a very serious violation, indicating that these counselor educators strongly believed that a professor and student should not have a romantic and/or sexual relationship while the student is in the program, regardless of whether the student is currently taking a class from the professor.

I believe that a professor has the responsibility to avoid a romantic relationship with anyone in the program. Counselor educators have a power differential over students, and students who are vulnerable may not have the ego strength to avoid such a relationship.

- **Scenario 3—a practicum supervisor's concern over a student counselor's poor work.** The student's poor work with practicum clients is a result of some unresolved personal issues facing the student. Once the personal concerns are discovered, supervision focuses on the student's personal issues for the remainder of the semester.

The majority of the students (56%) felt that only a minor violation had occurred, whereas 24% said no violation had occurred and 18% saw a moderately serious violation. The counselor educators concurred with the students across the continuum. The widespread ratings given to this scenario may indicate that there is confusion as to the role of the supervisor when supervisee self-disclosure and personal growth are involved. From the students' perspective, they might hesitate to be open for fear of being judged negatively by the supervisor. In addition, it is an ethical responsibility for counselor educators to see that students who are not emotionally ready to work as counselors are not permitted to complete the program without remediation. One student colleague told me that it was correct for the professor to recommend counseling, but it was not his task to be the counselor. She went on to say that if the professor provided personal counseling instead of supervision, at the end of practicum the student might be emotionally healthy but an ineffective counselor due to lack of supervision. My viewpoint is that it is our responsibility as students to be professional and willing to process our own unfinished business before we can be effective helping professionals. Counselors cannot help clients work through issues that they have not been willing to work on for themselves.

- **Scenario 4—grading in a group counseling class that includes an experiential group activity.** A student does B work on exams and other graded assignments but excels in group leadership. The professor gives the student an A in the course even though the syllabus indicates that group participation will not be graded.

Most of the student sample group (90%) rated this scenario as no violation or only a minor one. Some of my fellow students thought that the student in the scenario deserved to receive credit for her group performance. Others felt that the syllabus should have been changed only after a consensus vote by the class that would have effected the students collectively. The range of responses from professors leads me to wonder whether there is confusion among counselor educators as to how to evaluate group counseling courses and the purpose of training groups in the educational process.

- **Scenario 5—a sexual dual relationship.** A doctoral student attends a national convention at his professor's invitation so that he can assist her in presenting a workshop. During the convention, the professor and student enter into a sexual relationship. Upon returning to campus, the professor tells the student that the interlude was a mistake and they should both act as if it never happened.

Most of the students (85%) believed this was a moderately serious or very serious violation. Discussion with fellow students revealed that most of them believed the professor took advantage of the student because of the power differential. They also said that the violation was heightened by asking the student to forget the interlude ever happened. Surprisingly, 15% of the students felt that either no violation or only a minor violation had occurred. They reasoned that consenting adults can do whatever they choose. The response of the counselor educators was similar to that of the students in that 90% said the interlude was either a moderately serious or very serious violation.

- **Scenario 6—professor and student roles in an introductory skill-building course.** Students practice together in dyads. During review of an audiotape intended to evaluate the student "counselor's" skill development, the professor hears the student "client" reveal some personal problems that leads him to question whether the student should be pursuing a degree in counseling at this time. The professor discusses this concern with the student.

The majority of the responses from the students (85%) and from the professors (90%) stated that no violation or only a minor violation had occurred. Student discussion in reference to this vignette was diverse. Some thought the professor had overstepped his boundaries, but others believed the professor was correct in discussing his concern with the student client. I suspect that some students rated this scenario as serious because it is threatening to them: Either they have been unwilling to work on personal issues or they are concerned that their self-disclosure will be closely scrutinized by the professor and used against them. This vignette raises a real dilemma because the student is encouraged to self-disclose; but what if self-disclosure involves unresolved issues that may detract from the student becoming an effective counselor? How helpful is it for the student to go through the program and get to practicum or internship, and then during evaluation find out that remediation is necessary? By the time students get to practicum, they are seeing "real" clients. Who is it going to serve if the student counselor breaks down while with a client because he or she becomes overwhelmed by countertransference issues?

- **Scenario 7—bartering.** A counselor seeking her state licensure contracts with a supervisor who agrees to provide supervision for $40 an hour. When the supervisee later en-

counters some financial difficulties, they change their contract to an arrangement in which the supervisee provides
typing services in lieu of the fee.

The majority of both students (79%) and counselor educators
(95%) believed that no violation or only a minor violation had occurred. Although bartering is not explicitly prohibited by some
ethical codes, I think the supervisee is in danger of being exploited
here. Because typing is not worth $40 an hour, the arrangement
could evolve into a kind of indentured servitude. It also puts the
supervisor in a precarious position. What if the typing is not up
to the supervisor's standards? Can the supervisor be objective
when it comes time for evaluation?

One or more of these scenarios may seem familiar whether you
are a student or a counselor educator. I would like to thank Barbara Herlihy—with whom I have a beneficial dual relationship as
she is my adviser, major professor, and collaborator on this section of the book—for this valuable learning experience. There are
circumstances, such as this project, where it is beneficial to have
a dual relationship in the process of educating counselors. As
just demonstrated, however, there is much confusion and difference of opinion within our profession as to the role of dual relationships between counselor educators and students. It is my
intention, through this position paper, to generate thought and
conversation as to what we as professionals—both students and
educators—can do to improve our profession and maintain a level
of ethical professionalism that our clients and all who observe us
may model.

Gerald Corey's Commentary

*Like Susan Naas, I am surprised by some of the ratings by both
students and counselor educators. For example, in Scenario 1, most
of the respondents thought that either no violation or only a minor
violation had occurred in the case of the graduate student and professor who were involved in a joint writing project. The fact is that
the student did most of the work on the manuscript, yet the professor
claimed sole authorship. Not only did the professor exploit the student, but she also was dishonest.*

In the second scenario, Naas points out the reality that counselor educators have power over students, which makes romantic and sexual relationships inappropriate and unethical. It is this potential misuse of power that makes many forms of dual relationships problematic. It is the responsibility of counselor education programs to increase the awareness of students about the potential dangers of dual relationships. First, however, counselor educators themselves must be aware of and sensitive to the potential hazards and imbalances of power in educational and therapeutic relationships.

I fully agree with Naas when she contends that students have the responsibility to recognize and work through their own unfinished business that might block their effectiveness as helping professionals. Donigian (1991) rightly has stressed that a consumer's trust in the profession is violated if the counselor is not psychologically prepared for the rigors of the work. The data that Naas reported indicate that more clarity is needed as to the proper focus of supervision. When personal problems of students are identified, students have the responsibility to take steps to resolve their problems so that they do not project their conflicts onto their future clients. Counselor educators also have responsibilities both to the students and to future clients of these students. Although I do not see it as the job of supervisors and counselor educators to provide therapy for their supervisees and students, they do have a key role in challenging and supporting students to get the professional help they may need.

In Scenario 4 most students (90%) saw no violation or only a minor violation in the case of the professor who used a group experience as a basis for increasing a student's grade. First, I have trouble with using participation in an experiential group as a basis for a letter grade. But more importantly, the professor's behavior was inconsistent with the policy stated in the syllabus. Ethically, students have a right to expect that professors will follow through with what is written in the syllabus, and not doing so erodes the basis for trust. In the next chapter, I describe in greater detail my philosophy pertaining to teaching and evaluating group counseling courses.

I took the inventory under discussion myself, and I had difficulty with the stipulations that accompanied some of the rankings, such as "reprimand and corrective actions," or "permanent expulsion from AACD." The choices might been more simply stated as "no violation," "minor violation," etc. I administered this inventory to my ethics class and found that they also had some problems with the way the choices were presented. Nevertheless, the inventory did create some healthy exchanges in class, and it is a useful discussion tool. As Susan Naas indicates, I agree that the results add some weight to the argument that the topic of dual relationships deserves a central place in various courses in counselor education programs. The responses of the students on several scenarios indicate that they are unaware of some of the problematic aspects of certain dual relationships.

Barbara Herlihy's Commentary

Although the results of the survey that Naas reports are preliminary, they do illustrate the lack of consensus regarding a variety of dual relationship issues. Like Naas, I find some of the results distressing. I agree with her and with Corey that the professor in the first scenario (who allowed a student to do most of the work on a manuscript and then took full credit for it) exploited the student's eagerness to make a contribution. I, too, am surprised that 80% of the counselor educators who responded saw this as no violation or only a minor violation. Can the pressure to "publish or perish" be so strong that some counselor educators are willing to overlook their ethical responsibility to credit students' work? Or is there simply a prevailing expectation that student assistance in research projects— no matter how extensive—is to remain largely hidden from public view while professors take the credit? It appears that students may have this expectation because the majority of them (72%) also saw no violation or only a minor violation.

Naas expresses concern regarding respondents' reactions to other scenarios. In Scenario 5, a sexual liaison between a professor and student was rated as a "very serious" violation by only 65% of the counselor educators. I wonder whether those who responded differently were aware of the applicability of "patient/therapist sex syndrome" to sexual relationships between students and professors. The student in the scenario, who was told by the professor after they returned from the convention to "act as if it never happened," might well have felt denigrated and exploited.

Similarly, the results in the seventh scenario about a bartering arrangement surprised me. Sixty percent of the counselor educators saw no ethical violation when a supervisee arranged to provide typing services in lieu of a fee for supervision. Naas highlights some problems that could arise. What if the typing services were not adequate? What if the supervisee fell further and further behind in the amount owed because an hour of typing is unlikely to be of equal value to an hour of supervision?

With respect to Corey's commentary, I certainly agree with his conclusions. The division of opinion does add weight to our contention *that dual relationship issues need to be more fully addressed in counselor education programs. I can also see how Corey had some difficulty with the stipulations that accompanied the rankings. They do seem somewhat arbitrary, although they are based on the sanctions available to the AACD Ethics Committee. However, I think they serve the purpose of reminding us that ethical violations do carry consequences.*

- If you are a student in a counselor education program, what are your reactions to Susan Naas' opinions and to the data she presents? Does this sample of students represent your views? In what ways do you agree or disagree with Naas' statements?

POLICIES AND GUIDELINES

Given the controversy surrounding dual relationships between educators and students, we became interested in learning what graduate programs are doing to create policies or guidelines regarding this issue. Corey's interest stemmed from the fact that many of the instructors who teach in his program are part-time instructors (teaching one or two courses) who are employed full time by community agencies as counselors, social workers, or marriage and family therapists or who are engaged in private practice. When he began investigating what other programs have done to create policies or guidelines about dual relationships, he found little in the way of written policies. In fact, in researching this topic he concluded that most programs in his area were silent on these matters. He was told by some that the issues are so complex that it was best not to open up the matter for discussion. Some simply said that no formal policies or guidelines were available, but they expected the faculty to adhere to the ethical codes of their professional organizations. With this as a background, he plowed ahead with his attempts to forge a written policy that could provide clear guidelines for faculty who were considering the matter of accepting either current or former students as clients. He found a great deal of diversity among his colleagues and considerable opposition to the idea of developing a written policy with "teeth."

TEACHING STUDENTS ABOUT
DUAL RELATIONSHIPS

We conclude this chapter with a look at the issue of preparation of future counselors: What is the responsibility of counselor educators in teaching students about dual relationships? How can the issues best be raised and explored, and how can students be prepared to deal with dual relationship dilemmas?

In the ethics courses we teach, we spend considerable time discussing dual relationships. Our students show a great deal of interest in discussing the issues: Many of them have never really considered the potential risks or benefits of dual relationships, so the discussions serve to increase their awareness of potential ethical dilemmas. We examine dual relationship standards contained in the codes of ethics of the various professional organizations. We use case vignettes to introduce core ethical dilemmas, frequently role playing a vignette and then discussing possible courses of action. Students are encouraged to think about their values as these pertain to a host of dual relationship issues. The combination of reading codes and articles, enacting case situations, participating in debates, and being challenged to defend a position typically results in an increased awareness of the pervasiveness of dual relationships. Students begin to develop a sensitivity to the subtlety and complexity of the topic.

Borys and Pope (1989) developed a list of implications for the education and training of helping professionals. They asserted that through careful attention to program planning and evaluation, students could be helped to increase their sensitivity to dual relationships that are unethical and harmful. Their recommendations for training programs include the following:

- Programs should present literature in which the nature, causes, and consequences of dual relationships are explored.

- The ethical and clinical implications of both sexual and nonsexual dual relationships need to be reflected in virtually all clinical coursework, supervision, and other forms of education.

- There is a need for clear and explicit institutional standards regarding potential dual relationships between students and educators.
- There is a need for written, operationally defined procedures for avoiding conflicts of interest in monitoring and enforcing the institutional standards regarding dual relationships.

We concur with these recommendations and add the following specific points:

- When counselor education programs include a separate ethics course, ample time should be devoted to critical ex-aminination of dual relationship issues, both sexual and nonsexual.
- In all clinical coursework and coursework containing experiential components, the relevant dual relationship issues should be specified at the outset and carefully worked through as they occur on a case-by-case basis. The individual and group supervision sessions required by CACREP are an ideal place to deal with real-life dilemmas pertaining to the dual relationship issues that are bound to surface during students' practicums and internships.
- Because there is some reason to question the adequacy of counselor educators' training in ethics (Stadler & Paul, 1986) and their level of familiarity and comfort with ethical standards (Roberts et al., 1982), renewed emphasis should be given to professional development workshops on dual relationship issues.
- The heart of the matter, as Williams (1990) noted, is that actions speak louder than words: "By observational learning, counselor trainees learn to behave according to the conduct of professional role models. Therefore, it behooves counselor educators and supervisors to model what constitutes ethical behavior" (p. 113).

Thus the key to fostering ethical management of dual relationship issues lies in our own behavior. If we are unaware of the potential problems, we are likely to find ourselves involved in relationships that are harmful to both student and professor. If we—and our students—are clearly aware of the potential for conflict of interest, for being exploited, or for misusing power, then there are avenues to prevent these situations from happening.

CHAPTER 4

PREPARATION OF GROUP COUNSELORS

This chapter, which extends our discussion of dual relationship issues in counselor education, focuses specifically on the training of group counselors. We have devoted a separate chapter to this topic because there is considerable controversy regarding not only the ethical guidelines that apply to group work educators but also the question of how group counseling courses should be taught.

Most group work educators agree that there is a need for an experiential component in a group counseling course to assist students in acquiring the skills necessary to function as effective group leaders. It is common practice to combine the didactic and experiential aspects of learning. Yet there does not appear to be agreement on the goals for these experiences or on how students can best be evaluated (Forester-Miller & Duncan, 1990). Faculty who teach group courses often function in multiple roles as group facilitator, teacher, evaluator, and supervisor. In teaching the group courses, there is often a blending of educational and therapeutic roles and functions. Thus, there is the issue of potential dual role conflicts when instructors who teach group courses also provide an experiential dimension that focuses on self-awareness and self-exploration.

Questions addressed in this chapter include the following:

- What conflicts exist regarding dual relationships in codes of ethics and preparation standards? How can these conflicts be resolved?
- How can students' rights to privacy be protected in experiential coursework involving self-disclosure?
- How can group counseling skills best be evaluated?
- What are some ways to teach group counseling courses?

Several guest contributors present their views. George M. Gazda discusses some distinctions that can be drawn between *education* and *therapy* in group counseling courses. Holly Forester-Miller takes the position that counselor educators have an ethical obligation to require students to participate in a group counseling experience. Gerald Corey and George Williams present two models for teaching group counseling courses. Finally, George M. Gazda offers a commentary on issues raised in the chapter.

CODES OF ETHICS AND PREPARATION STANDARDS

The AACD *Ethical Standards* (1988) contain several statements in Section H (Preparation Standards) that are applicable to the teaching of group counseling. Although we have discussed some of these standards as they apply to counselor education in general, (in chapter 3), we repeat them here to frame our discussion of issues in preparing group counselors:

- Members in charge of learning experiences must establish programs that integrate academic study and supervised practice.

- Members, through continual student evaluation and appraisal, must be aware of the personal limitations of the learner that might impede future performance. The instructor must not only assist the learner in securing remedial assistance but also screen from the program those individuals who are unable to provide competent services.

- Members must ensure that forms of learning focusing on self-understanding or growth are voluntary, or if required as part of the educational program, are made known to prospective students prior to entering the program. When the educational program offers a growth experience with an emphasis on self-disclosure or other relatively intimate or personal involvement, the member must have no administrative, supervisory, or evaluating authority over the participant.

- The member will at all times provide students with clear and equally acceptable alternatives for self-understanding or growth experiences. The member will assure students that they have a right to accept these alternatives without prejudice or penalty.

The ASGW *Ethical Guidelines for Group Counselors* (1989) contain an explicit statement in the "dual relationships" section regarding the teaching of group counseling courses:

- Students who participate in a group as a partial course requirement for a group course are not evaluated for an academic
  grade based upon their degree of participation as a member in
  a group. Instructors of group counseling courses take steps to
  minimize the possible negative impact on students when they
  participate in a group course by separating course grades from
  participation in the group and by allowing students to decide
  what issues to explore and when to stop.

The preparation standards of the Council for Accreditation of Counseling and Related Educational Programs (1988) offer this guideline to counselor educators:

- During their programs, students are provided the opportunity
  to participate in a planned and supervised small group activity
  designed to promote and improve students' self-understanding,
  self-analysis skills, and interpersonal skills. The activity is NOT
  used or intended to provide "counseling" or therapy for
  students. . . .

The ASGW (1991) training standards state that core competencies should be obtained through satisfactory completion of a basic course in group theory and practice and through participating in a planned and supervised group experience. The implementation guidelines specify articulation of the ASGW standards with the CACREP standards that pertain to group work. The ASGW stan- dards specify that the planned group experience should conform not only to CACREP standards but should also be harmonious with the AACD and ASGW ethical standards about dual relationships.

Specialists in group work have identified conflicts within and among ethical codes and preparation standards. They disagree about how these conflicts might best be resolved. Some writers take the position that counselor educators must adhere to stated prohi- bitions against dual relationships, whereas others argue for chang- ing the standards to acknowledge and support counselor educators in fulfilling the multiple roles inherent in teaching group counseling.

Lloyd (1990) has pointed out that apparent conflicts between the ethical codes and the CACREP standards create an ethical dilemma for instructors of group counseling courses. He noted that counselor educators are required to offer a group activity to promote student self-understanding, self-analysis skills, and interpersonal skills but are not to provide their students with counseling in the process, which would create an unethical dual relationship. To help resolve the problem, he proposed (1) that operational definitions of *group activity* and *counseling* be clarified in the standards, (2) that the profession determine whether counselor educators who provide group activities for their students are involved in unethical dual relationships or whether these practices should be exempted, or (3) that CACREP standards clarify that group activities should be provided by a person who does not have supervisory, administrative, or evaluative authority over the students.

In the following statement, George M. Gazda offers a classification scheme that addresses the first of Lloyd's concerns: the need for operational definitions. He suggests that distinctions can be drawn between *education* and *therapy* in counselor education programs.

Dual Relationships in Teaching Group Counseling Courses

George M. Gazda

One of the primary obstacles facing the various professional societies that are attempting to develop guidelines for training and practice of group workers is the problem of deciding whether or not certain group procedures, such as T-groups and encounter groups, should be classified as *education* or as *therapy*. Considerably different conditions currently govern these different classifications. I am inclined to decide the issue based on the degree to which the goals for the individuals in a given group include self-disclosure in the affective domain. Based on my model for group procedures, only instructional, guidance, social/life skills training, and the traditional T-groups are clearly in the realm of education. All other groups are, in varying degrees, classified as therapeutic in intent and are therefore subject to ethical standards governing those in the helping professions. That is, in my classification scheme, all groups that involve remediation or rehabilitation are classified as therapy groups. Within this broad classification, however, different standards are recommended for training based upon the degree of responsibility that a given leader may have to assume for a given client. The greater the responsibility assumed, the greater the need for intensive training.

One needs to be mindful of the pertinent distinctions between therapy and training. Therapy focuses on pathology, aiming toward its resolution. Protection and freedom to explore private and subjective aspects of adjustment are indispensable to the objective of gaining health through the resolution or correction of defect. Not so with training. Fundamentally, training starts with a healthy individual and aims towards increments in diagnostic sensitivity and social skills of the kind that can increase personal effectiveness in group decision-making situations. Revelation, exposure, and confidences are inconsistent with the objectives of such training. It is up to the trainer, operating under his or her particular code of ethics, to make distinctions between training and therapy and keep the two separate based on the distinguishing characteristics of each. A trainer acting as a therapist with the same students he or she trains is essentially instigating and perpetuating a dual relationship.

Gerald Corey's Commentary

George Gazda urges us to be mindful of the pertinent distinctions between therapy and training, which I see as the core of his position statement. I think that group counselor educators have a responsibility to discuss some of the factors that differentiate a training group from a therapy group.

Recently I received a copy of guidelines for instructors who teach group therapy classes for the Graduate School of Education and Psychology at Pepperdine University. The guidelines for instructors emphasize the value of orienting students to the nature of experiential learning in a group process course. At the initial class meeting instructors present an Informed Consent Statement, which outlines the benefits and risks of participating in an experiential group. Course grades are based on lectures and discussions, but not on the experiential group. Instructors are expected to explain to the class members the goals of the experiential group and to clarify the differences between therapy and training. Students are involved in discussing and clarifying training goals that guide their participation in the group.

Gazda's point is well taken that trainers need to make distinctions between training and therapy, and need to keep them separate based on the distinguishing characteristics of each. The problem arises in actual practice when trying to make clear distinctions between training and therapy because there is some overlap.

The guidelines used by Pepperdine University state that experiential training is clearly a legitimate form of education about group process. This kind of training requires students to involve themselves in more active and personal ways than is generally true of cognitively focused and didactic learning. Experiential training and learning often involve role playing, skills training, giving and receiving interpersonal feedback, self-disclosure in the here-and-now, and interpersonal communication. The group process format often has therapeutic effects, even though it is not the aim to provide therapy. In a group process context, students are given opportunities to identify and express their feelings: They are able to clarify and challenge their beliefs and values, and they can examine their thinking and feeling patterns. The experiential group can serve as an interpersonal laboratory in which members can gain awareness of how they impact others. The interpersonal focus in these groups is based on a social microcosm view—that we can learn a great deal about how others affect us and how we affect others outside of the group by paying attention to what is going on inside the group. Thus, the group experience provides members with opportunities to view themselves as others do and to decide for themselves ways that they may want to change any patterns of thinking, feeling, and acting.

In contrast to training groups, therapy groups have different aims and often differ with respect to intensity of self-exploration, depth, techniques utilized, and the nature of the relationships among members and between the leader and the members. In Gazda's classification scheme, therapy groups involve remediation or rehabilitation; the focus is often on pathology with the aim of resolving personal problems. The guidelines for instructors at Pepperdine University indicate that it is easy for a group process format to turn into group therapy, and instructors of group course are cautioned to exert special care not to cross the line between experiential learning and therapy. Pepperdine's guidelines specify some areas that would be inappropriate for training groups: pressuring members to reveal embarrassing personal material; systematically attempting to dismantle defenses of members; engaging in interpretations designed to uncover unconscious conflicts, motives, or attitudes; utilizing techniques to treat emotional problems such as phobias, depression, and eating disorders; and attempting to work through deep-seated problems stemming from childhood traumas. Rightly, the Pepperdine guidelines encourage instructors to meet individually with those students who appear to need therapy and help them to find appropriate professional help outside of the training group.

In summary, it is often difficult to draw clear distinctions between what goes on in experiential training groups and in therapy groups. Although each group has different aims and often employs different techniques, the nature of the group process overlaps. Instructors/trainers need to monitor themselves by keeping the purpose of the group clearly in mind, and they also need to teach students how to make these distinctions. The two separate domains of training groups and therapy groups can be clarified through ongoing reflection and discussion.

Barbara Herlihy's Commentary

George Gazda draws some useful distinctions between education and therapy. His definition of training certainly applies to the participants in and the goals of a T-group. T-groups, or experiential components of a group counseling class, are composed of basically healthy individuals, and their purpose is to increase students' diagnostic sensitivity and social skills that will make them more effective group leaders.

Gazda seems to suggest that these training groups are exempt from the ethical guidelines that have created such a controversy. He suggests that other groups are "subject to ethical standards governing those in the helping professions." If this interpretation were accepted, the controversy regarding the group work educator's adherence to ethical guidelines would be resolved.

However, I question Gazda's suggestion that "revelation, exposure, and confidences are inconsistent with the objectives of such training." If T-groups are—as some of our literature suggests—a microcosm of the larger, outside world, then self-disclosures and the working through of some personal concerns are part of the T-group experience as they are in an "outside" group. If T-group participants are restricted from making revelations and sharing confidences, I think the result will be a stilted and artificial experience. I cannot see how students will learn what they need to know about dealing with the personal concerns and self-disclosures of clients in groups they will lead in the future. Yet, Gazda's point is well taken that T-groups are not intended to provide therapy. Because I do not draw the distinctions as clearly as Gazda does, I continue to struggle, in *teaching group counseling courses, with exactly where to draw the line between therapy and training.*

***

THE TRAINING DILEMMA:
VIEWPOINTS AND POSSIBLE SOLUTIONS

Some writers have taken exception to the seemingly restrictive nature of existing ethical guidelines pertaining to the dual role relationships of faculty persons who include experiential learning in their group counseling courses. Williams (1990) disagreed with the literal interpretation of the AACD guideline that seems to prohibit offering a group experience involving personal disclosures and involvement when the leader has administrative, supervisory, or evaluative authority over the participants. He maintained that counselor educators serve as role models to their students by participating in the various roles of teacher, supervisor, and group leader.

Other writers have suggested different solutions to the dual relationship dilemma in teaching group counseling. Donigian (1991) suggested that the ASGW standards should be revised. He asserted that ethical codes seem more concerned with protecting the student than the consumer of counseling services, and as the codes are currently written they can be used to excuse counselor educators from exercising their responsibility to evaluate students' emotional and psychological readiness to enter the profession. He stated that it may be necessary to "reassess our current ethical code and accept the fact that the risk of the dual relationship may be far less than the risk of placing ill-prepared counselors in the field" (p. 7).

Gumaer and Martin (1990) agreed with Donigian to some extent:

> Most counselor educators will admit that students who are regularly maladaptive or exhibit personal issues that inappropriately affect their clients can be potentially harmful counselors. This issue has been studiously avoided in the proliferation of ethical guidelines among the counseling professions. (p. 99)

Yet Gumaer and Martin also believed it is imperative that students who participate in group activities as part of a course not be evaluated academically for performance or participation in the activities.

Pierce and Baldwin (1990) viewed the dilemma as one of participation versus privacy. To ensure student privacy, counselor educators could comply with some ethical standards by not evaluating student participation in groups. However, to comply with other standards, counselor educators have to know students well enough to ensure that they are able to provide competent service or else remove them from the program.

Dye, in an interview conducted by DeLucia (1991) on perspectives on the field of group work, maintained that the AACD ethical codes pertaining to dual relationships are vague and desperately need revision. Dye alluded to the restrictions on being someone's friend and professor at the same time. He added, "You can't conduct any kind of group course in which students are graded because group experience requires disclosure, and when people are encouraged and/or even allowed to disclose, it is then unethical to be in an evaluative relationship" (DeLucia, 1991, p. 71). According to Dye, in the fields of training group workers and counseling supervision, dual role relationships between supervisors and graduate students are inevitable. For example, in supervising students in practicum, it is difficult to differentiate precisely between a trainee's personal life and how he or she is functioning with a client. Dye believed that we do not have good definitions of the parameters or the limits of relationships between educators/supervisors and students/trainees.

Clearly, the question of how to best prepare students to be effective group counselors is complex and controversial. Pierce and Baldwin (1990) reviewed options such as eliminating group counseling courses from counselor education programs, arranging for groups to be led by professionals who are not on the counselor education faculty, relying on role playing in the group experience, and structuring the group experience to limit student participation and self-disclosure to immediate here-and-now experiencing. They found these options to be an unacceptable abdication of the counselor educator's responsibility for assessing student competence. They offered a nine-step plan that both requires student participation and includes safeguards to protect student privacy.

Holly Forester-Miller agrees that it would be unethical and inappropriate to send group counselors into the field without a required group experience. In the following position paper, she presents a rationale for this requirement and offers several guidelines for providing such an experience.

Dual Relationships in Teaching Group Counseling

Holly Forester-Miller

In the past, counselor educators have debated whether it was ethical and/or appropriate to require students to participate in an experiential group as part of their training in group counseling. The current literature indicates that a group experience is an essential component of training group counselors (Corey & Corey, 1992; Forester-Miller & Duncan, 1990; Yalom, 1985). The Association for Specialists in Group Work concurs that it is an important aspect of training. The revised *Professional Standards for the Training of Group Workers* (ASGW, 1991) state "The practice domain should include observation and participation in a group experience, which could occur in a classroom group" (p. 5). It is apparent, because a group experience is such a necessary component of training, that it would be unethical and inappropriate to send group counselors out into the field without this very important part of training.

In teaching individual counseling skills, we demonstrate and role play counseling situations for our students. They also practice their skills on each other, for several reasons. First, it gives them a "safe" place to practice. Second, they can give each other valuable feedback based on their counseling knowledge. Third, it gives them the opportunity to experience the counseling process from the client's perspective. These same reasons are relevant to the practice of group counseling skills. In group counseling the process and dynamics are very different from individual counseling, and skills are of no value if the counselor does not understand the process and dynamics that are occurring. Students can read about group process, but until they experience it, I do not believe they can fully understand it. Students have told me time and again that they thought they understood what the book was saying about the stages of a group but that it was so different actually to watch the process occur in our personal growth group. This is especially true of the dynamics that occur during the stage we refer to as the transition or storming stage. For example, it is extremely helpful for students to see the leadership being challenged, to observe the nondefensive response of an experienced leader, and to be able to discuss that experience with the leader.

If the medical profession sent surgeons out to practice surgery who had only read about operations or seen videos, but who had never participated in a "real" surgical procedure, would we be willing to let one of those surgeons operate on us? It seems to me that, analogously, it is our ethical obligation to require students to participate in a group counseling experience. It is no longer a matter of *whether* it is appropriate. The question now is *how* this group experience can be offered in a way that is ethical and appropriate.

The personal growth group and/or training group experience built into group counseling courses is very different from a therapy group. The main differences lie in the intensity of the experience and the depth of sharing on the members' parts. Yet the stages of group and the leadership issues at each stage remain the same, thus offering a wonderful learning opportunity while minimizing the risks to the students. Keeping the grading process separate from the level of participation in the group removes a major source of risk to the students. As long as counselor educators do the proper planning for the group experience and, as with any group, design the experience always keeping in mind the purpose and objectives of the group, the risks of the dual relationship will be low.

Forester-Miller and Duncan (1990) recommended several guidelines and conditions under which the risks to students are minimized. Several that apply here and have not already been mentioned are (1) that the personal growth experience not be related to the process of program screening, whether for admission or for continuing in the program; (2) that students be evaluated only on their level of group skill acquisition; and (3) that students not be allowed to lead a group of their peers without the professional responsible for the group being present.

In addition to offering guidelines, we also provide four alternatives for providing a group experience to students that meet the conditions we suggest:

1. Having the master's-level group experience led by post-master's students under faculty supervision
2. Having the instructor lead or co-lead the group, but utilizing a blind grading system for assessing the students' learning and skill acquisition

3. Requiring that the students participate in a counseling group that is external to the academic setting
4. Having the instructor lead the group with the students utilizing the role-play technique.

These are all viable options open to the counselor educator who teaches group counseling. The one I prefer is to lead the group and utilize a blind grading system. This approach offers several benefits to the students. One major benefit is to experience the "real" thing firsthand, to be able to see the group process at work and at the same time experience it from the perspective of the client. This method also allows the students the opportunity to try on the leadership role in an ongoing group with the faculty member present to offer assistance and feedback. It provides the students with an effective leader role model in which the faculty member can feel confident of the skill level being demonstrated and the types of techniques being modeled. It also provides a common experience for the students and instructor to utilize in discussing group process and giving examples. This method provides a potentially unique experience for students by allowing them to see the faculty utilizing the skills and applying the strategies that have been discussed.

The benefits of such an experience certainly outweigh the risks, especially if the faculty member has planned the experience to minimize the risks. It seems to me that we owe it to our students and to their future clients to provide the best training possible, utilizing the most effective teaching methods available. Therefore, not offering a group counseling experience as part of group counselor training would be neglectful and unethical. Some dual relationships are not only ethical but beneficial.

Gerald Corey's Commentary

Forester-Miller focuses on a central issue in emphasizing the need for counselor educators to plan a group experience carefully, keeping in mind the main purposes and objectives of the group. If this planning is done and certain guidelines are followed, not only are the risks of dual relationships relatively low, but there are also benefits that outweigh the risks. As teachers of group counseling courses, we certainly need to be aware of the potential problems that stem from combining didactic and experiential approaches. Yet, as Forester-Miller implies, we ought not to be governed by a rigid rule against all dual relationships.

I applaud her stance that "not offering a group counseling experience as part of group counselor training would be neglectful and unethical." I would add that the crux of the matter is not the methods we use in teaching the group course, or even the structure used. Instead, the integrity, competence, and professionalism of the counselor educator are the best measures to prevent potential abuses that might be a part of dual relationships.

Barbara Herlihy's Commentary

My views are very similar to those of Holly Forester-Miller. It is difficult for me to imagine how students could learn group counseling skills without having the opportunity to practice those skills in a safe, supervised environment.

As a counselor educator who regularly teaches a group counseling course, I have struggled for years with the question of how to provide the best possible learning experience for students in the most ethical way. It is not difficult to keep grading separate from the experiential component of the course. In the program where I teach, we have implemented Forester-Miller's suggested policy that students' participation in the training group is not evaluated either as part of their grade or for admission or retention purposes. Students can clearly see that this policy exists by reading the student handbook and the course syllabus. However, I think it is important to respect that we ask a great deal of students when we ask them to trust that these procedures will in fact be followed and to act on that trust when they choose to self-disclose during the group experience. For the course instructor to violate that trust would be inexcusable. This underscores Corey's point that the integrity of the counselor educator is at the crux of the issue.

In her position paper, Forester-Miller suggests that having advanced students (rather than the course instructor) lead the group experience is one acceptable alternative to the dual relationship dilemma. It seems to us that this solution may create a different dual relationship concern. Consider the following vignette:

> As part of a master's degree training program for group counselors, students work under supervision facilitating an experiential group for the introductory course in counseling taken by all students in the program. Students who are just beginning their coursework are also required to enroll in a section of a self-exploration group as part of the introductory course. Some of them are wondering about the ethics of having other students in the role of facilitator. They oppose the idea of being expected to self-disclose in a group setting with student leaders, even though they are under supervision of a faculty person. The complaining students think that this is a dual relationship issue because their student leaders are enrolled in the same program.

- What do you think about the practice of using students to facilitate self-awareness groups for other students, assuming they are given adequate supervision?
- What potential dual relationship issues, if any, can you see? What safeguards can you suggest to protect both the student facilitator and the students who are members of such a group?
- If this group were conducted by a faculty member who teaches the groups course (and who is likely to have the students in his or her future classes), what issues need to be addressed?

No solution seems to be free of drawbacks. Because the questions involved in how to teach a group counseling course are so complex and controversial, we include in this chapter two models for teaching these courses. Gerald Corey describes an undergraduate course that he teaches. Then George Williams describes how he organizes and teaches a two-course sequence in the graduate program. Corey and Williams each present their viewpoints on the dual relationship issues that arise in teaching these courses.

The Teaching of a Group Counseling Course and the Training of Group Leaders

Gerald Corey

One of the undergraduate courses I regularly teach is Practicum in Group Leadership (see Corey, 1981). This course is taught in such a manner that students get a balanced experience of didactic material on group process and theories of group, opportunities to lead and co-lead self-directed groups in which they can apply what they are learning, supervised experience in group leadership, experiential learning involving working on their own personal issues in a group, and supervision sessions that are therapeutic as well as educational. Thus, in a single course the students are exposed to a variety of ways of learning about groups, both cognitive and experiential. I cite this class as an example of the many group leadership courses that typically combine academic learning with opportunities for personal learning.

Briefly, I will highlight some of the essential features of Practicum in Group Leadership, which is an undergraduate elective course in the Human Services Program at California State University, Fullerton. First, students are screened both individually and in a small group before they are allowed to enroll in the course. The course involves supervised experience in co-leading a group-oriented class on the campus. Students in the course meet for weekly supervision as a group with the faculty member who supervises their work as co-leaders. In addition, the students meet with me twice a week for regular class sessions. On Tuesdays there is a didactic focus: a short lecture on group process issues or consideration of a specific theory of group work as well as a demonstration group that I lead to illustrate the practice of a particular theoretical orientation. On Thursdays the class is divided into two groups of 12, each with an experiential focus. The students co-lead this group for the first 45 minutes of the session, which is followed by 30 minutes of processing time with a supervisor. Another faculty member assists me in supervising these Thursday groups. Although these groups remain the same for the semester, the other supervisor and I alternate with the supervision of these groups.

In addition to the regular class meetings twice a week, and the one time each week that they meet for group supervision with another supervisor, this class begins with a 3-day training and supervision workshop during the first weekend of the semester.

This residential workshop consists of many opportunities for the students to function as group members and as co-leaders of their own small group during the weekend. There are five other faculty members who function as supervisors during this weekend. Before the students enroll in this weekend workshop, they are informed of the nature, purpose, and structure of the class. They do get involved in self-exploration and in dealing with interpersonal issues that emerge in the group process. They each have two opportunities to co-lead their group during the weekend, and each of these sessions is directly supervised. The students co-lead for the first 45 minutes to an hour, and the next 45 minutes are devoted to discussion of group process with the supervisor of that particular session. (For additional details and a description of this weekend workshop, see Corey and Corey, 1986.)

At this point, let me explore what I see as some major ethical considerations in teaching this group course and briefly describe some of the safeguards I have developed to lessen the chances of negative outcomes. As I mentioned, students are screened prior to enrollment in the course. There is also a 4-hour premeeting (as a class) during the semester previous to enrollment. This meeting is held toward the end of each semester and provides detailed information to the students as to what they can expect to learn and what will be expected of them as participants. If they determine that they do not want to participate as a member of a group as well as learn about group facilitation, they are free not to enroll in the course. This is a measure to ensure informed consent. Students are given a detailed syllabus and are prepared for the weekend workshop and all of the academic and personal requirements associated with the course.

At this premeeting I discuss with the students some of the problems inherent in this course that combines both academic and personal learning. They are cautioned that the experience of leading groups, even under supervision, often touches them in personal ways and brings to the surface their own personal conflicts and struggles. They are also informed about the basis for grading and evaluation. For example, the weekend workshop is a credit/no credit course, and they are not graded in any way on the quality of their participation either as a group leader or as a member of their group. The Practicum in Group Leadership course is a graded one, and again their participation in their group as a member or as a leader is not a criterion for determining the grade. Two major papers and an objective final examination are the criteria for assigning the course grade.

One way many educators attempt to minimize the conflict entailed in being both a professor and a counselor is to avoid grading students on their participation in the experiential activities that are part of the course. This practice is consistent with the ASGW (1989) guidelines. In group courses that have an experiential component, I fully endorse the principle of not putting students in a bind by using their participation in the group as a factor in determining the course grade.

There are a number of factors in the design of this course that reduce the chances of students being harmed by the experience. These measures include the following:

- The screening, selection, orientation, and preparation process results in students who have a clear idea of the nature and requirements of the group leadership course they are considering. The premeeting is particularly useful in helping the students become acquainted with one another as well as become oriented to this form of experiential learning.
- The fact that this course is an elective allows for a more intensive learning experience than if it were required. Students take this kind of group course because they are genuinely interested in learning more about themselves as well as learning skills in facilitating a group.
- The fact that other professionals besides myself serve as supervisors for both the weekend workshop and also the entire semester offers students diverse perspectives on group process and leadership styles.
- Students in the course are informed that they can decide for themselves the nature and extent of their self-disclosure in the group. In fact, the focus of these groups is often on here-and-now interactions within the group context rather than an exploration of outside concerns of the participants. They have plenty to explore in reference to dealing with one another as they build a cohesive learning group, and therefore, it is not necessary that they delve into their "personal secrets."
- The basic rationale of the course is presented and clarified from the outset of the course. The assumption the course is built upon is that the best way to learn about group process is to participate in the group and learn firsthand about issues such as the creation of trust, dealing with conflicts, and challenging one's resistances. There is an integration

of conceptual learning about groups and the learning that grows out of actually experiencing a group and then focusing on key issues for discussion as they emerge in the learning group.

In examining the ethics of requiring group participation for students in a group counseling class, another question should be asked: Is it ethical for group leaders to consider themselves qualified to lead groups if they have never been group members themselves? I strongly endorse participation in a group as part of a leader's training. Learning from books and lectures is important but has its limitations; certain skills can be learned only through experimentation. Struggling with trusting a group of strangers, risking vulnerability, receiving genuine support from others, feeling joy and closeness, and being confronted are all vital learning experiences for future group leaders. If for no reason other than because it provides a deep understanding of what clients face in groups, I think that group experience for leaders is indispensable.

Certainly in a single group course there are many demands on both the students and the professor. It is not easy to focus on cognitive material at times, then focus on the anxiety of co-leading a group, and then at other times focus on personal exploration. Perhaps the greatest challenge is providing a balance between the focus on self-learnings and the focus on what makes a group work.

Dual Relationship Issues in Teaching a Group Leadership Course

George T. Williams

Most graduate-level programs in counseling and many undergraduate programs in psychology or a related human services field have a specific group course as part of the curriculum. A typical question among counselor educators is: What are the potential dual role conflicts for the instructors teaching the group counseling courses? Many counselor training programs are separating the small group experience from courses in group counseling and group process by either relegating responsibility to someone not employed as a full-time faculty or by separating students' course grades from participation in the group. In this paper, I present some of the major dual relationship ethical dilemmas I perceive to be inherent in teaching master's-level group leadership courses that are designed for the training and supervision of group leaders while using a combination of didactic and experiential components.

The master's-level graduate program in counseling at California State University, Fullerton, includes two required group courses: Counseling 519, Therapeutic Group Experience, a one-credit course; and Counseling 528, Groups: Process and Practice, a three-credit course. Each of these courses will be discussed in reference to the controversial issue of dual relationships.

Counseling 519, Therapeutic Group Experience, is an experiential group class that is designed to enhance a learning and self-development process for counseling students. The focus of the group is one of personal growth and increasing self-awareness as a counselor-in-training. The course typically is taken by students during their first semester of enrollment in the graduate counseling program and requires students to experience being a member of a group with approximately 16 students. Counseling 519 includes two major parts. The first part includes the group experience itself. Group therapists who are not full-time faculty in the department are hired to lead these groups, which are held over a 2-day weekend.

The second part of Counseling 519 requires students to write a paper that relates their course group experience to the assigned readings about group process and practice. Final course grades are determined exclusively by students' final written papers about their group experience, submitted after the group counseling experience. In an attempt to avoid bias in grading, all papers are identified by confidential code numbers to maintain student anonymity and are evaluated by a faculty member who is not the group leader for the class. Students are instructed not to break any confidentialities and to maintain the anonymity of group members and their group leader while writing their papers.

The other course, Counseling 528, is limited to 16 students. The course includes focused attention on the issue of how students can best learn group leadership skills and theoretical knowledge as well as acquire an increased awareness of themselves. The course is structured like the practicum course in group leadership described earlier by Corey, and the training/supervision workshop described by Corey and Corey (1986) in that "participants [students] acquire or refine group leadership skills by participating in a small group as both a member and a leader at different times" (p. 18). The major goals of this course are (a) to provide master's-level students with supervised group-leading skills training and theoretical knowledge pertaining to those skills and (b) to assist students in developing an increased awareness of themselves as group leaders and persons. Although the Counseling 519 course focuses on the student being a member of a group, the primary focus of Counseling 528 is for students to practice group leading skills. Students practice group leading skills from 10 different theoretical approaches to group work, and they also learn more about themselves as persons and develop their own integrated eclectic model for working with groups. The Counseling 528 class is structured so that the instructor functions in multiple professional roles including teacher, supervisor, evaluator, and group leader at times.

I disagree with the literal interpretation of the AACD ethical standard that prohibits members from having supervisory or evaluating authority over participants in a growth experience with an emphasis on self-disclosure or personal involvement. I believe counselor educators serve as role models to their students by participating in the various roles as teacher, supervisor, and group leader. It seems that the AACD and CACREP standards need to follow the leadership of ASGW in determining guidelines for dual relationships when training group leaders. The conflict among the AACD standards, the ASGW ethical guidelines, and the CACREP standards needs resolution for consistency in determining what constitute professional standards for the training of group counselors.

I am convinced of the benefits of the course instructor functioning in certain multiple roles. Hiring group leaders who are not full-time faculty at the institution to teach a class such as Counseling 519 serves the intended purpose of students learning more about group process and being a member of a group. However, Counseling 528, in which students are focused more on learning skills about how to apply different theoretical approaches to leading a group, requires that the course instructor function in multiple roles as teacher, supervisor, evaluator, and group leader. One might argue the benefits of hiring an outside faculty for teaching Counseling 528 as with the Counseling 519 class to handle the dual role conflict. But aren't full-time counselor educators hired to train students to become both individual and group counselors? I find it interesting that no questions seem to be raised regarding small group practicum classes in which the counselor educator serves multiple roles while supervising students to become individual counselors.

I do not believe counselor educators should be restricted from teaching group counseling courses just as I do not believe they should be restricted from supervising a group practicum class that focuses on individual and/or group counseling skills. One might argue that full-time faculty can teach group courses *as long as* they are not involved in any small group counseling experience. Such a response I believe limits the potential learning for students with such a class structure. The process of learning how to lead a group requires that there be a group of people with whom to practice the skills. From a perspective of logistics, it makes sense to have students learn their group leading skills by serving both as leader and member.

One might argue that it would be better to protect the students' privacy by not having them serve as members of the group where there is a focus on learning group leading skills. Such a stance may suggest having students lead groups containing members who are not students enrolled in the graduate counseling program. Does a faculty member have the time to directly observe and supervise so many different groups? I think not. I also believe this approach to avoiding dual relationships has other limitations. For example, there exists the potential risk of "doing harm." Important philosophical and moral questions need to be addressed: Should the course instructor enforce the principle of beneficence (i.e., acting in a proactive way to "do good") by removing a student from the class and the academic degree program in order to protect future clients from potential harm that is likely to be done by the student? Or should the instructor enforce the principle of nonmaleficence (i.e., the rule of "do no harm") and respect the student's integrity and personal privacy by not sharing with the student or others any concerns about the student (Beauchamp & Childress, 1983)? To answer these questions requires a value judgment. My bias weighs more heavily with the principle of beneficence, which I view as relating closely to the issue of screening for the profession. With respect to the AACD standards, I question how a counselor educator is to "screen from the program those individuals who are unable to provide competent services" without knowing more about the students than their academic performance. I believe the personhood of the counselor is one of the most important attributes for the professional counselor "to provide competent services." There have been instances in observing the in-class groups when I felt ethically obligated to refer a class member for outside professional help. However, I did not withdraw the student from the class. I believe that withdrawing a student under these circumstances could be emotionally damaging for the individual as well as damaging to the cohesion and trust of the group.

In conclusion, I concur with Lloyd (1990) who stated that "The ethical issue with dual relationships concerns the misuse of trust" (p. 85). I also agree with Lloyd's (1990) statement that "live demonstrations of counseling, role playing counseling skills, and numerous opportunities for self-disclosure are an omnipresent part of a counselor education program" (p. 86). The term *dual relationships* has received negative reactions among counselor educators and in the professional literature. I do not believe that all dual relationships in the teaching of a group leadership course have harmful effects on the student or the counseling profession. Perhaps a more appropriate term to convey what is damaging would be *exploitative dual relationships*. It seems that the rigidity of accreditation ethical standards has taken away some of the humanness.

<hr/>

Questions surrounding the preparation of group counselors are indeed complex. In the following commentary, George M. Gazda offers his response to some of the issues that have been discussed in this chapter.

Commentary on Dual Relationship Issues in Preparing Group Counselors

George M. Gazda

The issue is not whether or not students/trainees should be provided a "group" experience. Everyone agrees that they should. I do not think that one can always clearly differentiate one group from another in practice. There will always be some overlapping in practice between counseling/therapy and education/training groups. All the more reason to avoid the probability of this happening by not placing the leader and trainees in an experiential group in the beginning! The issue is who should provide this experiential part of their training in order to avoid unethical dual relationships. Dual relationships are either ethical or unethical. One cannot have it both ways, i.e., ethical for counselor educators and unethical for others. To conclude that "it is not difficult to keep grading separate from the experiential component of the course" and "participation is not evaluated either as part of their grade or for admission or retention purposes" is to raise the question, How does one protect the public if the information gleaned is not utilized? And Herlihy, Corey, Forester-Miller, Donigian, and Williams all have taken the position that they do it to protect the public from incompetent group counselors/leaders. If evaluations and screening/retention decisions are not being made based on these required class/group experiences, how can these same teachers protect the public? Are we to conclude that they know who these incompetent student/trainees are, but to avoid the dual relationship ethical issue they do not give them lower grades or deselect them from the program through whatever means?

If these group educators would use the group counseling practicum experience to do their supervision of the student/trainees' group leadership skills, they would not need to create a situation rife with opportunity for unethical dual relationship possibilities, namely requiring students to participate in a "growth" experience with the instructor as leader/facilitator. (Part of the difficulty is definitional. Corey and Williams seem to define *group practicum* as a personal growth experience for the student/trainee rather than the more generally accepted definition of the student/trainee leading a group of authentic help seekers or clients. Williams concludes "logistics" prevent the use of the more accepted definition of group practicum from being used in his program. Logistics cannot be used as an argument for or against ethical training.) Others not involved in student evaluation can provide a growth group experience much better and more authentically. You see, there is also the ethical responsibility of giving the student/trainee the opportunity to experience what a *true* group counseling/growth experience is like without the fear of *potential* evaluation.

All of the reasons that are presented for requiring classroom-linked experience, such as protection of the public and opportunity to model for the student/trainee, can be accomplished in the group counseling practicum in which the teacher can, on occasion, co-lead the student/trainee group and model for the trainee while still observing the student's leadership skills throughout the life of the group.

It is puzzling to me why those counselor educators who insist that their group trainees must have a group experience with them as part of their group counseling course at the same time do not insist that the trainees have an individual counseling experience with them as part of their individual counseling course. Does not the public need the same protection from possibly incompetent individual counselors?

- If you are a counselor educator who teaches group counseling courses, where do you stand on the issues raised in this chapter? What safeguards do you believe are necessary to protect both your students and the public they eventually will serve?

- If you are a student in a counselor education program, what are your reactions to this controversy? What kinds of learning experiences do you think you need in order to become an effective group leader?

CONCLUSIONS

Indeed there is controversy about dual relationships in the preparation of group counselors. As the issue has been framed in the literature, conscientious counselor educators are caught in a "no-win" ethical dilemma. On one hand, if we remove ourselves from what many consider to be problematic dual roles—such as combining didactic and experiential learnings by performing multiple functions that may include any combination of instructor, supervisor, group leader, consultant, and counselor—we are vulnerable to charges that we have abdicated our responsibility to the profession and the public to assure competent service. On the other hand, if we do teach by combining roles, we are vulnerable to charges that we have abdicated our responsibilities to uphold ethical standards and to respect the privacy of student self-disclosure and personal growth.

It seems obvious to us that counselor educators need to work to clarify the question of how group counseling courses can best be taught. It is equally obvious that no consensus exists on this question. We do believe that if counselor educators choose to keep group experiences free from evaluation, then other procedures need to exist within the program to screen out unsuitable candidates.

Coursework that prepares students to conduct group work does not present the only opportunity for screening/evaluation. At this point, there is a wide range of choices that counselor educators can make in preparing students to be group counselors. We each must choose according to our own stance on the issues, balancing our responsibilities to our students, to the profession, and to consumers of counseling services.

CHAPTER 5
SUPERVISION

Our final chapter in part II, Issues in Counselor Preparation deals with supervision. Supervision of counselor trainees occurs primarily in counselor education programs, although counselors in the field also work under supervision toward their licensure or certification. The nature of the supervisory relationship raises some unique dual role issues. In this chapter, we draw upon the available literature, share our own views, and include the guest contribution of L. DiAnne Borders along with our commentaries. Rex Stockton has also sent us his views on various issues in supervision, and we have included these throughout the chapter. Questions that guide our discussion include these:

- What guidance do codes of ethics offer supervisors? Do various codes conflict with each other?
- Is it ever appropriate to integrate both counseling and supervision? What are the problems involved in blending the two roles?
- How can supervision include exploration of the supervisee's personal issues as well as of cases?
- What are guidelines for developing boundaries in supervisory relationships?
- How can the issue of supervisor countertransference be dealt with in supervision?
- What are the ethical and legal ramifications when the supervisee does not perform competently? How can this situation create role conflicts for the supervisor?

ETHICAL CODES AND GUIDELINES

Although supervision has been presumed to be the "watchdog" of counseling services provided to the public (Slovenko, 1980), until recently little work has been done on ethical issues within the supervisory relationship (Newman, 1981; Upchurch, 1985). In the past few years, more attention has been given to these issues, as is evidenced by the publication of such excellent resources as the *Handbook for Counseling Supervision* (Borders & Leddick, 1987), *Supervising Counselors and Therapists: A Developmental Approach* (Stoltenberg & Delworth, 1987), the *Standards for Counseling Supervisors* (ACES, 1990), and *Counselor Supervision: Principles, Process, and Practice* (Bradley, 1989). Another resource that will soon be available is the *Curriculum Guide for Training Counseling Supervisors: Rationale, Development, and Implementation* (Borders et al., in press), which has been prepared by the ACES Working Group for Supervisor Training. Supervisors can thus now find guidance regarding dual role relationships by consulting both the literature and the standards.

The ACES *Standards for Counseling Supervisors* (1990) consist of 11 core areas of knowledge, competencies, and personal traits. The standards specify that "The supervisor's primary functions are to teach the inexperienced and to foster their professional development, to serve as consultants to experienced counselors, and to assist at all levels in the provision of effective counseling services. These responsibilities require personal and professional maturity accompanied by a broad perspective on counseling that is gained by extensive, supervised counseling experience."

Another standard pertains to the importance of establishing a mutually trusting relationship with the supervisee by providing an appropriate balance of challenge and support. This standard states that "Professional counseling supervisors demonstrate conceptual knowledge of the personal and professional nature of the supervisory relationship and are skilled in applying this knowledge."

Supervisors should also demonstrate conceptual knowledge of supervision methods and techniques. According to the ACES standards, supervisors must be able to do the following:

- State the purposes of supervision and explain the procedures to be used.
- Negotiate mutual decisions regarding the needed direction of learning experiences for the supervisee.
- Perform the supervisor's functions in the role of teacher, counselor, or consultant as appropriate.
- Clarify their roles in the supervision process.

- Interact with the counselor in a manner that facilitates the supervisee's self-exploration and problem solving.

It is clear from reviewing this list that the ACES standards imply that supervisors possess the personal and professional maturity to play multiple roles in the supervision process. Supervisors have a responsibility to clarify their role and to explain the purpose and procedures of supervision. However, the boundaries are not always clear, as supervisors need to perform a variety of roles, including that of teacher, supervisor, counselor, and consultant. It appears that there are some contradictions between these ACES standards and the AACD *Ethical Standards* (1988) (which explicitly prohibit functioning in multiple roles of counselor, educator, supervisor, administrator, and evaluator). As we have stated earlier, our preference for reconciling this contradiction is that the AACD *Ethical Standards* be revised to reflect the inevitability of certain types of role blending.

BOUNDARIES OF THE SUPERVISORY RELATIONSHIP

Several of the focus questions that we asked at the beginning of this chapter are so interrelated that they cannot be discussed separately. Here we explore boundary issues in supervision. Is it ever appropriate to integrate both counseling and supervision in the same relationship? What are the problems involved in blending the two roles? How can supervision include exploration of the supervisee's personal issues as well as of cases? The following vignette illustrates how some of these issues may arise:

Andrew is a counselor educator and supervisor who regularly teaches an internship seminar. Andrew makes it clear to students at the initial class meeting that he conducts his internship seminar using a group supervision format that focuses on the counselor as a person. He informs his students that "The main emphasis will be on your own dynamics and reactions to your clients—not on an analysis of your clients, counseling skills and techniques, or case management strategies. Of course, you will learn various alternatives for dealing with your clients, but our primary concern will be on how your attitudes and behaviors may be influencing your clients. Thus, you will be expected to examine your needs, motivations, and most of all your potential sources of countertransference in these group supervision sessions."

Andrew's chairperson questions him on the appropriateness of his style of teaching this seminar. Other instructors focus on teaching specific skills and interventions and do a great deal of case management work. The chairperson thinks that Andrew is opening himself to the possibility of blurring his role as an educator by focusing on the personal dimensions of his supervisees. She suggests that he recommend to his students that they seek personal counseling apart from the program and that he focus his course more on skill development. In his defense, Andrew claims that he is not conducting group therapy, but rather he is asking his students to look at how their own dynamics influence their interventions with their clients. He deals with personal problems of his supervisees only to the extent that these problems appear to be influencing their work. He sees it as his job to help them become aware of the ways that they are impacting their clients.

- Do you think that Andrew's chairperson has legitimate reasons for her concerns that he is getting involved as both therapist and educator for his supervisees?

- What are your thoughts about Andrew's approach to group supervision? Do you think that supervision can be therapeutic, even though the focus is not therapy for supervisees?

- What do you see as the appropriate balance between teaching supervisees about their own dynamics and the dynamics of their clients? What is the balance between focusing on supervisee self-awareness and teaching skills?

- What are some potential benefits and risks to the supervisees in Andrew's class? Would you want to be a student in the class?

Ethical questions related to dual relationships are particularly difficult in the practice of supervision (Stoltenberg & Delworth, 1987). Although a dual relationship occurs when a supervisor becomes the supervisee's counselor (Bernard, 1987), in practice there are few guidelines for supervisors to help them distinguish between the two roles (Whiston & Emerson, 1989). The goals of supervision have been variously defined along a wide continuum from *personal* growth for the supervisee to acquisition of skills with a focus on the supervisee's *professional* development. As we have seen, the ACES standards acknowledge that supervision entails a multiplicity of roles, including that of counselor.

It can be extremely difficult to determine when a supervisory relationship has become a counseling relationship. Although the therapeutic aspect of the supervisor's role and the role of the counselor are not synonymous, the distinction between the two is not well defined (Whiston & Emerson, 1989). When supervisees have personal problems, supervisors may be tempted to counsel them. For counselor educators, this temptation may be enhanced by a belief that the student's personal growth takes precedence over the possibility of compromising the professor/student relationship (Roberts et al., 1982), or supervisors may naturally fall back on their counseling training when problems arise (Whiston & Emerson, 1989). Nonetheless, personal counseling of a supervisee may cloud the supervisor's objectivity and interfere with the ability to supervise adequately (Cormier & Bernard, 1982).

Some writers believe that distinctions can and should be made between the roles of counselor and of supervisor. Wise, Lowery, and Silverglade (1989) contended that the primary goal of supervision is to protect the welfare of the client, and this precludes making the supervisee's personal growth a primary focus. Thus, supervision cannot provide the supervisee with the intensive personal growth experiences that counseling can provide.

It seems clear to us that unless the nature of the supervisory relationship is clearly defined, both the supervisor and supervisee may be put in a difficult position at some point in the relationship. If supervisors overextend the boundaries of a supervisory relationship, there is the potential that the supervisor's objectivity will be impaired and that the supervisee will be inhibited from making full use of the supervision process. For instance, if the supervisor is not clear about the primary purpose of supervision, at some later point supervisees might request personal therapy when they become aware of problems that interfere with their ability to counsel effectively.

Of course, if a sexual relationship becomes a part of a supervisory relationship, then this confounds the entire process. It is doubtful that supervisees will be getting the supervision they need for their cases if they are also involved in a romantic relationship with their supervisor. The Ethics Committee of the American Psychological Association has clarified that "Romantic or sexually intimate relationships between clinical supervisors and supervisees constitute, by fact and by definition, dual relationships. Psychologists should make every effort to avoid such sexual relationships" ("Ethics," 1988).

Our guest contributor Rex Stockton (personal communication, December 21, 1990) notes that the power differential is another factor that needs to be considered:

> There is a marked inequality of power in the relationship. It is the supervisor who has the power to pass or fail a student, to write or not write a letter of recommendation, and so on. The student's recognition of this inequality may hinder his or her self-disclosures and, thus, stifle personal growth. The student's failure to recognize this may lead to personal disclosures that could unfairly jeopardize his or her class standing.

There seems to be some agreement that supervision should concentrate on the supervisee's professional development rather than personal concerns, and that supervision and counseling are not the same. However, there is confusion about the *degree* to which a supervisor can ethically deal with personal issues. The question remains: To what extent should supervision include exploration of supervisees' personal issues?

Stockton (personal communication, December 21, 1990) believes quite strongly that the roles of counselor and supervisor cannot be blended. He states that "attempts to merge these two roles may result in the supervisee receiving a soured experience, emotional harm, or academic penalty." Nonetheless, he acknowledges that supervisors do commonly encounter beginning counselors who exhibit above-average levels of anxiety due to inexperience. He adds that

> Acceptable and sometimes helpful supervisory efforts to reduce such heightened anxiety may include acknowledging its presence, providing positive feedback for what the student is able to do, and couching constructive feedback in facilitative terms. Supervisors can use their skill as counselors to normalize counselor anxiety and somewhat reduce its adverse impact, but to jump fully into the counselor mode would constitute a dual and conflicting relationship. Admittedly, though the extremes and their ramifications can be clearly drawn, there is much gray area with which to contend.

From our perspective, effective supervision focuses on the impact of the counselor on the counseling process. We think that it is a mistake for supervision to focus exclusively on client cases or problem-solving strategies regarding how to deal with clients. Thus, supervision can be useful in helping students become aware of personal limitations or unresolved problems that intrude into effective helping. However, there is a difference between helping students identify and clarify those concerns they need to explore versus converting supervision into an in-depth personal therapy session. For instance, if a student becomes aware of an unresolved issue with his mother that is being played out in his counseling sessions with "motherly" women, it is appropriate to focus on how his personal limitations are blocking effective counseling, but we doubt that it would be appropriate to abandon the supervisory focus for a therapy experience. In such cases, students will hopefully be encouraged to find a resource where they can get the therapy they need for themselves personally and professionally.

Distinguishing where the appropriate boundary lies between supervision and counseling can be difficult. If you are a counseling supervisor, where do you stand on these issues? Do you believe that the supervisory and counseling roles are separable? Or do you think that some role blending is inevitable? How would you defend your position if a colleague challenged your views?

If you are a graduate student working under supervision, or a counselor working under supervision toward your licensure or certification, what do you think about these issues? Where do you want your supervisor to draw the line in dealing with any personal concerns you may be facing?

A final boundary issue concerns social relationships. Stoltenberg and Delworth (1987) suggested that friendships and social relationships between supervisors and supervisees should be avoided when possible. They recommended that if such relationships are entered into, possible ramifications should be openly explored. Harrar, VandeCreek, and Knapp (1990) admitted that it is inevitable that supervisors will encounter trainees in social settings and community activities. They advised that a supervisor need not shun supervisees on such occasions, unless the supervisor believes the professional relationship will be compromised. However, they did caution against attempting to supervise relatives, spouses, friends, former clients, or others with whom they might find it difficult to be candid about performance.

GUIDELINES FOR SUPERVISORS

Given the confusion that exists over whether and how the supervisory and counseling roles can be blended, what guidelines exist to help the ethically conscientious supervisor? Informed consent is vitally important in supervision. First, supervisees have a right to know the nature and purposes of supervision, their rights and responsibilities, and what they can expect from their supervisor. Second, clients of supervisees have a right to know that they are receiving services from a trainee. Harrar et al. (1990) noted that clients have the right to elect not to receive services under these conditions, and that failure to inform a client of a trainee's status could expose the supervisor and supervisee to possible lawsuits.

Supervisors are also advised to document their supervisory work. Harrar et al. (1990) recommended that supervisors document with consideration for (1) quality of care given the client, (2) quality of training given the supervisee, and (3) ethical and legal issues involved if a complaint should be lodged. They noted that courts often follow the principle that "what has not been written has not been done" (p. 38).

Several writers have offered models to assist supervisors in working through the supervision process with their boundaries intact. Wise et al. (1989) have suggested a stage-oriented approach:

- *Presupervision.* This stage encompasses the student's entry into and adjustment to graduate school. Because it is a stressful period and because students have not yet begun to see clients, it may be a good time to recommend personal counseling.
- *Self-focus.* Students begin to see clients but lack knowledge and experience. Supervision is most helpful when it concentrates on skill development, clarifying student concerns, and providing structure.
- *Client focus.* Students have increased interaction with clients, become aware of inadequacies in their knowledge and expe-

rience, and feel confused or ambivalent. They typically increase their initiative and become less dependent on their supervisors. The supervisor continues to concentrate on skill development and case conceptualization. Personal counseling might be recommended only if the student remains too dependent on the supervisor or is not making adequate progress due to personal issues.

- *Interpersonal focus.* Students become more comfortable with their skills and shift their focus from issues of competence to issues of self-awareness. This may be the most appropriate time to recommend personal counseling to promote the students' greater openness and awareness of themselves and their relationships with others.

- *Professional focus.* Students now have begun to develop a therapeutic personality and a sense of professional identity. A consultation model of supervision is most appropriate, and personal counseling should be recommended only to deal with "blind spots" in specific areas or life stressors that are impeding performance.

We think this provides a useful decision-making model for supervisors to help them determine the supervisee's stage of development and to use that knowledge to decide on the appropriateness of personal counseling.

Whiston and Emerson (1989) took a somewhat different approach. They suggested that Egan's (1990) three-stage model can provide a practical method for distinguishing between supervising and counseling. According to these writers, supervisors should limit their work to Egan's first stage of exploring and clarifying a supervisee's personal problems when those problems are impeding his or her work. After the supervisor has identified the personal issues, the supervisee then has the responsibility for resolving them. If the supervision process moves into Egan's second and third stages—establishing goals and taking action regarding the personal problem—supervision then becomes counseling. Whiston and Emerson recommended that counseling be provided by an independent counselor while the supervisor continues to focus on the supervisee's professional development.

We believe that, as is the case with any professional relationship, it is essential that the supervisory relationship be grounded on a clear contract so that both the supervisee and the supervisor have an understanding of their respective roles and so that both are guided toward the achievement of clearly understood and agreed-upon goals. The topic of boundary issues ought to be explored if and when there are concerns. Stockton (personal communication, December 21, 1990) stresses the importance of maintaining objectivity and keeping clearly in mind that the primary role of a supervisor is to ensure competence on the part of the supervisee. His thoughts are as follows:

> The supervisor must have a clear standard for supervisee competence, an acceptable method of assessing the supervisee's approximations of that standard, and a formulation as to how to best work within the educator/supervisor role in facilitating supervisee competence. In this regard, relative objectivity is of great importance.
>
> Though certainly a complex concept, the supervisee's competence may be distilled down to three broad domains: (1) repertoire of appropriate counseling techniques, (2) theoretical foundation, and (3) personal level of human functioning. Supervisors are, of course, trained as counselors, and often the temptation is to try to help the supervisee resolve his or her own personal issues. This is a serious mistake that sets up not only dual but, in some ways, conflicting roles. When human characteristics of the supervisee interfere with counseling tasks, the educator/supervisor is advised to refer out to another professional rather than trying to help the supervisee develop in ways that are beyond the role of the educator.
>
> I do not believe dual relationships are helpful for supervisees in the long run because there is the potential to impair supervisor objectivity and impede the supervisee's ability to participate fully and freely. It is difficult to be guided by one's roles when they conflict, and the likelihood of objectively assessing each competency reduces as the supervisor becomes increasingly involved in the student's personal life.

Thus, although many gray areas remain when supervisors attempt to differentiate between their supervisory and counseling roles, it seems clear that a supervisory relationship should not be allowed to become a counseling relationship. Supervisors can use these criteria to help them determine when to refer a supervisee for counseling: the supervisee's stage of professional development,

Egan's model of the counseling process, and expected standards of competence.

There is one final consideration related to the decision to refer a supervisee for counseling that we have not yet explored. When a supervisor recommends personal counseling for a supervisee, this may infuse an emotionally charged issue into the relationship. The supervisee may feel threatened and believe he or she has been judged to be incompetent. The supervisory relationship could become strained and the supervisee might be less open about his or her own experiencing in discussing cases with the supervisor. Wise et al. (1989) have captured the essence of this concern: "Whether the student approaches the suggestion of personal counseling as a criticism or as a helpful addition to supervision will depend on the supervisor's attitude, tact, and timing in making the recommendation" (p. 334).

> If you are a supervisor and were faced with the need to recommend counseling for a supervisee, how might you go about it? What factors might you consider in making your recommendation, and what might you tell the supervisee? If you are a supervisee, how might you react if your supervisor made such a recommendation to you? Might this change the nature of the supervisory relationship, from your perspective?

FOCUS ON THE SUPERVISOR: COUNTERTRANSFERENCE ISSUES

Supervisor countertransference is a phenomenon that is bound to occur in some supervisory relationships, when supervisors have intense reactions to certain supervisees. Stockton (personal communication, December 21, 1990) has clear views regarding where the responsibility rests in such cases:

> Supervisor countertransference is a useful issue to face because it does occur. However, it should be incumbent upon the supervisor to resolve such issues either through his or her own efforts, therapeutically, or as is more often the case, through brief professional consultation. This is a burden that should not be placed upon the supervisee's

shoulders. The duality that results, along with the inequality of power, would place the supervisee in a very uncomfortable and vulnerable position.

We hope that supervisors monitor their countertransference, and that when these issues arise that they seek their own supervision or, at the very least, consult with a colleague. A point we wish to make is that countertransference does not have to be viewed negatively—as something that necessarily gets in the way of supervision. Indeed, by monitoring our countertransference in the supervisory process, we can learn some important lessons about supervisees. Our reaction to supervisees can tell us something about them as well as telling us about ourselves. We suggest that supervisor countertransference be dealt with in a manner very similar to therapist countertransference. First of all, it is important to be aware of our countertransference reactions. It is crucial that we understand our needs and how they may be triggered by certain supervisee behaviors. This is especially true when a supervisor finds himself or herself sexually attracted to a certain type of supervisee. What is crucial is that supervisors do not exploit supervisees for the purpose of satisfying their needs and that they do not misuse their power over supervisees. When a supervisor has unmet needs that interfere with effective supervision, the supervisee is placed in a difficult position. As supervisors, it is important that we recognize our countertransference issues and seek consultation. We also have an obligation, when we are unable to successfully resolve our issues, to take further measures to protect our supervisees. These might include seeking personal therapy, referring the supervisee to another supervisor, or inviting a colleague to cosupervise sessions if the supervisee agrees to this.

SUPERVISEE INCOMPETENCE: ETHICAL AND LEGAL RAMIFICATIONS

Supervisors are both ethically and legally responsible for the actions of those they are supervising. If a client of a supervisee, for example, commits suicide, the supervisor is likely to be more vulnerable than the supervisee from a legal standpoint. The reality of the fact that supervisors are responsible for all of the cases of their supervisees does place special pressures on the supervisor that could create a conflict. If the supervisor becomes aware that the supervisee lacks basic relationship skills or lacks personal maturity, what is he or she to do? Is it appropriate to bring this to the attention of the faculty? Should a determination be made of whether or not the supervisee is personally qualified to remain in the program? The legal ramifications of the supervisor's responsibilities when the supervisee is not functioning competently underscore the importance of clearly defining the nature of the supervisory relationship from the outset. Students should know about the consequences of not competently fulfilling their contracts. To be sure, the supervisor has a duty to do what is in the best interest of the supervisee, yet he or she also has a responsibility to the welfare of the clients who are being seen by the supervisee. This matter deserves a full discussion at the outset of the supervisory relationship.

Stockton (personal communication, December 21, 1990) describes the difficulties that can arise when the boundaries of the supervisory relationship have not been clear and the supervisee does not perform adequately:

> When one has to say to a supervisee, "I'm sorry. You are not measuring up to my standards of competence," it is far better not to have had a counseling relationship with that student. A supervisor can remain both ethically and legally clear when such a dual relationship has been avoided. The same cannot be said when this is not the case. Consider the following example:
>
> A supervisor assesses her supervisee as having a human problem that interferes with his ability to perform his counseling tasks. Rather than referring him, the supervisor develops a counseling relationship in hopes of therapeutically addressing the human problem. At the end of the semester the student is deemed by the supervisor as incompetent to counsel and is given a failing grade. Feeling betrayed, the student seeks an academic hearing, charging that it is the instructor who is incompetent in her counseling skills and thus has no appropriate basis by which to measure his competency. So, who is incompetent? The student, the instructor, or both? We have no way of answering that question. However, it is very likely that had the instructor not added counselor to her supervisory role, that question would never have been asked.

Further ideas and a different perspective are offered by L. DiAnne Borders, who discusses the implicit duality within the supervisory relationship in the following position statement.

Duality Within the Supervisory Relationship

L. DiAnne Borders

A number of writers have addressed dual role relationships in supervision and have begun the difficult task of differentiating between healthy and harmful relationships (e.g., Bernard & Goodyear, 1991; Kitchener, 1988; Ryder & Hepworth, 1990). Several problematic dual roles are clearly recognizable, such as sexual and counseling relationships between supervisor and supervisee. More subtle forms of duality, however, are less easily identified and avoided.

Within the supervisory relationship itself, duality (if not paradox) is implicit. On the one hand are factors that encourage the development of a fairly intimate partnership. The universal goal of increased self-awareness necessitates that some attention will be given to supervisees' personal development. In fact, advanced supervisees are eager to discuss personal issues that are affecting their clinical work (Heppner & Roehlke, 1984; Rabinowitz, Heppner, & Roehlke, 1986). Within these discussions, supervisors quite naturally might self-disclose about similar events during their own development.

On the other hand, however, are factors that mitigate against the formation of a close and open relationship. The power differential between supervisor and supervisee, for example, can generate a good deal of anxiety for both persons, although supervisee anxiety is more frequently noted (Borders & Leddick, 1987). The hierarchical nature of the supervisory relationship also can elicit individual issues related to power and authority. Supervisors and supervisees bring developmental histories with a variety of "authority figures" (e.g., parents, previous supervisors) that influence their interactions (Alonso, 1983). Each person also is driven somewhat by individual motivations, such as needs for approval, affiliation, and control (Alonso, 1983; Robiner, 1982), and their unique perceptual frameworks (e.g., gender-related expectations, Nelson & Holloway, 1990). These intra- and interpersonal dynamics suggest that transference and countertransference are quite likely to occur (Doehrman, 1976).

A recent case study of one supervisory dyad illustrates several aspects of duality within the supervisory relationship. Martin, Goodyear, and Newton (1987) reported that both the supervisor (male) and supervisee (female) indicated that their second session was the "best" during the semester. This session was focused primarily on personal issues of the supervisee, who reported that the supervisor "affirmed me and connected what I was experiencing personally as countertransference onto clients" (p. 227). The supervisor believed that this session was an important test of both him and the boundaries of their relationship. He also noted how the supervisee had linked him with her father, who had strong and critical opinions about the supervisee's plans.

The "worst session" for the supervisee (the 10th session) also was focused on personal issues. In this session, however, the supervisor took on the client role, revealing personal information concerning his son. The supervisor reported he felt relaxed in the client role and was unconcerned that the session was being taped (for purposes of the study). In contrast, the supervisee said she felt disengaged, vulnerable, and insecure. Quantitative and qualitative data verified her report. Martin et al. (1987) noted that the role reversal in this session created a double-bind for the supervisee, who was told by the person in charge (supervisor) to take charge (as counselor).

As this case study illustrates, boundaries of the supervisor-supervisee relationship are somewhat ambiguous and can be easily violated, however unintentionally. Supervisors may not realize that they have created a dual role within the supervisory relationship and may be unaware of negative effects on the supervisee. Such awareness could be blocked by the supervisor's developmental history, individual needs, and perceptual frameworks. Nevertheless, it is clearly the *supervisor's* responsibility to monitor the potential for such duality and to correct any debilitating effects (Borders & Leddick, 1987).

Given the complexity of dual roles, it seems unlikely that supervisors can effectively monitor themselves and the supervisory relationship on their own, despite their most sincere efforts to do so. Clearly, there is a need for training that sensitizes supervisors to duality within the supervisory relationship. Such training should emphasize development of self-awareness regarding the variety of personal factors that may lead to a violation of relationship boundaries. Supervisors should identify those factors that could unconsciously influence their behaviors in the supervisory relationship. With this awareness, supervisors could more effectively monitor their interactions with supervisees.

Because needs change over time and because manifestations of those needs are often quite subtle, self-monitoring also should be supplemented by ongoing supervision case conferences. Currently such conferences are quite rare, except (perhaps) for doctoral students in supervised training experiences. It seems clear, however, that practicing supervisors also could benefit from systematic consultation with colleagues.

The exercise of "due care" (Kitchener, 1988) regarding dual role relationships is a critical challenge for supervisors. Increased self-awareness and the challenge and support of colleagues are first steps toward ameliorating effects of dual roles that typify every supervision relationship.

Gerald Corey's Commentary

I take issue with DiAnne Borders' comment that "it seems unlikely that supervisors can effectively monitor themselves and the supervisory relationship on their own, despite their most sincere effort to do so." It seems to me that a mark of professionally mature supervisors is that they are aware of their own dynamics and the dynamics of the relationship between their supervisees and themselves. It seems that unless supervisors are able to monitor themselves in their relationships with supervisees, the supervisors could benefit from supervision themselves. I am certainly in agreement with Borders when she calls for training of supervisors that sensitizes them to the potential problems of duality within the supervisory relationship. Her point of using colleagues for challenge and support as a way of increasing self-awareness of supervisors is well taken.

A point that I find interesting in Borders' paper is the power differential between supervisor and supervisee, which often leads to supervisee anxiety. Many students do indeed experience struggles related to authority of supervisors and educators. Supervisees often strive for approval and confirmation by their supervisors. This struggle can be fruitfully explored in the supervision session, especially if this dynamic affects the supervisee's functioning with clients. Borders mentions a case study in which one of the best sessions was focused mainly on personal issues of a female supervisee and a male supervisor. If the supervisee, for example, has unresolved is-

sues with her father, she may be looking to her supervisor for affirmation that she wanted from her father. If her father was critical and always expected more than she delivered, then the supervisee might treat the supervisor as a critical father. The supervisee can benefit from an exploration of her transference, if this is done with sensitivity and awareness of the boundaries of the supervisory relationship. This example shows that the lines are sometimes thin between self-exploration and supervision.

Barbara Herlihy's Commentary

I agree with Borders that it seems unlikely that supervisors can effectively monitor themselves on their own. Despite our best efforts, we are only human and are bound to have blind spots in our self-awareness. Borders makes this point quite clearly when she cites the study by Martin et al., in which the "worst" session was when the supervisor was self-disclosing. I agree with Borders' statement that there is a need for more training for professionals who take on supervisory roles. The ACES Standards for Counseling Supervisors accentuate the need for supervisors to have had extensive experience. Yet what I see in actual practice is that many professionals who work as supervisors are trained and experienced as counselors but not necessarily as supervisors. Specific training in how to do supervision is not readily available outside doctoral programs, and many if not most supervisors out in the field are master's-level practitioners. I share Borders' concern and offer these recommendations:

- That standards for supervisors be extended to include specific training in supervision, and that such standards be adopted by state counselor licensing boards to ensure that supervisors are fully qualified.

- That experienced supervisors at least occasionally supplement their self-monitoring with ongoing supervision case conferences, as Borders suggests.

- That, as might be possible in group supervision, cosupervision (two supervisors working conjointly with a group of supervisees) sometimes be arranged. (In my own work, I conduct an ongoing supervision group for counselors seeking their state licensure and do this with a trusted colleague. I find her feedback to be invaluable for my continuing self-awareness and professional growth.)

Supervision requires different skills than counseling, and there is no guarantee that a good counselor will make a good supervisor. According to the ACES Standards for Counseling Supervisors, an effective supervisor needs to be comfortable with the authority inherent in the supervisor role; needs to be able to function in multiple roles as teacher, counselor, and consultant; and needs to possess the personal and professional maturity that come with experience. When we add to these qualifications the need to deal competently with the implicit duality of the supervisory relationship, we are asking a great deal of our supervisors. I hope our profession will move more actively to help supervisors be the best they can be. Perhaps the American Association for Counseling and Development could add supervision training to its repertoire of professional development workshops held each year across the country. When coursework in supervision is offered, the forthcoming Curriculum Guide for Training Counseling Supervisors *(Borders et al., in press) provides an excellent, comprehensive resource.*

CONCLUSIONS

In this chapter, we have highlighted the implicit duality that exists in the supervisor/supervisee relationship and have noted the difficulties in determining where the boundary lies between supervision and counseling. Because supervision involves a tripartite relationship among supervisor, supervisee, and clients of the supervisee, supervisors have multiple loyalties. They have obligations not only to the supervisee but also to the clients of the supervisee, the supervisee's employer, and ultimately to the profession. When these loyalties conflict, supervisors are confronted with difficult ethical dilemmas.

This chapter also concludes part II, Issues in Counselor Preparation. In three chapters, we have examined issues in counselor education, in the preparation of group counselors, and in supervision. In part III, we turn our focus to issues in counseling practice. We explore specific dual relationship questions that confront practitioners in a variety of settings in their work as counselors and consultants with individual clients, couples and families, and groups.

PART III:
ISSUES IN COUNSELING PRACTICE

CHAPTER 6
PRIVATE PRACTICE

In this chapter, we explore a wide range of dual relationship issues that private practitioners encounter in their work. Two guest contributors also share their views. Larry Golden highlights some of the more subtle dilemmas faced by counselors in private practice. Karen Strohm Kitchener focuses on an issue that has been the subject of considerable controversy: whether posttherapy relationships are ever appropriate. Questions that frame our discussion include the following:

- What do codes of ethics say about dual relationships in private practice?
- Is bartering for goods or services unethical? What are the potential risks in this practice?
- Should a counselor ever counsel a friend? A social acquaintance?
- Should a private practitioner ever accept a gift from a client?
- Should private practitioners ever socialize with clients?
- What potential problems exist when the counselor has a home office?
- What are the limits of self-disclosure, and how could overextending the limits create a dual relationship dilemma?
- Can one become friends with a former client? Have a romantic relationship with a former client?
- What dual relationship issues arise in marriage and family therapy?

ETHICAL STANDARDS

Private practitioners who provide counseling services to individuals work under various licensures and titles, including counselor, psychologist, social worker, and psychotherapist. In chapter 1, we noted that cautions against dual relationships are contained in ethical codes for counselors (AACD *Ethical Standards,* 1988), psychologists (APA *Ethical Principles for Psychologists,* 1989), and social workers (NFSCSW *Code of Ethics,* 1985).

Another code of ethics that is relevant to our discussion here is that of the American Mental Health Counselors Association, the division of AACD with which many private practitioners are affiliated. This code states as follows:

> • Mental health counselors are continually cognizant both of their own needs and of their inherently powerful position vis-à-vis clients, in order to avoid exploiting the client's trust and dependency. Mental health counselors make every effort to avoid dual relationships with clients and/or relationships which might impair their professional judgment or increase the risk of client exploitation. Examples of such dual relationships include treating an employee or supervisor, treating a close friend or family relative, and sexual relationships with clients. (AMHCA, 1987)

As we have discussed in previous chapters, despite ethical codes practitioners are often left to their professional judgment in attempting to distinguish between harmful nonsexual dual relationships and those that are benign. In the absence of specific guidance, we are left with many gray areas. Situations will arise that call for our best judgment. In the position statement that follows, Larry Golden describes some incidents that involve rather subtle distinctions.

Dual Role Relationships in Private Practice

Larry Golden

It is likely that when people concern themselves about dual relationships, sex between counselor and client comes to mind. That such violations continue testifies to the possibility that a small number of members of our profession are not troubled by ethical prohibitions. Actually, the issue of sex between counselor and client should not pose a dilemma for the ethical practitioner. The boundaries are clearly marked.

There are certain types of dual relationships, however, that can put even a mentally healthy and well-intended counselor in a bind. A dual relationship occurs whenever the counselor interacts with a client in more than one capacity (Bennett, Bryant, VandenBos, & Greenwood, 1990). The remainder of this discussion focuses on some of these more subtle "nonsexual" problem areas by examining four incidents and the important questions they raise.

Incidents, Questions, and Commentary.

Incident 1: The client is a single parent who cannot afford the counselor's fees. However, she is an expert typist. Therapy is exchanged for typing at an agreed-upon rate.

Question: Is it ethical to barter goods or services in exchange for therapy?

Commentary: To date, the American Association for Counseling and Development has not ruled on bartering as an ethical issue. However, the American Psychological Association strongly advised against this practice (APA Ethics Committee, 1988), as did the Association for Specialists in Group Work (ASGW, 1989). Although the counselor may be motivated by concern for a client who cannot afford to pay for services, Kitchener and Harding regarded bartering as "fraught with potential traps" (1990, p. 152). The counselor becomes the client's employer, creating a dual relationship. How much typing is worth an hour of psychotherapy? What if the typing is free of errors but the psychotherapy is not?

Incident 2: A marriage counselor is approached by a fellow church member who says, "Sandra and I need your help. . ." The counselor and the individual asking for help are not personal friends, although they are acquainted through various church activities.

Question: Is it ethical to counsel a mere acquaintance?

Commentary: The AACD *Ethical Standards* (1988) caution against "dual relationships that might impair the member's objectivity and professional judgment (e.g., as with close friends or relatives). . ." This standard does not quite answer the counselor's question, so that she must rely on her own judgment. Will shared church membership interfere with objectivity? Will her clients be less forthcoming with personal information for fear that their "dirty linen" might be aired amongst the congregation?

Incident 3: The counselor is going through a divorce. He is under great stress. When one of his clients reveals her upset feelings about her impending divorce, the counselor discloses that he is in the midst of a similar situation.

Question: What are the ethical limits of self-disclosure?

Commentary: Counselors hurt too. Should we tell our clients about our pain? Might it not be therapeutic, or at least honest, for clients to know that we have "feet of clay?" This is another situation that challenges the counselor's good judgment because ethical standards are nonspecific. The AACD standard that best applies states that "the counselor is aware of the intimacy of the relationship and avoids engaging in activities that seek to meet the counselor's personal needs at the expense of that client." This counselor must wrestle with issues of when and how much (if anything) he should disclose. If the counselor's personal pain proves to be a distraction, a frank discussion with the client is appropriate and may well lead to a referral.

Incident 4: The counselor offers a "nonsexual" hug to her client by way of saying goodbye at the end of a session.

Question: Is it ethical for a counselor to hug a client?

Commentary: Of course, hugging is not unethical. However, to hug or not to hug must be a conscious decision with consideration for each of our clients. Could the touch be misperceived? Could it arouse feelings of sexual attraction? Could a hug feed a client's romantic fantasies?

Conclusions. The unique relationship between client and counselor in the private practice setting holds much promise. Our clients may be befuddled by their emotions or may be unaware of what they are feeling. Our objectivity and perception can shed light on the client's confusion and help to set the client on the path of self-mastery. However, the work is fraught with ambiguities and potential pitfalls. Even a hint of duality could cut into our odds of success.

When private practitioners find themselves in waters that are not clearly charted by our profession's ethical standards, they must be guided by an internal ethical compass. Following are suggestions for those who wish to safely navigate the shoals of dual entanglements:

1. Get peer supervision. The lack of supervision is the Achilles heel of private practice. Consult with your colleagues about difficult cases.

2. Get therapy. Counselors are well advised to regard inter-mittent psychotherapy as a type of personal in-service training throughout their professional lives.

3. Avoid even the appearance of a conflict of interest. It takes years to build a solid professional reputation, yet one mis-calculation could tear it down.

Gerald Corey's Commentary

Larry Golden states that "When private practitioners find them-selves in waters that are not charted by our profession's ethical standards, they must be guided by an internal ethical compass." I like both the idea here and the way Golden puts the matter. The core of the issue for me is making sure that "our internal ethical compass" is functioning properly. How do we monitor our tendencies toward self-deception? We may convince ourselves that we are behaving ethically in questionable situations, yet we could be deceiving our-selves. If our compass is faulty, then we are bound to get lost, to the detriment of both our client and ourselves. I like Golden's suggestion of seeking peer supervision. Perhaps it would be a good practice for us to arrange for regular supervision sessions with colleagues for the purpose of focusing on our practices. More than merely discussing client cases, it would be good to focus on ourselves in relationship to our clients. Rather than focusing on the client's transference to-ward us, we might focus on our countertransference toward a par-ticular difficult client. Supervision that focuses on our reactions to our clients can teach us about some of our unresolved personal con-flicts, our needs, and our motivations.

Greenburg, Lewis, and Johnson (1985) suggested that private practitioners can be helped to deal with stress, isolation, and burnout by becoming involved in a peer consultation group. Such a group can assist private practitioners in dealing with problematic feelings to-ward clients, can enable them to maintain ethical principles and professional standards, and can provide emotional support and prac-tical help in dealing with many problems that arise in private practice. In a national survey of peer consultation groups for psychologists in private practice, Lewis, Greenburg, and Hatch (1988) found that 61% of the sample would like to belong to a peer consultation group if one were available. Of the 23% of the sample who were currently in a peer consultation group, the findings indicated a high degree of sat-

isfaction with membership. Borders (1991) has advocated structured peer groups as a way to enhance skill development and provide self-monitoring. According to her, such groups are valuable resources for counselors throughout their careers. Peer consultation groups can help practitioners to clarify their views about dual relationship issues that they may encounter.

Barbara Herlihy's Commentary

It could be that the "lack of supervision is the Achilles heel of private practice," although I think the Achilles heel is more probably isolation. Independent private practitioners work under many frustrations, including fluctuations in income, client cancellations and no-shows, and hassles with third-party payers. Without regular opportunities to interact with peers, and to consult about difficulties and dilemmas that arise, private practitioners may be more vulnerable to the temptation to meet their personal needs in inappropriate ways. They may be tempted to be overly self-disclosing or to socialize with clients if they lack these outlets with peers. Although I have framed the rationale somewhat differently than Golden, I do agree that peer supervision and consultation are important for private practitioners.

Golden raises the issue of nonsexual hugging, and I wish he had further explored this issue in his commentary. In my view, giving a hug may be inappropriate with some clients, for example, those who have strong ambivalence or fantasies about the therapist, or those whose culture interprets hugging in a different way than my own culture. The timing of a hug is another important consideration. For instance, I avoid hugging a client when the gesture might tend to interrupt a therapeutic flow of tears or when it might detract from a client's sense of self-support.

In the remainder of this chapter, we will explore some specific dual relationship issues that impact counselors in private practice. These include bartering, counseling a friend or acquaintance, accepting gifts from clients, socializing with clients, problems inherent in working out of a home office, limits of self-disclosure, and relationships with former clients. At the end of the chapter, we focus specifically on unique dual relationship dilemmas in marriage and family therapy.

BARTERING FOR GOODS OR SERVICES

The *Ethical Guidelines for Group Counselors* (ASGW, 1989) state that "Group counselors do not barter (exchange) professional services with group members for services." Bartering is considered unethical by the American Psychological Association (APA Ethics Committee, 1988). The proposed revision to the APA code of ethics includes a statement on bartering that affirms the rationale for avoiding the practice but also delineates circumstances under which a psychologist might participate in a bartering arrangement:

> Psychologists ordinarily refrain from accepting goods, services, or other noncash remuneration from patients or clients in return for psychological services because such arrangements create inherent potential for conflicts, exploitation, and distortion of the relationship. A psychologist may participate in bartering only if (1) the patient or client requests this method of payment, (2) unusual circumstances make it the only feasible option, (3) it is not clinically contraindicated, and (4) the relationship is not exploitative. When the client or patient is providing services as barter, the time required of them must be equitable. ("Draft," 1991, p. 32)

Aside from the standards of these two professional associations, most codes of ethics are silent on the issue of bartering. Thus, many private practitioners are left to rely on their own judgment. There seems to be little consensus among professionals about bartering. Among the findings of Borys' (1988) study was the following:

- On the question of accepting a service or product as payment for therapy, 51% of the ethics questionnaire respondents reported the *belief* that this practice was either "never ethical" or "ethical under rare conditions," and nearly 97% of the practice-form respondents reported that they engaged in this *practice* not at all or only with a few clients.

Interestingly, during the hearing that was held in California in 1990 to discuss proposed draft regulations on dual relationships, no witnesses raised the issue of bartering, including trading services. Nevertheless, Leslie (1991) reported that licensing boards "look askance at barter arrangements, especially those that require the patient to 'work off the debt.' "

Kitchener and Harding (1990) cautioned that there are potential problems in bartering, even though the practice may be motivated by an altruistic concern for the welfare of clients with limited financial resources. They pointed out that the services a client can offer are usually not as monetarily valuable as counseling. Thus, clients could become trapped in a sort of indentured servitude as they fall further and further behind in the amount owed.

Generally, we are inclined to think that the practice of bartering opens up more problems than it is worth. Take a client who pays for therapy by working on the therapist's car: If the service is less than desirable, the chances are good that the therapist will begin to resent the client on several grounds—for having been taken advantage of, for being the recipient of inferior service, and for not being appreciated. Another potential problem is on the client's part. What criteria do we use to determine what goods or services are worth an hour of the therapist's professional time? If it takes a client 6 hours to pay for a 1-hour therapy session, or if the client believes the therapy is of poor quality, the client might begin to feel exploited and resent the therapist. Feelings of resentment, whether they build up in the therapist or in the client, are bound to interfere with the therapeutic relationship.

Although we can see many potential problems in bartering, we think it would be a mistake categorically to condemn this practice as unethical. In some cultures or in some communities, bartering is a standard practice, and the problems just mentioned may not be evident. For instance, rural environments may lend themselves more to barter arrangements. We know a practitioner who worked with farmers in rural Alabama who paid with a bushel of corn or apples. Within their cultural group, this was a normal way (and in some cases, the only way) of doing business. Leslie (1991) noted that many different kinds of barter arrangements could arise and that some might not be exploitative. There are also alternatives to bartering, such as using a sliding scale or doing *pro bono* work.

What is your own stance toward bartering? If you see it as unacceptable for yourself in your own practice, do you think it is acceptable for others? What alternatives to bartering might you consider with your clients who are unable to pay your fee?

COUNSELING A FRIEND OR ACQUAINTANCE

As is the case with bartering, practitioners seem to be divided over the issue of counseling a friend. In a study of the beliefs and behaviors of therapists conducted by Pope, Tabachnick, and Keith-Spiegel (1987), 48% of the respondents considered it unethical to provide therapy to one of their friends, and 70% said they had never engaged in the behavior.

Some writers have cautioned against counseling a friend. Keith-Spiegel and Koocher (1985) have noted that counseling friends involves "faulty expectations, mixed allegiances, and misinterpretation of motives" (p. 269) that can lead to disappointment, anger, and dissolution of the relationship. Kitchener and Harding (1990) pointed out that counseling relationships and friendships differ in function and purpose, and that frustration and confusion result when there are role conflicts.

We agree that the roles of counselor and close friend are generally incompatible. Friends do not pay their friends a fee for listening and caring. It could be difficult for a counselor who is also a friend to avoid crossing the line between empathy and sympathy. It hurts to see a friend in pain. Because being a counselor as well as a friend to the same person creates a dual relationship, there is always the possibility that one of these relationships will be compromised. It may be difficult for the counselor to switch roles from friend to professional and to confront the client for fear of damaging the friendship. It may also be problematic for clients, who may hesitate to talk about deeper struggles for fear that their counselor/friend will lose respect for them. Counselors who are tempted to enter into a counseling relationship with a friend might do well to ask themselves whether they are willing to risk losing the friendship.

Because many private practitioners conduct groups as a significant part of their work, it may be worth noting here that the Association for Specialists in Group Work's code of ethics also addresses the issue of counseling friends. The code states that "Group counselors do not admit their own family members, relatives, employees, or personal friends as members to their groups" (ASGW, 1989).

A question remains, however, as to where to draw the line. Is it ethical to counsel a mere acquaintance? A friend of a friend? A relative of a friend? We think we might be going to absurd lengths if we were to insist that counselors should have *no* other relationship—prior or simultaneous—with their clients. Often, clients seek us out for the very reason that we are not complete strangers. A client may have been referred by a mutual friend, or might have attended a brief seminar given by the counselor as a public service. A number of factors may enter into the decision as to whether to counsel someone we know only slightly or indirectly. Borys (1988) found that male therapists, therapists who lived and worked in the same small town, and therapists with 30 or more years of experience all rated dual professional roles (as in counseling a friend, relative, or lover of a client) as significantly more ethical than did their comparison groups. Borys speculated that men and women receive different socialization regarding the appropriateness of intruding on or altering boundaries with the opposite sex (men are given greater permission to take the initiative or otherwise become more socially intimate). In a rural environment or a small town, it is difficult to avoid other relationships with clients, who are likely to also be one's banker, beautician, store clerk, plumber. Perhaps more experienced therapists believe they have the professional maturity to handle such dualities, or it could be that they received their training at a time when dual relationships were not the focus of much attention in counselor education programs. At any rate, whatever one's gender, work setting, or experience level, these boundary questions are bound to arise for the private practitioner.

Perhaps the question we need to ask ourselves is whether the nonprofessional relationship is likely to interfere, at some point, with the professional relationship. Sound professional judgment is needed to assess whether objectivity can be maintained and role conflicts avoided. Yet we need to be careful not to overstress the value of "objectivity." In our view, being objective does not imply a lack of personal caring or of subjective involvement. Although it is true that we do not want to get lost in the client's world, we think that we do need to enter this world in order to be effective.

A special kind of dual relationship dilemma can be created when a counselor needs counseling. As therapists, we are people too, with our problems. Many of us would want to go to our closest friends, who might well be therapists, to hear us out and help us sort out our problems. Our friends can be present for us in times of need, yet not in a formal way. We would not expect to obtain long-term therapy with a friend, nor should we put our friends in a difficult position by requesting such therapy, no matter how skilled they may be as therapists.

ACCEPTING GIFTS FROM CLIENTS

Borys' (1988) survey included two items relevant to the issue of accepting gifts from clients:

- On the question of accepting a gift worth under $10, 16% of the ethics questionnaire respondents reported the *belief* that this was "never ethical" or "ethical under rare conditions," and slightly more than 50% of practice-form respondents reported they had engaged in this *practice* not at all or only with a few clients.

- On the question of accepting a gift worth over $50, 82% of the ethics questionnaire respondents reported the belief that this was "never ethical" or "ethical under rare conditions," and slightly more than 98% of the practice-form respondents reported they had engaged in this *practice* not at all or only with a few clients.

Apparently, the price of the gift is a major factor in determining whether it is ethical to accept it. We think that there are other factors that should be examined besides the price tag of the gift. First of all, the motivation of the client needs to be considered. Certainly, if the giving of a gift is an attempt to win the favor of the therapist or is some other form of manipulation, it is best not to accept the gift. In addition to the motivation of the client, the relationship that has developed between the therapist and the client must be considered. As is true of so many ethical dilemmas, one possibility is for the therapist to discuss his or her reactions with the client about accepting a gift. It might very well be the client's way of expressing appreciation. If the therapist were to simply say, "I cannot accept your gift," the client might feel hurt and rejected. Rather than using a price tag to determine the ethical quality of accepting gifts, it is important to have a full and open discussion between the client and the therapist.

One way to avoid being put in the awkward position of having to refuse a gift is to include a mention of policy in the counselor's disclosure statement. Herlihy, in her private practice, routinely gives new clients a disclosure statement that includes the information that although the sessions may be intimate and personal, the relationship is a professional one and does not allow her to accept gifts. Although being clear with clients at the outset of the relationship does prevent some later dilemmas, Herlihy also recalls that one of her clients was a homemaker who occasionally brought her a jar of homemade jelly. Another brought a potted plant to their termination session as a way of saying "thank you" for the work they had accomplished together. She thinks it would have been churlish of her to have refused to accept those small gifts in the spirit in which they were offered. By contrast, one of her clients was a corporate executive who offered her a stock tip based on his insider's knowledge. When she explained to him why it was improper for her to profit from information gained in a counseling session, this led to a productive exploration of business ethics and the client's conflicting feelings about his involvements in some "shady" dealings.

Thus, we believe that a number of factors need to be considered in the decision of whether or not to accept a gift from a client. These include the worth of the gift, the stage of the counseling relationship, the motivations of the client in offering it, and the motivations of the counselor in accepting or rejecting it.

> In your own practice, have you ever accepted a gift from a client? Have you ever had to refuse the offer of a gift? How do you deal with this issue in your own work?

SOCIAL RELATIONSHIPS WITH CLIENTS

Borys' (1988) survey included several items related to social relationships with clients:

- On the question of inviting clients to a personal party or social event, 92% of the ethics questionnaire respondents reported the *belief* that this practice was never or rarely ethical, and 99% of the practice-form respondents reported they engaged in this *practice* not at all or with only a few clients.

- On the question of going out to eat with a client after a session, 81% of ethics questionnaire respondents reported the *belief* that this practice was never or rarely ethical, and 98% of practice-form respondents reported they engaged in this *practice* not at all or with only a few clients.

- On the question of inviting clients to an office/clinic open house, 51% of ethics questionnaire respondents reported the *belief* that this practice was never or rarely ethical, and 92%

of practice-form respondents reported they engaged in this *practice* not at all or with only a few clients.

- On the question of accepting a client's invitation to a special occasion, 33% of ethics questionnaire respondents reported the *belief* that this practice was never or rarely ethical, and 92% of practice-form respondents reported they engaged in this *practice* not at all or with only a few clients.

These findings suggest that the majority of practitioners avoid social relationships with clients in their actual practice, although they are divided on whether they consider some social relationships to be unethical. We think that it is important for therapists to be clear about the boundaries of the counseling relationship. If therapists are unclear, clients are likely to be even more unclear. The intimacy of the counseling relationship can easily lead clients to view the counselor as a "special type of friend" and to invite the counselor to participate in their lives outside the counseling sessions. When these invitations are declined, clients may feel hurt and rejected. One way to avoid these situations might be, as with accepting gifts, to include a policy about social relationships in the counselor's disclosure statement.

One important factor in determining how therapists perceive social relationships with clients may be the therapist's theoretical orientation. Borys (1988) found psychodynamically oriented practitioners to be the most concerned about maintaining professional boundaries. Among her findings:

- One of the most consistent findings was that psychodynamically oriented clinicians affirmed the unethical nature of dual professional, financial, and social involvements that have been explicitly prohibited by the APA *Ethical Principles* (1989) to a significantly greater degree than clinicians of other orientations.

- A reason given for the psychodynamic practitioners' opposition to dual role behaviors was the nature of psychodynamic training that promotes greater awareness of the importance of clear, nonexploitative, and therapeutically oriented roles, boundaries, and tasks. Their training stresses the subtle but potentially far-reaching consequences of violating these norms. It is also true that, in the psychodynamic view, transferential phenomena give additional meaning to alterations in boundaries for both client and therapist.

- A further explanation is that psychodynamic theory and supervision stress an informed and scrupulous awareness of the role the therapist plays in the psychological life of the client—namely, the importance of "maintaining the frame of therapy." This orientation focuses on the therapeutic implications when the professional role is altered, blurred, or distorted. Psychodynamic training focuses on the needs and motivations of the therapist, which has the potential for enabling psychodynamic practitioners to recognize and avoid exploitative relationships.

In summary, the counselor's stance toward the issue of socializing with clients depends on several factors. One is the nature of the social function: It may be more appropriate to accept a client's invitation to a special event than to invite a client to a party at the counselor's home. The orientation of the practitioner is also a factor to consider. Some relationship-oriented therapists might have no difficulty attending a client's graduation party, for instance, yet a psychoanalytic practitioner might feel uncomfortable accepting an invitation for any kind of out-of-the-office social function. This illustrates how difficult it is to come up with blanket policies to cover all situations.

In chapter 1, we gave an example of a situation in which a marriage counselor attended the renewal of wedding vows ceremony and reception of a couple she was seeing. We labeled the counselor's behavior as *benign* because no harm was done. Others might disagree with our views. Some might argue that attending the ceremony was an appropriate and desirable adjunct to the work done in therapy. Others might contend that the counselor took an unnecessary risk in attending the reception when she wasn't prepared to deal with the possibility that someone might ask her how she knew the couple.

What are your views about socializing with clients? How would you describe your theoretical orientation, and how do you think that orientation influences your views?

POTENTIAL PROBLEMS IN A HOME OFFICE

Private practitioners who use their personal residences for their offices may need to exercise particular care in keeping their personal and professional lives separate. Although having a private practice in one's home is not an ethical issue in itself, it is essential that clients are protected from interruptions and that therapists create a professional atmosphere when their office is in their home.

Setting up a practice in one's home opens up some potential dual relationship issues that can affect the client-therapist relationship. It appears that using one's home for one's office is becoming more acceptable, or at least more common. Richards (1990), in his book about private practice, made an excellent point that the needs and rights of the therapist's family should receive equal consideration to those given the client in a home office situation. It is not fair to children to banish them from the house, yet it is certainly not fair to clients to subject them to interruptions and normal noises. If we do use a home office to see clients, we must design a private space for our work with them. They should not have to contend with any interference during their therapy hour.

Therapists should realize that by using their home as their office, they are revealing a good deal of information about themselves and their lifestyle. Richards (1990) made the following observations:

> Clients have a need to know their therapist and identify with them. Therapeutically, this involves a variety of issues such as self-disclosure, transference, and countertransference. This means that if the therapist decides to have a home office, the effect that the house and the practitioner's lifestyle have on the public image and on the counseling relationship should be considered. (p. 59)

Practitioners also need to assess what clientele are appropriate—or not appropriate—for a home office practice. For example, clients who are potentially dangerous should not be seen in such a setting. Therapists need to consider the safety of themselves and their families when they work with intrusive or dangerous clients.

LIMITS OF SELF-DISCLOSURE

Borys (1988) found that 65% of her respondents to the ethics questionnaire believed it was never or rarely ethical to disclose details of current personal stressors to a client, and 91% of the practice-form respondents reported that they had done so not at all or with only a few clients. The wording of this item may have led a vast majority of respondents to claim that they did not engage in the practice: Going into detail about one's own stressors is certainly less appropriate than some other forms of self-disclosure. The *purpose* of self-disclosure in therapy should be kept clearly in mind. As therapists, when we disclose personal facts or experiences about our lives, it should be appropriate, timely, and done for the benefit of our client. If we are in tune with our clients, they will give us indications of how they are responding to our disclosures. If we go into great detail in disclosing the nature of our personal lives, we need to ask ourselves about our intentions and whether we are meeting our needs at the expense of our clients.

Clients are seeking our help for their problems, not to listen to our stories about our past or present struggles. This is such a subtle matter that it becomes difficult to put clear limits to therapist disclosure. Although we might carefully weigh how much and what we disclose of our personal lives to our clients, it might be very therapeutic to share our reactions to our client during the therapeutic hour. How are we affected by being with our client? What are our immediate reactions to being a part of this relationship? Again, the manner in which we share our reactions, the timing, and the client's readiness to hear our reactions are critical. Self-disclosure is a means to an end, not a goal in itself. As therapists, if we lose sight of the appropriate professional boundaries with our clients, the focus of therapy might well shift from the therapist attending to the client to the client becoming concerned about taking care of the therapist. In the preceding chapter, Borders noted in her position statement that the worst session between a supervisor and supervisee was the one in which the supervisor was self-disclosing. This is a good illustration of the dual role conflict that can arise. When a therapist takes on the role of client, the client is placed in the position of caretaker to the therapist. Clients, like the supervisee in Borders' example, are likely to feel vulnerable and insecure.

A key ingredient in maintaining appropriate boundaries of self-disclosure is the mental health of the counselor. If we are not being listened to by our significant others, there is a danger that we might use our clients as people who can understand the situation. If we are using our clients to satisfy our needs for attention, then we have an ethical problem. Our clients might become substitute parents, children, or friends, and this kind of reverse relationship is certainly not what our clients need.

In group counseling situations, a counselor might be inclined to be more self-disclosing than is true in individual counseling. This is not necessarily problematic, but counselors who lead groups should keep in mind that their primary purpose is to facilitate interpersonal communication and help the members use the group process to obtain their personal goals. Group leaders who use their groups as a way to work out their personal problems are behaving inappropriately. The ASGW *Ethical Guidelines* (1989) state clearly that "personal and professional needs of group counselors are not met at the members' expense" and that "group counselors avoid using the group for their own therapy."

RELATIONSHIPS WITH FORMER CLIENTS

Borys (1988) found that 53% of respondents to the ethics questionnaire believed it was never or rarely ethical to become friends with a client after termination, and 96% of practice-form respondents reported that they had done so not at all or with only a few clients. In the Pope et al. (1987) study of the beliefs and behaviors of therapists, 42% of the respondents said that they never formed social friendships with a former client, and only 6% considered it to be unethical. Practitioners seem to be divided about the ethicality of this behavior.

Does the therapeutic relationship ever end, so that other relationships become possible and appropriate? Karen Strohm Kitchener presents a thoughtful discussion of this issue in the following position statement.

Posttherapy Relationships: Ever or Never?

Karen Strohm Kitchener

One of the most confusing issues facing counselors and their clients is the nature of the relationship once the therapeutic contract has been terminated. Often clients fantasize that their counselors will somehow remain a substantial part of their lives as surrogate parents or friends. Counselors are sometimes ambivalent about the possibility of continuing a relationship, recognizing that there are real attributes of clients that under other circumstances might make them attractive colleagues, peers, or even sexual partners. In small towns or subculture communities in which contact is unavoidable, this becomes particularly problematic.

For the most part this issue remains unaddressed by the AACD *Ethical Standards* (1988) or the ethical codes of AACD's divisions, although all mental health organizations recognize that the responsibility to maintain confidentiality does not end just because the counseling relationship is over. In fact, the presumption of most ethical codes is that, other things being equal, maintaining confidentiality is a lifelong responsibility. We do not share clients' secrets just because they are no longer paying us. In other words, the codes acknowledge that mental health professionals have some ongoing responsibility to their former clients.

It is my position that there are other responsibilities, particularly when engaging in posttherapy relationships. The welfare of the former client and the gains that have been made in counseling are at risk when new relationships are added to the former therapeutic one. In other words, the risk of ethical complications is high, and counselors should avoid such relationships when they put the welfare of the former client at risk. Because the probability of harm from engaging in posttherapy sexual relationships is very high, they should always be considered unethical.

Ethical Responsibility. Many (Beauchamp & Childress, 1989; Kitchener, 1984; Stadler, 1986; Steere, 1984) have argued that when ethical codes are silent on issues that have potential ethical relevance, more fundamental ethical principles come into play. Specifically, the two principles that are consistently mentioned as fundamental in counseling are the responsibility to not harm clients and to bring some kind of benefit to them. In fact, we would not be in business as counselors if we did not believe that ultimately the core value in counseling and therapy is to help or in some way improve the lives of those we counsel. Taking someone into therapy implies that we have a contract to help them. If we harm those we have agreed to help, we are undermining the foundation of our profession (Kitchener, 1984).

Once someone has terminated his or her counseling relationship with us, our contract to help them ends. No one would suggest that because we have once seen a person in therapy we have a lifelong obligation to help them. But it is equally implausible to suggest that just because our contract has ended we ought willfully to engage in activities that will undo the benefits that have accrued from our services. If counselors were generally to engage in such activities, they would be promoting for themselves an endless supply of clients. Fix someone, hurt them, fix them again, and so on. Both our obligations to avoid hurting and to help our clients would be violated.

The question then becomes: Do posttherapy relationships undo the good we have done? Evidence is accruing that in particular sexual encounters with former clients have a variety of harmful consequences for the client, the counselor, and the profession (Vasquez, 1991). Two characteristics of the client-counselor alliance make such relationships difficult. The first is that there are vast differences in roles between therapist and lover. Because the former client's initial experience of the therapist is as a person who is committed to attend to and help him or her, it may be disconcerting to discover that the former therapist may not be the idealized person about whom the client fantasized. In fact, Geller, Cooley, and Hartley (1981–1982) have presented evidence that clients create an internalized "image" of their therapists and that the continuation of this image is associated with ongoing improvement after therapy is ended. Although there is no direct evidence, it is not hard to imagine that the image of the helper would be drastically altered should a sexual encounter occur. Consequently, therapy benefits could be truncated or destroyed. Further, Vasquez (1991) reported studies that suggest that memories of the therapeutic relationship remain important for extended periods after termination, and that many clients consider reentering therapy with their former therapists, an option that is closed if other relationships have ensued.

The second characteristic of the therapeutic alliance that makes posttherapy sexual relationships difficult is the power differential between therapist and client. Acknowledged or not, therapists because of their prestige and personal characteristics and because of transference issues often have considerable power over their clients. This power does not necessarily end with the end of therapy and may limit a former client's ability to make clear, rational, and autonomous choices about entering into a relationship with a former therapist. Choices that are not free initially often end up being resented and, thus, have the potential to cloud the impact of the former therapeutic alliance, or worse, they may be experienced as victimization and deeply traumatize the former client.

On the other side of the issue, such relationships are also fraught with dangers for therapists. Often they create unanticipated dynamics such as dependency that limit the equality of subsequent interactions (Kitchener & Harding, 1990). In addition, they may set up legal liabilities because in some states sexual relationships with former clients are illegal.

What about other posttherapy relationships with clients? Obviously, many of the same dynamics may be operating in nonsexual posttherapy relationships as in sexual ones. Former clients may be disillusioned with their therapists or feel exploited by them. However, nonsexual relationships lack the intensity or emotional vulnerability of sexual encounters and so have less of an immediate potential for damaging the prior therapeutic gains or recreating earlier trauma of sexual exploitation. Perhaps the final word ought to be "Let the counselor take care." Ultimately, because they are professionals whose services are committed to helping others, counselors have a strong ethical responsibility to avoid undoing that which they have worked so hard to accomplish.

Gerald Corey's Commentary

Karen Strohm Kitchener highlights an important message—that mental health counselors have an ongoing responsibility to their former clients. Perhaps it is this point that makes posttherapy relationships, especially of a social, romantic, or sexual nature, particularly problematic. Kitchener contends that the probability of harm from engaging in sexual relationships after terminating a therapeutic relationship is high, and that therefore, they should always be considered unethical. Personally, I do not go as far as asserting that such relationships "should always be considered unethical." Although Kitchener's argument seems somewhat extreme to me, I grant that it has merit. This is especially true in those cases in which therapists terminated the professional relationship with the motivation of beginning a personal relationship. Ethics committees have indicated that if it seems that termination occurred to give the appearance of compliance with an ethical guideline, the committees will find a clear ethical violation.

Regarding posttherapy relationships, I am in agreement with Akamatsu (1988) when he suggested that guidelines are necessary, but that they should delineate contingencies or circumstances that might be considered in determining the ethics of a particular case. He called for clearer guidelines, but he favored the individual handling of each case.

Kitchener raises a question that is good material for debate and discussion: Do posttherapy relationships undo the good that we have done? She presents a good argument that supports that sexual relationships with former clients have potential consequences. One factor that makes these new relationships difficult is that there are major differences in the roles played by a therapist and by a lover. Another factor that makes posttherapy sexual relationships difficult is the power differential between therapist and client.

The topic of posttherapy personal relationships with clients is one that I expect will continue to be debated among professionals for some time to come. If the practitioner works in a state where such relationships with former clients are illegal, this reduces the potential for meaningful debate. Even though there may be no legal mandate against such relationships, the ethical issue still looms large as to exploiting the power of the therapeutic role for the personal benefit of the therapist.

Barbara Herlihy's Commentary

It seems clear to me that there is sufficient rationale for prohibiting sexual relationships with former clients, and I think Kitchener does a fine job of elucidating that rationale. I agree that such relationships "should always be considered unethical" when the professional relationship involved personal counseling. I am reluctant to extend an outright ban to include brief-term career counseling or to some other "counseling" relationships (for instance, if the client was a member of a counselor's group when the group was primarily educational in nature).

With respect to nonsexual relationships with former clients, including friendships, some of the dangers that apply to sexual relationships do not apply. Kitchener does make an excellent point, though, when she states that posttherapy personal relationships close the door to the client's reentrance into therapy with the former counselor. Counselors are relieved of their obligation to continue helping when the therapeutic relationship ends, but it is questionable as to whether clients should be denied the opportunity to ask for our help again in the future. I do believe, however, that we make a mistake when we draw the boundaries of the professional relationship too narrowly. In my private practice, I do not want my clients to gain the impression that I care about them only during the therapeutic hour or only for the duration of the formal relationship. I routinely follow up with my clients after termination and enjoy hearing from them, even though I do not convert professional relationships into social relationships. Despite my concern regarding too rigid an interpretation of boundaries, I am impressed by the impact of Kitchener's final statement—that ethically conscientious counselors must be careful to avoid undoing what they have worked so hard to accomplish.

ISSUES IN MARRIAGE AND FAMILY COUNSELING

Because many marriage and family therapists are in private practice, we conclude this chapter with a look at some specific dual relationship issues that arise in marriage and family therapy.

Marriage and family therapists, like professionals in some other counseling specializations, have given increased attention to dual relationship issues in recent years. The revised *AAMFT Code of Ethics* (AAMFT, 1991) contains several standards pertaining to dual relationships. Under Responsibility to Clients, the code states as follows:

- Marriage and family therapists are aware of their influential position with respect to clients, and they avoid exploiting the trust and dependency of such persons. Therapists, therefore, make every effort to avoid dual relationships with clients that could impair professional judgment or increase the risk of exploitation. When a dual relationship cannot be avoided, therapists take appropriate professional precautions to ensure judgment is not impaired and no exploitation occurs. Examples of such dual relationships include, but are not limited to, business or close personal relationships with clients. Sexual intimacy with clients is prohibited. Sexual intimacy with former clients for 2 years following the termination of therapy is prohibited.

Under Professional Competence and Integrity, the code states as follows:

- Marriage and family therapists do not engage in sexual or other harassment or exploitation of clients, students, trainees, supervisees, employees, colleagues, research subjects, or actual or potential witnesses or complainants in investigations and ethical proceedings.

Finally, under Responsibilities to Students, Employees, and Supervisees, the code repeats the admonition against dual relationships and adds the following:

- Examples of such dual relationships include, but are not limited to, business or close personal relationships with students, employees, or supervisees. Provision of therapy to students, employees, or supervisees is prohibited. Sexual intimacy with students or supervisees is prohibited.

Some writers have taken exception to certain portions of this code. Ryder and Hepworth (1990) contended that extending the dual relationship prohibition beyond sexual misconduct is undesirable. They were concerned, in particular, with the dual relationship rule as it applies to graduate student supervision and training. They argued not only that certain aspects of dual relationships are ubiquitous and impossible to eliminate but that eliminating them is a bad idea. They suggested that supervision can be viewed as a process of helping a beginning therapist evolve into a colleague and perhaps even a friend. They pointed out an essential difference between therapy and supervision: Termination of therapy is the end of a relationship, but termination of supervision may involve a transition into a collegial relationship or friendship. They suggested that a good supervisory relationship emphasizes ambiguity, contradiction, and complexity. They concluded that "We think the blanket admonition to avoid nonsexual dual relationships with supervisees is a bad idea. We think it is a bad idea because we should stand for dealing effectively with inevitable complexity in relationships, and we should not stand for trying, quixotically, to legislate simplicity into relationships" (p. 131).

The revised *AAMFT Code* (1991) is one of the few codes that attempts to place a time limit on sexual relationships with former clients. In chapter 2, we stated that we wondered what was "magical" about a 2-year limit. Ryder and Hepworth (1990) have asked the same question. Again, they have argued against oversimplification, pointing out that "it is absurdly concrete that an act prohibited on one day can become permitted on the next" (p. 128).

The views of Ryder and Hepworth are illustrative of the phenomenon that seems to be occurring regarding dual relationships in the counseling profession more generally. Each time that a point about dual relationships is codified, a counterpoint seems to emerge that challenges it. Clearly, our profession faces further debate before consensus is reached regarding dual relationships.

> If you are a marriage and family therapist, what is your reaction to the revised *AAMFT Code?* Do you support the attempt to define and prohibit problematic dual relationships? Or do you believe, like Ryder and Hepworth, that it is a mistake to attempt to legislate such relationships?

It seems to us that some boundary issues apply in a special way in marriage and family therapy. A counselor's loss of boundaries in couples or family counseling can create inappropriate alliances and render the therapy ineffective. Consider this example:

> Paul, an intern, was counseling a married couple who came to therapy to work out problems in their marriage. Paul increasingly came to view the wife as overbearing and rigid. As the supervisor observed a session, she noted that Paul's responses to the husband were generally supportive, whereas his responses to the wife's verbalizations were often challenging or nonempathic. When the supervisor met with Paul and asked him what he was experiencing in the session, Paul replied, "I don't see how he can stand being married to her!"

> In this example, Paul colluded with the husband, in effect lining up with him against the wife. If you were Paul's supervisor, how might you work with Paul? Might you point out that Paul had, in effect, created an implicit and unacknowledged dual relationship as the husband's defender and advocate?

Dual relationships can arise for marriage and family therapists in other, more obvious ways. When the therapist has a prior relationship with either a husband or a wife, or with one member of a family, marriage and family therapists recognize the inadvisability of entering into a counseling relationship with the couple or the family. Social relationships with couples or families who are currently in counseling are generally to be avoided. When an individual has been in counseling, and then wishes to change the focus of the counseling to marriage or family therapy, some therapists refer the case to another professional. The prior individual therapeutic relationship might present some difficulties for the newly entering spouse or family members who might not feel on an equal footing. Yet these difficulties could be acknowledged and openly discussed.

In marital and family practice, a therapist may see a wife in individual therapy, then at some point the husband may join the sessions for couples therapy, and at times the entire family may be seen. Some therapists may not be comfortable with this practice, and they may have difficulty in sorting out primary allegiances. Confidentiality questions may arise. Some therapists are willing to see each spouse individually and to honor information divulged in the sessions as confidential (that is, it is not brought into joint sessions or individual sessions with the other spouse without explicit consent). Other therapists make it a policy to refuse to keep secret information that is shared in an individual session. Their view is that secrets and hidden agendas are counterproductive to family therapy. Perhaps the key is to practice in ways that are congruent with our values and our therapeutic style. It is essential that policies regarding confidentiality be explained to couples entering therapy.

Systems theory is based on a different orientation than individual therapy. In doing individual therapy, we may be sensitive to how an individual's changes affect his or her family, and we may explore ways in which the client's family is now influencing him or her, but the primary focus is on the individual's dynamics. From a systems perspective, one part of the system affects the whole system, and the system affects the individual. Margolin (1982) argued that complex dilemmas can arise when family members are seen together in therapy. Some interventions that serve one person's best interests might burden another family member or even be countertherapeutic. Margolin summarized the multiple responsibilities of the family therapist:

> Attempting to balance one's therapeutic responsibilities toward individual family members and toward the family as a whole involves intricate judgments. Since neither of these responsibilities cancels out the importance of the other, the family therapist cannot afford blind pursuit of either extreme, that is, always doing what is in each individual's best interest or always maintaining the stance as family advocate. (p. 790)

The systems perspective does raise a range of possible conflicts. All of these need to be addressed by the ethically conscientious practitioner.

CONCLUSIONS

Private practitioners confront myriad dual relationship issues in their work, some of which we have not covered in this chapter. For example, is it ever ethical to have a business relationship with a client? To sell a product to a client? To counsel an employee, or employ a client? We encourage you to read Borys and Pope's (1989) article that addressed some of these questions. Some issues that arise in private practice as well as in other settings are addressed in other chapters (e.g., we discuss counseling an employee in the next chapter). Issues that affect counselor educators who also have private practices were examined in chapter 3.

We hope, however, that this chapter has provided a thought-provoking discussion of some of the dual relationship issues that are most problematic for private practitioners and that they encounter most frequently in their work. It is clear that some issues are complex and that situations will arise about which there is no consensus. Golden summarized nicely when he stated that counselors must be guided by an internal compass in such situations.

CHAPTER 7

COLLEGE PERSONNEL WORK

Sue Spooner, in her position paper in this chapter, asserts that "the potential for dual relationships is everywhere within higher education." We think she states the situation quite accurately. In chapter 3, we examined some of the complex dilemmas that arise when counselor educators play multiple roles with their students. Similar issues arise in college and university counseling centers because many professionals who work in these counseling centers perform multiple functions—as counselors, supervisors, administrators, course instructors, and colleagues to faculty and staff. There is considerable potential for conflict among these roles. College student personnel workers who work in residence halls face yet another set of dual relationship dilemmas.

Hayman and Covert (1986) found that counselors employed in college and university counseling centers reported facing four types of ethical dilemmas. Although dilemmas related to confidentiality (including client dangerousness) were reported to occur with the greatest frequency, dual relationship issues were also cited by the study's respondents. These issues included "role conflicts" (because the counselor functions in multiple roles vis-à-vis the client, for example as counselor and personal friend, counselor and evaluator, or counselor and supervisor) and "conflicts with employer and institution" (because the counselor believes limitations on services imposed by the employer are not in the client's best interests or because there is pressure to alter a student's status). The authors of this study also asked college counselors what resources they used to resolve ethical dilemmas. They found that the counselors made little use of resources available to them—such as consultation or ethical standards—and most often resolved ethical dilemmas by relying on their own common sense.

We wonder whether the respondents to Hayman and Covert's study are typical in their failure to consult ethical standards. Hopefully, college and university counselors are aware that the American College Personnel Association (ACPA) *Statement of Ethical Principles and Standards* (1989) contains several standards pertinent to dual relationship issues.

In the section on Professional Responsibility and Competence, four standards caution student affairs professionals:

- Abstain from sexual harassment.
- Abstain from sexual intimacies with colleagues or with staff for whom they have supervisory, evaluative, or instructional responsibility.
- Refrain from using their positions to seek unjustified personal gains, sexual favors, unfair advantages, or unearned goods and services not normally accorded those in such positions.
- Ensure that participation by staff in planned activities that emphasize self-disclosure or other relatively intimate or personal involvement is voluntary and that the leader(s) of such activities do not have administrative, supervisory, or evaluative authority over participants.

The section on Student Learning and Development repeats the strictures against sexual harassment and sexual intimacies, and further cautions student affairs professionals:

- Avoid dual relationships with students (e.g., counselor/ employer, supervisor/best friend, faculty/sexual partner) that may involve incompatible roles and conflicting responsibilities.

It seems clear that when ACPA undertook to revise its ethical standards 2 years ago, those responsible for the revisions were very much attuned to the pervasiveness of dual relationship dilemmas in college personnel work. However, these standards—like all ethical codes—can not and do not provide answers to every specific ethical dilemma that college personnel workers might encounter. Some questions that may arise and that we discuss in this chapter are these:

- What role conflicts are inherent in counseling faculty and staff members? In counseling an employee?
- What potential role conflicts exist when college counselors also serve as course instructors?

- What are the role conflicts when a college counselor also functions as an administrator? When a student client is the subject of a campus discipline matter?
- Is it ever acceptable for college counselors to refer to themselves when they also have a private practice? How do college counseling centers develop a referral base?
- What dual relationship issues are involved in residence life?

Before we examine each of these issues, it may be useful to present an overall perspective. In the following position statement, Sue Spooner realistically argues that dual relationships are sometimes unavoidable and calls for awareness and careful judgment.

Dual Relationship Issues in College Student Personnel Work

Sue Spooner

The potential for dual relationships is everywhere within higher education. They are unavoidable, and they are not in all cases problematic. Counselor educators and counseling center staff are frequently approached by colleagues in the college or university environment who are seeking help for personal concerns. Other student affairs staff may or may not be trained as counselors. For those who have clinical skills, it would be ridiculous to ask them not to utilize those skills in the service of others. The lines separating consultations, supervisory sessions, and psychotherapy are rarely clear. Avoidance of all conflict is unlikely, and demanding it is apt to create more anxiety and guilt than the issue warrants.

It is easy to say that one should always refer such requests to someone outside the university, but in practice that may not be feasible for a variety of reasons. Community resources may not be available. Many colleges and some universities are situated in small towns where private practitioners are scarce. The cost of such services may not be covered by insurance and may be too expensive for the help seeker. The colleague may have had great difficulty in approaching us and may lack the courage to speak to anyone else. The colleague is indicating a degree of confidence that is not only flattering but also bodes well for a successful outcome.

If one's administrative role as supervisor of the help seeker, or as supervisor of one who in turn supervises that person, brings us in direct conflict, that should be discussed and understood. I believe that it is nearly impossible to adhere to a hard and fast rule about avoidance of all dual relationships in the higher education environment. Instead, I believe we should strive to be aware of the potential conflicts inherent in them and use our careful and considered judgment in deciding whether to offer help to a colleague.

In deciding whether or not to offer that help, one must consider not only the ethical issues involved but also the consequences for the colleague of offering or not offering such help. Up-front discussion of confidentiality and its limits is always necessary in these instances. Indeed, our reputation for that confidentiality may be one of the factors that brought the person to us. Much of what one hears and learns in the course of confidential conversations must disappear down that "deep well," which I call *the habit of silence.*

In situations that involve conflicts between two or more colleagues, an inside consultant who can serve as mediator is often more useful than an outsider, and outsiders are rarely, if ever, called in to these situations in higher education. The insider may have information that is pertinent to the situation and may also learn things best kept under wraps. Again, proper training helps us to forget we know.

The many situations that arise in the residence halls are particularly illustrative of the dual relationships that occur in student affairs work. Residence hall directors and their staffs tend to become melded into tightly knit working units. They are thrown together 24 hours a day. It is impossible for people in these networks not to know details of the private lives of others. The ages of the people involved make it likely that romantic relationships will develop between members of the staff, and they also sometimes occur between staff and student residents. Although we may officially frown on such developments, it would be flying in the face of human nature to try to prohibit or prevent such relationships from developing. Higher education is no more immune than any other work environment to conflicts such as those created by the office romance. When the boss is dating or even living with one of the staff, there are endless difficulties, not the least of which ensue when the relationship gets into trouble. Biased employee evaluations, charges of preferential (or prejudicial) treatment in work assignments, and even fights in the office over problems in the relationships are just some of the issues that get tangled up in such dual relationships. Again, it is wise to discourage them but impossible to prevent them. In most cases, we all agree that the practice of professional staff entering into romantic relationships with students is—and should be—prohibited by our ethical codes. But increasingly, many of our students are adult learners, with lives apart from their student status. When consenting adults enter into mutually chosen relationships, it is unlikely that we can enforce that prohibition.

Residence life staff typically are aware of problems their students and other staff members have with drugs and alcohol, with school work, with family ties, and myriad other elements of the lives of the young professionals and the young adult students they serve. They are frequently the best sources of help for both students and colleagues experiencing problems of various sorts. They also know about referral and tend to use their referral sources wisely and well.

Much the same can be said for other areas of student affairs in which dual relationships may exist. The key is not to avoid them at all costs but to be aware of the issues and conflicts that can arise and be prepared to deal with them as ethically and professionally as possible.

The young professional who works in student activities may be best friends with one who is on the staff of the academic advising center. They are apt to discuss situations that arise for either of them around students, staff, and the general ebb and flow of the institution. Perhaps a student who is overinvolved in activities to the detriment of studies and grades needs help. It is likely that both can be helpful, and this collaboration can be extremely effective. The residence hall staff member who knows and trusts a counseling center staff member who has been helpful in dealing with his or her own needs is more likely to seek consultation and make appropriate referrals to this known and trusted colleague. If properly alerted to conflicts and issues that hold the potential for hazards within their dual relationships, staff can avoid most of them and seek supervisory or consultative assistance for those that are unavoidable.

Finally, in the case of help for a colleague, there is the question of how long and how deeply to be involved. The decision must be based on knowledge of one's own limitations, the seriousness of the issues, and whether other help is available and appropriate.

Personally, I consider it simply part of my obligation to my institution to be of help to colleagues who seek me out. I do not charge for my services, but I am not in private practice. If I were, perhaps I would see this matter in a different light. I do not enter into long-term psychotherapeutic relationships with colleagues, and often the help I give is not even formalized into what others would recognize as a counseling session. But I do not feel that I can ignore a plea for help, so I offer whatever assistance is appropriate and seek consultation or make a referral if the ethical or clinical issues are complex.

Gerald Corey's Commentary

Spooner points out that dual relationships are sometimes unavoidable. For her, the core ethical concern is not to avoid dual relationships at all costs but to be aware of the issues and conflicts that often arise and to be prepared to deal with them as ethically and professionally as possible. I agree with her contention that they are not always problematic. She makes a useful point that rigid rules may not be appropriate in dealing with dual relationships in a higher education setting. I found myself wishing that Spooner had spelled out some other specific ways to reduce the problematic aspects of such relationships.

She rightly suggests that there are not always clear lines separating consultations, supervisory sessions, and counseling. Perhaps one way of sharpening these lines is to consider the primary purpose of each of these activities. True, there are areas of overlapping methods and purposes between supervision and counseling, yet each of these activities has different goals. From my perspective, keeping clearly in mind the main purpose of the activity—be it consultation, counseling, or supervision—is a way to assess the appropriateness of some of the dual relationships that might occur.

I appreciated Spooner's comments on the value of an up-front discussion of confidentiality and its limits involving dual relationships in higher education settings. Certainly, in some of the examples she gave (of a college counselor providing counseling to a colleague), the parameters of confidentiality need to be addressed prior to the decision to get involved in a helping relationship.

*Spooner observes that it is wise to discourage romantic involve-
ments between professional staff and students. She contends that
when consenting adults enter into these relationships, it is unlikely
that we can enforce our prohibition. It still seems that it is our professional responsibility to take steps to make professional staff
aware of the dangers of such relationships and to consider some
measures to take when such prohibitions are ignored. For instance,
if we know of a colleague in the university counseling center where
we work who makes it a practice to become romantically involved
with former clients (or even current clients), are there no procedures
that we are expected to follow? If we confront our colleague and he
or she maintains that there is no problem because all parties involved
are "consenting adults who are entering into mutually chosen relationships," what is our professional obligation?*

*Realizing that Spooner is working under space considerations, her
article does indeed raise even more questions than it answers. I think
that she has presented her position in a concise and convincing
manner. She emphasizes that we need not only to consider the ethical
issues involved in dual relationships but also to examine the consequences that sometimes follow when we deny help to a colleague or
student strictly because of dual relationship constraints.*

Barbara Herlihy's Commentary

*I agree that some dual relationships are unavoidable in the higher
education setting, and that awareness of issues and conflicts helps
us prepare to deal with them as ethically as possible. Spooner is
quite realistic in pointing out a number of reasons why it is not wise
for a college or university counselor to automatically refer every request for help that a colleague might make. She considers it simply
part of her obligation to her institution to be of help to colleagues who
seek her out, although she does not enter into long-term psychotherapeutic relationships with them. This seems to me to be a reasonable
stance, and one that I would appreciate if I were a faculty member
at her institution.*

*Spooner is also being realistic when she states that romantic re-
lationships are likely to develop in residence halls, given the ages of
the people involved. Spooner believes that it would be flying in the
face of human nature to try to prohibit and prevent relationships from
developing between staff and student residents. This might well be
true, but I think that we have an ethical obligation to at least attempt*

to avoid these problematic dual relationships. Information about ro-
mantic and sexual dual relationships can be presented during ori-
entation sessions for residence hall staff, so that they understand
the importance of avoiding such relationships. Spooner is correct in
noting that there may be little we can do to enforce stated prohibitions
when consenting adults enter into mutually chosen sexual relation-
ships, but we do have a responsibility to raise awareness of the
risks and potential harm that can occur.

CONFLICTS IN THE COUNSELOR ROLE

College and university counseling centers generally have a broad
mission to provide supportive services to students, faculty, and
staff. Although counseling services are provided primarily to students, what should college and university counselors do when a
faculty or staff member seeks counseling from them? Role conflicts
are certainly possible if college and university counselors accept
faculty or staff members as clients, and the potential problems that
arise from this arrangement deserve a full and open discussion
before establishing a therapeutic relationship. The question might
be raised of whether there is a difference between seeing a faculty
member or staff member for a limited number of sessions (say not
to exceed three sessions) as opposed to an ongoing therapeutic relationship. College or university policies may exist that spell out the
services that the center's counselors may offer to faculty and staff,
and of course in these cases counselors must adhere to policy.
Nonetheless, potential dual relationship issues can develop in subtle ways, as the following vignette illustrates:

> Li-Sung is a counselor in a college counseling center. She regularly
> offers workshops for faculty on stress management techniques
> and burnout prevention. Her focus is to help faculty members
> recognize and cope with stresses associated with teaching. At
> times, faculty members have approached her and requested in-
> dividual sessions to talk about their experiences in the workshop.
> Li-Sung is wondering if she might be getting involved in dual
> relationships by seeing her colleagues for these individual ses-
> sions. She seeks your advice on this matter.

- What are you inclined to say to Li-Sung regarding seeing faculty members for concerns pertaining to their work environment?
- Do you see any dual relationship concerns in agreeing to an individual session to process a faculty member's reactions to the workshop? What if the session uncovers deeper concerns that would require extended counseling?

Situations could arise in which an employee requests counseling. Practitioners seem to be divided regarding whether such a practice is ethical. In a study of the beliefs and behaviors of therapists conducted by Pope et al. (1987), 80% of the respondents claimed that they had never provided therapy to one of their employees, and 55% of them considered such behavior to be unethical. In the Borys (1988) study, 58% of ethics questionnaire respondents believed that providing therapy to an employee was "never ethical."

From our perspective, there are more problems involved in counseling an employee than there are potential benefits. One of the main ethical binds in this practice pertains to the power of the therapist/employer to hire and fire and to make or deny recommendations for promotion.

What might you do if a department secretary were to ask you to provide personal counseling? Assume that you are a trained therapist who also happens to be the director of the college counseling center. One day your secretary asks you if you would be willing to talk with her about her problems with her husband. She adds that the only reason that she is making this request of you is because she knows and trusts you and that "it is not like her to talk to anyone about her personal life."

We can think of many risks if clear boundaries are not established and maintained in this case. A few questions that come to mind are: When would the counseling sessions take place? Would this be a part of her time on campus as a secretary? What if the counseling went poorly? What are the implications for the work rela-

(continued on next page)

tionship? What if the secretary discloses an abusive relationship with her alcoholic husband? What if she begins going to a shelter when he threatens to become abusive, as you have suggested, and misses work on these occasions? Although you are sympathetic, you are also responsible for disciplining her for her absences, and you are upset when she falls behind in the work she does for you.

We can think of many reasons to avoid establishing a professional therapeutic role with a secretary, whether one donated the professional time or charged a fee. Although we might be willing to listen to her personal concerns about her home situation as we would with a neighbor, we would exercise caution in encouraging her to go into much detail about her problems. Instead, we would reflect our immediate reactions and encourage her to consider getting the professional help that she may need.

CONFLICTS IN THE INSTRUCTOR ROLE

Potential role conflicts exist when college and university counselors also serve as course instructors. Assume that a college counselor also teaches part time in a counselor education program. Are there any ethical binds in this practice? We do not see any new problems for this counselor besides those facing any other part-time faculty person who also has a private practice. We generally do not think it wise for the faculty person to accept a student as a client. But what if the student is a client first—who then enrolls in the instructor's class? Is the instructor/counselor free to prevent the student from enrolling in his or her class? What if there is only one section of a particular course that the student is required to take? In cases such as this we think that it is a good policy that the instructor seek consultation. One alternative is to have another instructor determine the student's grade. What if the course is a supervision class for fieldwork, which is not graded? Does this pose a problem? Clinicians in the Borys (1988) survey who responded to the ethics questionnaire generally believed it was "never ethical" (44%) or "ethical under rare circumstances" (31%) to provide therapy to a current student or supervisee. In the same study, 39% of the respondents felt that it was "never ethical," and 28% felt that it was "ethical under rare circumstances" to allow a client to enroll in one's class for a grade. It appears that practitioners are generally opposed to providing therapy to current students, but slightly less so when the class is not graded.

One of the faculty members at Corey's institution drafted the following position paper that is relevant to this discussion of a college counselor who is also an instructor. This faculty member's main recommendation is to maintain clear, appropriate, and well-defined boundaries:

> First, I agree it is probably not possible to avoid all dual relationships, and in fact I believe an attempt to do so would result in rigidity. Rigidity in this field is generally very nonproductive. I also agree that not all dual relationships are harmful. The difficulty is obviously in where to draw appropriate boundaries. I have been approached by students to see them or family members in counseling. And inevitably students will bring personal issues into our office hours, as these issues sometimes relate to their grades or some other aspect of their progress in the course.
>
> When entering this field of study, I think students learn a great deal about themselves through papers, meetings with instructors, peer groups, and classes. This results in self-exploration and personal growth and disclosure, which we encourage, and means that consequently we are going to see people struggle and grow, and they are often going to pursue an instructor with whom they have developed a relationship. Even if the instructor is unaware, I believe students look to us and attach to us, just in the classroom alone. I think for an instructor to serve as a mentor is part of good education, but to serve in a therapeutic role on or off campus is inappropriate. I think we need to be very sensitive to the already existing dynamics of this relationship between instructor and student as one similar to that between therapist and patient, particularly regarding the distribution of power. I see the students here as feeling empowered with all of their new awarenesses, yet being vulnerable in the midst of this process. I do see it being our responsibility to prevent further boundary confusion by avoiding therapy relationships.

College and university counseling center professionals who also serve as instructors might be able to avoid some problems by having clear policies in place. For instance, students who work in the counseling center might be prohibited from taking a class with the professional who supervises their work. Or students who are currently in counseling might be prohibited from taking a class from the instructor who is also their counselor. Although such policies could not possibly cover every contingency that might arise, their existence if known to students could help those students make informed choices.

CONFLICTS IN THE SUPERVISORY ROLE

What are the potential role conflicts when the college or university counseling center serves as an internship site for students in the counselor education program? What about a paid employee who has completed her degree and is employed under supervision for final licensing hours? We see these as fairly common practices that do not necessarily create problems. However, in the case of an intern, it is helpful to have a clear contract and understanding with the intern and with the faculty from the graduate counseling program about what is expected. If the supervisor is asked to be a part of the committee that makes an evaluation of the intern to determine whether he or she should be allowed to continue in the program, this could create difficulties. Ideally, the supervisor might want to separate evaluative functions so that he or she could be fully present for the intern as a supervisor. However, as we discussed in chapter 5, the supervisory role does include evaluation. Supervisors have responsibilities not only to the interns they supervise but also to the interns' clients. In addition, supervisors perform the gatekeeping function, by allowing only those interns who can provide competent services to progress on out into the field. The key here, as already stated, is to have clear boundaries marked at the outset, with full understanding of those boundaries on the part of the intern, the supervisor, and the faculty of the counselor education program.

Are there potential problems in hiring an intern after he or she graduates? If the intern proves to be an exceptionally competent counselor and could fit ideally into a job position, what would be the problem in hiring this person? As long as due procedures are used to hire the best candidate for the position, we do not see an ethical problem. However, once the person is hired in the counseling center, he or she is no longer a supervisee but a colleague. This shift in roles can involve a difficult transition for both the former supervisor and the former intern and might necessitate some open discussion, sensitivity, and awareness.

CONFLICTS IN THE ADMINISTRATIVE ROLE

The director of a college or university counseling center functions in the role of an administrator, and it is unrealistic to assume that such a person could or should avoid any type of counseling activity with students. Here is an example in which one person must carry out at least two roles: that of counselor and that of administrator. The main potential role conflict we can see is when the administrator has an evaluative capacity. If this is the case, alternatives need to be worked out before establishing therapeutic relationships. In such a case, consultation with colleagues is a good practice.

Are there potential role conflicts when a student is involved in a campus discipline matter? Gerald Corey recalls an incident that occurred when he was a counselor in a college counseling center:

> The director of the center informed me that my client was being suspended from the college because of stealing expensive lab equipment. Fortunately, I was not asked to disclose to the director the details of what we had discussed in our sessions. However, the director asked me to continue seeing the student even though he was to be on probation. This particular student never told me anything about stealing property from the college, but what if he had disclosed this? I can see a potential role conflict that could emerge if he discussed his intended plans or his current behavior. My hope is that I would have clearly specified at the outset the limits of confidentiality and those areas where I would be required to report certain information. In this way, my client would understand both his rights and responsibilities, and he would also realize that I had certain responsibilities as his counselor.

As was noted in cases in which counselors also serve as instructors, having clear policies in place can help to avoid difficult situations. For instance, referral sources on campus (such as the dean who might refer students involved in discipline matters or the university's health center) should be clearly informed as to what information they will and will not receive about the students they have referred for counseling.

PRIVATE PRACTICE AND REFERRAL ISSUES

We know several counselors who work in university counseling centers who also have part-time independent private practices. Is it ever acceptable for these counselors to refer to themselves in their private practice? To refer to their colleagues who may also have independent private practices?

Our immediate reaction is that it is not acceptable for college or university counselors to refer their student clients to themselves in private practice. It is important for these counselors to follow the guidelines and policies of the counseling center where they work, which are likely to address this issue. To refer clients to one's private practice can easily be seen as a conflict of interest. However, let's consider the situation in which the college counseling center has a limitation on the number of times (say, six sessions) that a student can be seen by a counselor. Assume that at the sixth session the student says, "I feel that I am just beginning to make some progress, yet I realize that the college has a policy that ongoing counseling cannot be provided by the counseling center. I know that you have a private practice, and I would be willing to see you in your practice because I feel that we have an excellent working relationship and I really do not want to stop at this point."

> If you were this counselor, how might you respond? What might you say to the college counselor if she were to consult you for your advice in this matter? Would it make any difference if the counselor were to offer a discounted fee to the student? Is it realistic to suggest a referral? What if the counselor did suggest a referral and the student resisted, making it clear that he wanted to continue seeing the counselor with whom he began? What if other professionals were not willing to adjust their fee schedules to accommodate this student? What if the geographic location was one in which there were no other therapists within a range of 100 miles?

These questions show how complex this situation really is. Although we question the ethics of the college counselor who regularly draws his or her clientele for private practice from the college counseling center, we do not want to make a blanket statement that to accept a student in one's private practice is unethical. An emergency situation could arise, for instance if a suicidal client were seen by the college counselor for the limited number of sessions allowed. The counselor might assess the risk in attempting to refer this client as being higher than the risk involved in continuing to see the client in the counselor's private practice. Some nonemergency situations call for common sense judgments: Perhaps a client needs only one or two additional sessions to complete his or her work in counseling. Referring the client to another counselor does not seem to be the best option, especially since starting over with a new counselor might involve additional expense to the client.

Whether or not college and university counselors have their own private practices, it is likely that they will need to refer some clients whose needs they cannot meet due to constraints of the setting. How do these counselors develop a referral base? A counselor who does not have a private practice may have a colleague in the counseling center who does have one. We believe it is prudent policy to avoid referring to this colleague. Rather, the referral base should include practitioners in the community for whom it is clear that no conflict of interest exists. It certainly could include community practitioners whom the college counselors know and trust, so long as these practitioners do not have other ties to the university that could create a conflict of interest. Competent community practitioners should at least be afforded an opportunity to apply to be included on the referral list because limiting the list too narrowly to one's friends or associates could raise the issue of restraint of trade.

SUMMARY AND CONCLUSIONS

Dual relationship issues are truly pervasive in higher education, including college student personnel work. The ACPA *Statement of Ethical Standards* (1989) contains several statements that pertain to dual relationships, although there is some evidence that college and university counselors make little use of the code. Numerous forms of role conflicts are possible in college and university personnel work because of the multiple roles that are played—as counselor, administrator, course instructor, supervisor, and colleague to faculty and staff. Some practitioners, such as Spooner, counsel a realistic response to dual relationship issues in the recognition that not all dual relationships are avoidable or harmful. Spooner may be correct in asserting that the key is not to avoid them at all costs but to be aware of the issues and conflicts that could arise. College and university personnel workers, like professionals in other settings, must navigate carefully through some uncharted waters.

CHAPTER 8

SCHOOL COUNSELING

School counselors do not seem to have been much concerned with dual relationship issues. The *Ethical Standards for School Counselors* (American School Counselor Association [ASCA], 1984) make no specific mention of dual relationships, and very little has appeared in the school counseling literature about the topic. This lack of attention may be due to the fact that many dual relationship issues do not apply to working with children or to the school setting. For instance, the issue of posttherapy social relationships is more pertinent to working with adults, and the issue of bartering for goods or services does not apply to counselors who are salaried employees.

Nonetheless, we believe that school counselors need to be aware of dual relationship issues and that they do encounter dual role conflicts in their work. Although the ASCA code of ethics does not specifically address dual relationships, ASCA members are also bound by the *Ethical Standards* (1988) of AACD, the parent organization, and therefore by its standards on dual relationships. Questions that we explore in this chapter include these:

- In what ways can dual relationship issues arise for school counselors?
- What are the role conflicts inherent in working with minor clients?
- How can school counselors avoid dual relationship conflicts with teachers? Parents? Administrators?
- What issues arise when the school counselor functions as a consultant?
- What are the potential dual relationship issues in child abuse cases?

We present our own ideas regarding these questions, and A. Michael Dougherty identifies some roles and duties commonly assumed by school counselors that can create dual relationship conflicts.

ROLE CONFLICTS

Dual role conflicts can arise in subtle and sometimes unexpected ways for school counselors. Consider these two scenarios involving DeWayne and Angelica, both school counselors:

- After school, a teacher drops by DeWayne's office. DeWayne and the teacher are friends. DeWayne casually asks, "How's it going?" The teacher's response comes out in a rush. She is feeling tremendously stressed by the demands of raising a child with a handicapping condition, caring for an aging parent, and going to graduate school. When DeWayne suggests that she might want to consider seeking counseling, the teacher says, "Where on earth would I find either the time or the money for that! I hope you won't mind if I 'bend your ear' occasionally."

- Angelica is conducting a parenting skills group one evening per week. During the fourth session, one of the parents relates an anecdote about the discipline methods he uses. It seems clear to Angelica that these methods are abusive.

These two situations seem quite dissimilar, but they both raise potential dual role relationship conflicts. In DeWayne's case, the teacher hopes to receive—and clearly needs—some free counseling. It might be relatively easy for DeWayne to convince himself that it is okay just to "listen occasionally," and that it is his job to serve the teachers as well as the students. Yet DeWayne's friendship with the teacher prohibits him, ethically, from entering into a counseling relationship.

Angelica, too, might be torn by conflicting wishes. Although she knows she is legally and ethically required to report the child abuse, she foresees the difficulty in attempting to serve both as the parent's ongoing group leader and as reporter of the abuse. She is loathe to destroy the parent's trust and perhaps to disrupt the group. She is tempted to avoid or postpone reporting in the hope that the parent will learn nonabusive discipline methods by continuing in the group.

If you were in DeWayne's place, what would you do? How might you respond to your friend's request, in a way that both preserves the friendship and assists your friend to get the help she needs? What might you do if you were Angelica? How could you balance the requirements of the law, the needs of the child, the needs of the parent, and the needs of the group?

Both of these examples illustrate that potential dual relationship issues can arise unexpectedly and can create dilemmas for conscientious school counselors.

The situation in which DeWayne found himself is not at all uncommon. Friendships between teachers and school counselors are a natural outgrowth of their similar interests and daily contacts. In addition, many school counselors were teachers before they became counselors, and sometimes they counsel in the same school where they taught. When the transition first occurs from teacher to counselor, difficulties can arise. Teachers who are accustomed to the open sharing that occurs among colleagues may resent that the counselor, in his or her new role, has a different perspective on student concerns and seems less forthcoming with certain kinds of information due to the need to protect student confidentiality. These transitional difficulties can probably best be resolved through open communication in which the counselor clearly defines his or her new role.

Another problem relates to school counselors who are also teachers. Can they balance both roles? Being a teacher actually might help them in being a better counselor, yet their role as teacher could get in the way of forming counseling relationships. We recommend that when a professional must serve simultaneously as a teacher and a counselor, every effort be made to have a caseload consisting only of counselees who are not currently enrolled in the classes taught by the teacher/counselor.

Inevitably, school counselors will have friends who are also parents. This can create an uncomfortable dual role conflict when a friend's child attends the counselor's school and is assigned as a counselee. The counselor must keep separate boundaries around the professional relationship with the child and the personal relationship with the child's parents—an extremely difficult task!

Particularly in small towns and rural communities, it is difficult for school counselors to avoid some overlap between their personal and professional roles. When the counselor's friends are also the parents or teachers of his or her student clients, some role conflicts may be inevitable. For example, Gerald and Marianne Corey recently consulted with school counselors in Alaska. Many school counselors in that state fly from one school to another in very remote villages that are accessible only by plane. Thus, the school counselor serves many schools. Often the school counselor performs many functions and is even a relative of many of the school children. This example reminds us that the dual role relationship issues pertaining to school counseling need to be considered within the context of the community.

MULTIPLE RESPONSIBILITIES

School counselors serve multiple constituencies. ASCA's *Ethical Standards for School Counselors* (1984) spell out the counselor's responsibilities to pupils, parents, colleagues and professional associates, school and community, self, and the profession. We have noted that as the responsibilities and expectations of one role diverge from those of another role, the potential for harm increases. School counselors often encounter situations in which the expectations of their student clients, parents, teachers, and administrators all differ.

The main role conflict that we see school counselors as facing pertains to confidentiality issues. Conflicts about confidentiality often arise when school counselors try to balance their responsibilities to pupils with their responsibilities to parents (Huey, 1986). Counselors are legally responsible to the parents but ethically more responsible to the students. According to Wagner (1981), the younger the client, the greater the counselor's allegiance needs to be to the parent. Yet minor clients have a right to know what information they reveal will be kept confidential and what may be shared with parents (or teachers or administrators). One way to lessen the chance of unproductive role conflicts is to conduct sessions with the student and his or her parents in those situations in which the parent wants information about the child.

School counselors are often faced with difficult ethical dilemmas if their roles are not clearly defined, or if school policies exist that impinge on their effectiveness. Is the counselor serving the student, the student's parents, the community, or the school? It seems that if counselors are expected to carry out disciplinary functions, their capacity to serve as effective personal counselors is severely restricted. If they are expected to report drug abuse situations to parents or administrators, this will impact their ability to form counseling relationships with many students. If counselors are required to inform parents about details in cases concerning birth control or abortion, some students may do their best to stay away from the counselors. Sometimes school counselors are asked to suspend and expel students, monitor tardiness and truancy, police the restrooms, enforce school policies, and serve as supervisors at school events. Some of these functions may get in the way when school counselors attempt to establish personal counseling relationships with students.

In the following position statement, A. Michael Dougherty suggests that school counselors should avoid roles that conflict with their primary role as counselor and offers some strategies for taking a proactive stance in defining their roles.

The School Counselor's Role

A. Michael Dougherty

School counselors are often asked as part of their everyday duties to take on roles that might possibly conflict with their primary role as counselors, for example, such non-counseling-related duties as disciplinarian and lunchroom monitor.

I believe that school counselors should avoid roles such as disciplinarian, substitute teacher, and lunchroom/bathroom/bus monitor that conflict with their primary role as counselors to students. The unique role of the counselor in the school makes the taking on of such roles highly questionable as they are likely to violate some of the basic tenets of the counseling relationship (e.g., confidentiality). As a consequence, new counseling relationships with students may be inhibited and existing ones may be compromised.

School counselors often engage in both preventive and remedial efforts as part of their overall counseling program. Preventive aspects of the program include group guidance, consultation with teachers and administrators, advocacy, and membership on student support teams. The primary elements of the remedial role of the counselor include individual and group counseling.

Emphasis on the preventive aspects of the school counselor's role has increased in the past decade. Preventive interventions frequently assume an acceptance of the school counselor as "one of us" by other staff members. One important way to be accepted in such a manner is to engage in the same day-to-day activities in which other staff engage. Unfortunately, many of these activities jeopardize the counseling role of the school counselor. A critical issue for school counselors, then, is to gain acceptance by staff and at the same time not engage in roles that jeopardize counseling relationships with students. It is tempting for school counselors to give in and take on roles such as bus duty, particularly when there is strong pressure from administrators and teachers for them to do so. When school counselors assume roles such as these, undesirable dual role relationships may be created. When school counselors engage in such activities as bus duty, lunchroom duty, and bathroom monitoring, they increase the probability of placing themselves in the position of disciplinarian or informant. The dual roles of disciplinarian/informant and counselor, even when entered into only briefly, certainly put a counselor in a conflict of interest situation. Consider the following scenario as an illustration:

> Maria Sanchez, a middle school counselor, is currently conducting a counseling group for children of divorce. Vanessa is one of the students in the group. As a member of the school staff, Ms. Sanchez has accepted bathroom monitoring as part of her duties. One day, as she is monitoring the girls' bathroom, she encounters Vanessa smoking a cigarette. Ms. Sanchez is now in the situation in which she must report Vanessa to the school administration for misconduct.

If you were Ms. Sanchez, how would you handle this situation so that you hold to your commitment to monitor the bathroom and at the same time not damage the counseling relationship with Vanessa?

Even this very simple example dramatically points out the necessity for caution on the part of school counselors in taking potentially conflicting roles with the students they counsel. By reporting Vanessa to the administration, Ms. Sanchez could seriously damage the counseling relationship. Other students who hear of this counselor who "asks you to trust her at one time and turns you in at another time" could keep prospective clients from seeking out Ms. Sanchez as a counselor.

School counselors often think of their roles in terms of the "three C's": counseling, consultation, and coordination. But the reality is that there are many other potential roles that the counselor might assume. Smaller roles like that of taking on bus duty may seem inconsequential. However, when counselors engage in roles that are incompatible with the primary role of counselor, the resulting dual role relationships with students can have an adverse impact and should therefore be avoided.

School counselors, then, at the outset of each school year need to clearly and publicly state their roles to school personnel as well as to students. When staff and students alike realize the counselor's unique role in the school, then the counselor is much more likely to be able to avoid dual relationships that adversely affect counseling relationships with students. At the same time the school counselor can be accepted as "family" by staff by taking on additional duties that do not create the potential for inappropriate dual role relationships, such as working in the concession stand or running afterschool parent groups. By engaging in activities such as these, counselors can demonstrate to teachers and other staff that they too are carrying their load.

⸙

Gerald Corey's Commentary

Often school counselors are asked to suspend and expel students, monitor tardiness, take care of truancy concerns, police the restrooms, enforce school policies, function as substitute teachers, sit in study halls for students on detention, and serve as supervisors at school events. Some of these functions may get in the way of school counselors who hope to establish personal counseling relationships with students. I agree with Dougherty's contention that many of these day-to-day activities jeopardize the counseling role of the school counselor. As he indicates, it is difficult to fulfill the dual role of both counselor and disciplinarian/informant.

When counselors in a school setting take on roles that are incompatible with their primary roles as counselors, their relationships with students are bound to be adversely affected by attempting to balance multiple and conflicting roles. I see it as the responsibility of school counselors to educate both administrators and teachers as to their primary role. If school counselors assume roles that are directly oppositional to the spirit of the counseling process, they are indeed lessening their effectiveness in providing both preventive and remedial assistance. Counselors need to assume a proactive stance in establishing their professional identity, and they need to resist the pressures to be all things to all people. It is up to the counselors to decide on their priorities and then do the work of letting people know of their professional functions. They can help others appreciate their professional role by making personal appearances. It helps to talk to parent groups, to go into classrooms and talk to the students, and to meet in groups with teachers and administrators. Counselors might consider that if they do not define their own identity as professionals, other groups such as administrators will define their work roles for them.

Barbara Herlihy's Commentary

Michael Dougherty shows a keen sensitivity to the demands that are often placed on school counselors. With respect to multiple roles and duties, school counselors may feel as though they are in a "no-win" situation. If they object to taking on inappropriate duties such as monitoring restrooms or hallways, they risk being seen as uncooperative by administrators and as "privileged" by teachers. If they agree to take on such duties, they risk jeopardizing their counseling relationships with students.

Dougherty recognizes that school counselors want acceptance and to be seen as "family" by the school staff. I agree that counselors are more effective in their work when they are an integral part of a team. Yet I think that school counselors sometimes allow themselves to be taken advantage of because of their need to "people-please" and be accepted. In such cases, they would do well to remember what they tell their student clients: It is okay to say no to inappropriate requests.

Some noncounseling assignments create potential dual role conflicts, and Dougherty rightly argues that these should be avoided. I agree that it is up to school counselors to educate their constituencies about their proper role. It is also up to counselor educators to prepare prospective school counselors to manage this task. School counselors sometimes fault counselor education programs for presenting an idealized picture that ill prepares them for the struggles they face. I think this criticism has some validity. Counselor educators generally do a fine job of teaching the three Cs, but the real world of the school counselor is much more complex. If we expect school counselors to be proactive in defining their roles, then we as counselor educators have two obligations: (1) to give prospective school counselors realistic information about their future world of work, with all its complexities, smaller roles, and potential conflicts, and (2) to teach them effective strategies for proactively defining their roles.

School counselors are indeed hard-working, contributing members of the school staff who offer a unique set of services. The more that teachers, administrators, and parents understand what counselors can and do accomplish, the less pressure there will be for them to take on additional, inappropriate roles.

If you are a school counselor, when are you asked to take on noncounseling duties that could conflict with your counselor role? How do you handle such requests? What do you see as the advantages and disadvantages of taking on extra roles and responsibilities?

To sum up, we think that perhaps the best way to minimize dual relationship conflicts is for counselors to be clear as to their primary role and function as counselors and to communicate this to teachers, parents, administrators, and most important of all, to the students. Students have a right to know, before they get involved in a counseling relationship, the limits of this relationship and especially the limits of confidentiality.

Some children may need intensive personal counseling or family counseling, yet it might well be beyond the scope of the school to provide this assistance. If the school counselor attempts to offer this kind of counseling, he or she may be doing a disservice to the student in the long run. School counselors need to be aware of their limitations, especially in cases when they have a large number of students to whom they are responsible. If a counselor has a case load of 500 students, this does not allow for a great deal of intensive personal work with individual students. Furthermore, the school policy might be to refer students who need psychological assistance. To avoid becoming embroiled in role conflicts, it is a good practice for school counselors to develop a network of referral resources within the community.

THE CONSULTANT ROLE

School counselors are increasingly being expected to serve as consultants to teachers, administrators, and parents (Dougherty, Dougherty, & Purcell, 1991; Ferris & Linville, 1985). This role can create conflicts, as can all tripartite relationships. The counselor role assumes that the counselor's primary function is to establish a therapeutic relationship with the student's welfare as the first consideration. Yet the consultant role emphasizes the process of consulting with "other professionally competent persons when this is in the interest of the client" (ASCA, 1983, p. 6). Ferris and Linville (1985) raised some important questions: How can counselors uphold responsibility for the student's best interest if they are working only indirectly with the student in a consultant role? What are the ethical implications of giving a measure of responsibility for intervention and treatment to consultees (parents, teachers) who are not trained as counselors?

In their role as consultants, school counselors are most likely to encounter ethical issues pertaining to dual role relationships when they are involved in situations where boundaries are not clearly drawn. Being aware of the issues involved in the consultant/consultee/client relationship, and the rights of consultees, can enable counselors to identify and deal with ethical problems that may arise. Caplan (1970) has noted that consulting is not the same as counseling and that the two roles should be kept separate. Turning a consultant relationship into a personal counseling relationship is a mistake.

The consultant role pertains to issues such as maintaining a work-related focus, avoiding dual role relationships, and providing freedom of choice to consultees. According to Dougherty (in press), school counselors who function as consultants need to develop a well-defined set of mutually agreed-upon expectations regarding the nature of consultation. The focus must be on work-related concerns. For instance, school counselors should avoid discussing the personal concerns of a teacher or an administrator during consultation with that person. Due to their training, school counselors may have a tendency to move toward exploring the personal problems of their consultees. Therefore, they need to assess the potential harm that may arise before they engage in a dual relationship with their consultees. Ethical practice dictates that school counselors monitor their interventions so that they avoid creating dependency, using manipulation, or misusing power in consultation relationships. They should strive to create and maintain a collaborative relationship.

> If you are a school counselor who functions as a consultant, how do you deal with these issues? What steps do you take to ensure that student confidentiality is preserved and that students' best interests are served in these situations? If you are interested in learning more about how to manage the consultant role, we invite you to read chapter 11 for further information.

DEALING WITH CHILD ABUSE

Perhaps in no arena is the potential for dual role conflicts greater than in cases of child abuse. All counselors are bound by the law. When school counselors become aware of situations involving suspected child abuse or neglect, they are required to report it. The school counselor's role, however, is rarely limited to making a report. In fact, school counselors may find themselves involved in multiple roles as informant, continuing counselor to the child victim, employee of the school, liaison with other agencies, and witness in court.

The counseling relationship with the child can be endangered when a counselor files a report. Although children should be informed of the limits of confidentiality, a child may have conflicting reactions when the counselor reports the abuse. The counselor may be viewed as an ally in putting a stop to the abuse. Or the child may feel betrayed and angry, particularly if retribution against the child occurs in the home or if the child is removed from the home and perhaps from the school (to go to foster care) as a result of the counselor's action. It is more likely, however, because most abused children are left in their parents' custody, that the counselor will have the task of providing ongoing counseling to the child. Treatment of abuse victims can be a lengthy process that severely strains the counselor's resources. A problem can also develop when a counselor does not maintain appropriate boundaries. For instance, some counselors may attempt to become the friends of such children, or they may attempt to "adopt" them. Counselors need to recognize their limits and not allow themselves to become overly involved to the extent that they lose their capacity for objectivity.

Counselors also need to follow procedures that have been established in their school systems. Some systems require that the principal be notified before a report is made. Teachers may also need to be informed. It is difficult to maintain boundaries of confidentiality in these instances, and counselors must be careful to inform only those who have a need to know and to avoid relating specific material that the child has disclosed in confidence.

Once a counselor has made a report, he or she is involved with the court system until a final adjudication is made. The counselor will need to work with child protective services caseworkers, the police, and perhaps with attorneys. If the case goes to trial, the counselor may be required to testify as a witness. Considerable time demands can be involved, and counselors must tread carefully through the series of confidentiality questions that will arise. The multiple roles played by school counselors involved in child abuse cases can severely test the counselor's ability to handle conflicting demands and keep the client's welfare foremost.

SUMMARY

The work of the school counselor involves many ethical dilemmas, some of which involve dual role relationships and the conflicts that arise when counselors serve in multiple roles with various constituencies. Demands made by principals, teachers, parents, and outside agencies can sometimes run counter to student clients' best interests. These situations can be stressful. Parr (1991) offered some ideas for coping with these stressors. Some of them include consult with colleagues, clearly define and publicize your role and function, network with others, and practice personal stress management. We think these are all good suggestions. Dual role conflicts will arise for school counselors, and preparedness and good judgment are the keys to dealing with them effectively.

CHAPTER 9

REHABILITATION COUNSELING

Rehabilitation counselors who work in both the public and private sectors confront some unique dual relationship dilemmas. Perhaps in no other counseling specialization is there greater potential for divided loyalties and conflicts of interest. Rehabilitation counselors serve multiple constituencies. Each of these constituencies has a vested interest in the outcome of counseling, and these interests are often competing and contradictory.

Rehabilitation counselors facilitate the personal, social, and economic independence of persons with disabilities and, more specifically, help these persons find or return to employment. Traditionally, most rehabilitation counselors have worked in the public sector in federal and state government agencies such as rehabilitation facilities, state vocational rehabilitation programs, and Veterans Administration hospitals. More recently, private, for-profit rehabilitation companies have emerged to provide services, particularly in workers' compensation and the insurance industry. Public and private sector rehabilitation have much in common, although there are some differences in goals and emphasis. Public agencies espouse a long-term goal of maximizing human potential, whereas the private rehabilitation provider has the more results-oriented goal of returning the client to gainful employment, preferably in the same or a similar job with the same employer (Mitchell & Sink, 1983).

The accelerating growth in private sector rehabilitation has changed the structure of rehabilitation counselor training, job roles, and work functions. Other trends are for rehabilitation counselors to be involved with school-to-work transition, traumatic brain injury, and services to people with life-threatening illnesses (Fagan & Jenkins, 1989). Children with handicapping conditions make up approximately 10% of the school-age population; thus, rehabilitation service providers are becoming more involved in the school setting. Some writers (Humes, Szymanski, & Hohenshil, 1989; Lombana, 1989) have suggested the need for a transdisciplinary approach involving coordination among special education, school counseling, and rehabilitation providers.

In this chapter, we examine dual relationship dilemmas that arise for public and private sector rehabilitation counselors, using these questions to guide our discussion:

- What guidance is offered to rehabilitation counselors by codes of ethics?
- How can rehabilitation counselors balance competing commitments to their clients and to their employers?
- How can counselors serve as gatekeepers to services as well as serve as counselors?
- How can counselors serve as evaluators and expert witnesses and as counselors to their clients?

ETHICAL CODES

Certified Rehabilitation Counselors (CRC) are guided in practice by their *Code of Professional Ethics for Rehabilitation Counselors* (American Rehabilitation Counseling Association [ARCA], 1987). This code clearly states that "the primary obligation of rehabilitation counselors is to their clients. . . . Rehabilitation counselors shall endeavor at all times to place their clients' interests above their own." The CRC code has been adopted by several professional rehabilitation organizations including the American Rehabilitation Counseling Association, the National Rehabilitation Counseling Association, and the National Council on Rehabilitation Education. This code specifically addresses the dual relationship issue:

- Rehabilitation counselors will be continually cognizant of their own needs, values, and of their potentially influential position, vis-à-vis clients, students, and subordinates. They avoid exploiting the trust and dependency of such persons. Rehabilitation counselors make every effort to avoid dual relationships that could impair their professional judgments or increase the risk of exploitation. Examples of dual relationships include, but are not limited to, research with and treatment of employees, students, supervisors, close friends, or relatives. Sexual intimacies with clients are unethical. (ARCA, 1987)

Other codes exist that are more specific to the counselor's work setting. Ethical standards for the private sector rehabilitation professional are provided by the National Association of Rehabilitation Professionals in the Private Sector (NARPPS). Because of the special nature of private-for-profit rehabilitation counseling, the NARPPS code addresses the issue of competing interests more specifically. These NARPPS *Standards and Ethics* (1981) state that "When there is a conflict of interest between the disabled client and the NARPPS member's employing party, the member must clarify the nature and direction of his/her loyalty and responsibilities and keep all parties informed of that commitment."

The Certified Insurance Rehabilitation Specialists (CIRS) *Code of Professional Ethics* (1986) makes a similar statement:

- CIRS engaged in industry, education, private practice, and public agency work in which conflicts of interest may arise among various parties, as between management and labor, referral source and client, client and employer, or between CIRS and their principals must clearly define for themselves the nature of their loyalties and responsibilities and keep all parties concerned informed accordingly.

It should be noted that despite conflicts of interest that may arise, all codes of ethics for rehabilitation providers have client advocacy at the heart of the standards. The CRC code (ARCA, 1987) states that "Rehabilitation counselors shall serve as advocates for people with disabilities." The NARPPS code contains a section on advocacy that includes the statement that the "role of the NARPPS member as an advocate is to protect and promote the welfare of disabled persons to maximize control over circumstances that interfere with their obtaining vocational independence," and CIRS members are exhorted to respect the integrity and protect the welfare of clients, which includes resisting "arrangements that would result in the exploitation of clients."

In the position paper that follows, Mary Ellen Young suggests that the context in which rehabilitation counseling occurs makes some role conflicts inevitable. She identifies the conflicts that arise for professionals in the public and private sectors.

Role Conflicts in Rehabilitation Counseling

Mary Ellen Young

Rehabilitation counseling is a discipline practiced in an arena of service delivery systems with varying philosophical and legal mandates. Inherent conflicts in the work of the rehabilitation counselor create ethical dilemmas. To understand these inherent conflicts, three factors must be examined: (1) the legislative underpinnings of vocational rehabilitation practice, (2) the role of rehabilitation counseling in social service delivery systems, and (3) the impact of the medical rehabilitation model on the practice of rehabilitation counseling.

First, rehabilitation counseling exists as a counseling specialty because of congressional actions in adopting the Vocational Rehabilitation Act Amendments of 1954 (Rubin & Roessler, 1987). As part of this Act, in order to expand rehabilitation services, Congress authorized funds for training master's-level students in rehabilitation counseling. This mandate, along with continued support for training and services for almost four decades, has resulted in a cadre of trained professionals whose goal is to facilitate the development of persons with disabilities to their maximum vocational potential. To meet this goal, rehabilitation counselors in the public sector are gatekeepers for rehabilitation funds. They administer case service budgets that are used to purchase medical, psychological, educational, or vocational services.

Second, vocational rehabilitation is an integral part of a complex social service delivery system that includes both the public sector (Social Security Disability Insurance, Medicare, Medicaid, welfare) and the private sector (medical insurance benefits, long-term disability payments, personal injury claims, workers' compensation). The complexities of this social "safety net" create potential ethical dilemmas because of the competing ethical principles that guide the various programs. Two recent articles have framed the relationship between rehabilitation service delivery systems and ethical principles. According to Dougherty (1991) and Rubin and Millard (1991), beneficence is the principle that underlies society's willingness to provide direct payments to persons with disabilities to alleviate their suffering. These programs are substantial in terms of dollar amounts and are designed as entitlement programs. Persons who meet the eligibility criteria are entitled to the benefits of the program regardless of the program's financial limitations or the financial standing of the beneficiary. Sometimes in conflict with the principle of beneficence is the principle of autonomy. Autonomy, which is a commitment to helping the individual reach his or her maximum vocational potential or level of independent functioning, is an essential part of the underlying philosophy of most rehabilitation programs. These programs, however, are funded at a level that is only a fraction of the budget of the entitlement programs and the funds needed for provision of services. These budgets are managed by the rehabilitation counselor. Further complicating this picture is the principle of justice, within which the rehabilitation counselor has to make judgments about the fair distribution of his or her case service monies.

Third, rehabilitation services are provided within a medical rehabilitation framework. Caplan (1988) described the conflicts inherent in the medical, contractual, and educational models of rehabilitation. The medical model is the traditional model of the relationship between physician and patient, in which it is assumed that the doctor is the expert and has the wisdom and knowledge to make decisions for the patient. In the contractual model, which is more prevalent in medicine today, patient autonomy is maintained through the practice of informed consent. The individual has the right to accept or refuse any treatment and must be fully informed of the risks and benefits of that treatment. Informed consent is transferred only when the patient is a minor or is judged legally incompetent to give such consent. According to Caplan, this contractual model may be inappropriate in rehabilitation because the person may not be capable of understanding all of the ramifications of a traumatic injury or illness but is still not incompetent by legal standards. By contrast, the principle of the educational model is that the patient or client will be taught the benefits of the rehabilitation program—"interventions aimed at restoring or maximizing autonomy rather than simply presuming its existence" (Caplan, 1988, p. 6).

Thus, rehabilitation counselors must first decide the philosophical model upon which they will base decisions and actions, knowing full well that the resources available are indeed inadequate to assist all persons with disabilities to reach their maximum potential.

Dual Relationships in Public Sector Rehabilitation. The philosophy of rehabilitation counseling places a high value on the individual and the potential of that individual to make a contribution to society through work or maximum independent functioning. It is a premise of rehabilitation counseling that persons with disabilities who are capable of working should be working, and that the techniques of the profession are effective in helping persons with disabilities achieve their goals. Within this value system, the rehabilitation counselor in the public sector is the agent of the state/federal rehabilitation program, charged to spend case service monies wisely for the maximum benefit of society and persons with disabilities.

Thus, when a rehabilitation counselor in the public sector sits down with his or her client for the first time, the counselor is acting within a system that is neither value free nor value neutral but is based on preconceived ideas about the desired outcome of the interaction. In fact, the counselor is evaluated on how many successful closures (job placements) he or she makes in a given year. The counselor has a budget of case service money, but it is inadequate to meet the needs of everyone who needs or requests services. In addition, the counselor must follow the rules of the rehabilitation agency in establishing eligibility, developing realistic vocational plans, and documenting progress toward goals.

The client also brings differing needs, expectations, and desired outcomes to the first counseling session. He or she may or may not be primarily interested in going to work or becoming a "productive" member of society. The initial referral may come from another social service agency or from the client's parent or relative. It may be in the interest of society or of the client's family that the client undergo successful rehabilitation, but it is often the responsibility of the counselor to convince the client of the worthiness of such an action. Also working against the goal of vocational independence are the benefit systems (the entitlement programs previously mentioned). These programs have traditionally created a disincentive to return to work because return to work may result in a possible loss of income and medical benefits. So the client may enter the relationship with the idea that the counselor may pay for certain medical expenses, education, or training; may provide equipment such as wheelchairs or hand controls for vehicles; or may provide job placement services. These are all services the counselor *may* provide but is certainly not *required* to provide. The client may be fearful of losing secure benefits for the riskier—although potentially more rewarding—independence that successful work brings. Coupled with these expectations are physical and emotional reactions to traumatic injury or disabling illness, which contribute to an uncertainty about what to expect from and how to proceed with the counseling relationship.

So the rehabilitation counselor and the client begin their counseling process by negotiating the rehabilitation plan. This plan is a formal, written contract between the client and the rehabilitation agency. The counselor is bound professionally by ethical guidelines to avoid dual relationships that occur in other counseling situations, despite the potential conflicts of interest inherent in the rehabilitation system.

The following case illustrates the possible conflicts in this relationship:

> Jeremy is a 20–year-old man who injured his spinal cord in an automobile accident resulting in quadriplegia. Jeremy dropped out of high school at age 16 and went to work as a construction laborer. His automobile insurance policy has paid for his medical expenses and his initial stay in a rehabilitation hospital, but vocational services are not covered by the insurance. He was referred to the state rehabilitation agency by his social worker at the rehabilitation hospital. His social worker had talked about his going back to work, and one of his friends in the hospital had told him that the vocational rehabilitation agency might buy a van for him that he could learn to drive with hand controls. He has a vague idea that he wants to go back to work at some future time, but he has no idea what he could do with his disability. He believes that when he goes to the vocational rehabilitation agency, his counselor will have a good idea about what jobs someone with his type of disability can do and will give him some job leads. Jeremy started receiving Social Security Disability Insurance payments several months after his injury, and he is also eligible for Medicare to pay for his medical expenses. Although he used to live in his own apartment before the accident, he now lives with his parents. They provide some financial assistance as well as personal care assistance for him in dressing, bathing, and bowel and bladder care.

> When Jeremy meets with Deborah, his vocational rehabilitation counselor, she asks him a lot of questions about his injury, his education, his former work experience, and his rehabilitation goals. She also asks him how he is coping with his disability. He is pleased that she seems to care about him and what has happened to him. He discusses how frustrating it is to depend on his parents all the time. He shares his hope that the rehabilitation agency will buy a van for him. He is very disappointed when she tells him that it is unlikely that the agency will do this. She describes in detail what steps she needs to take to determine his eligibility for services and develop a plan for his

return to work. He leaves her office with an appointment with a vocational evaluator who will spend several days giving him some tests to see what he can do. The idea of taking tests makes him nervous because it is a lot like school, which was not a good experience for him. The more he thinks about keeping that appointment, the more anxious he becomes, and he is angry because he is not going to get a van. He does not keep his appointment for vocational evaluation.

This vignette illustrates some of the inherent conflicts that exist in the relationship between public sector rehabilitation counselors and their clients. First, they may have differing goals for the counseling process. The counselor has the predetermined goal of helping the client return to work or to maximum independent functioning. This goal evolves from the counselor's value system but is also driven by the fact that successful closure of the case will improve the counselor's evaluation. The client, however, may have differing needs and expectations because a return to work often means a loss of income and medical benefits. A dual relationship conflict is built into this situation: The counselor has simultaneous obligations to the provider of rehabilitation funds (to spend limited monies wisely), to his or her employer (to close the case successfully), to society (to maximize client productivity), and to the client (to foster autonomy and independence). Within this inherent conflict, the potential for harm increases as the client's expectations of the counseling relationship diverge from those of the counselor.

Thus, it is imperative for Jeremy's rehabilitation counselor to understand her choices and actions in the framework of the principles of beneficence, autonomy, and justice. Taking Caplan's position that autonomy cannot be assumed, she might work from the premise of beneficence, so that her decisions are based on teaching Jeremy the values of the vocational rehabilitation program to him and to society. This paternalistic attitude may result in a shifting of responsibility for the success of the rehabilitation program from the client to the counselor. Instead, it is important that the counselor emphasize that Jeremy is free to make his own decisions about whether or not to participate in the program. The vocational assessment that she is recommending is for him to use to explore his options and make choices based on the information given him. Although it is true that she will also make decisions based on the fair allocation of the resources at her disposal and on the evaluation results documenting his potential to benefit from services, he will have to be granted the freedom to choose based on all the information at his disposal. By compromising his autonomy, she risks damaging the counselor/client relationship to such an extent that future progress could be seriously jeopardized.

Dual Relationships in Private Sector Rehabilitation. Private sector (for profit) counselors walk a tightrope, balancing their commitment to their clients with their allegiance to the company that employs them and the company (usually an insurance company) that pays their employer as well as benefits to their clients. As if this situation were not already complicated enough, litigation is often a further confounding element. In private sector rehabilitation, at least three parties are involved: the client (injured worker on whose behalf the counselor is employed), the counselor (person who gives professionally competent advice), and the payer (third-party person or organization who pays the bills). This tripartite relationship can create role conflicts and divided loyalties. The private sector counselor must consider the needs and wishes of others involved in the rehabilitation process—attorneys, insurance representatives, workers' compensation boards—rather than focus exclusively on the needs of the client (Mitchell & Sink, 1983). Taylor (1985) gave a clear picture of the conflicting interests with which the private sector rehabilitation counselor must contend:

> In the workers' compensation system as well as other insurance and government systems, the rehabilitation counselor (and often the client) is continually buffeted by often contradictory vested interests. The state wants to protect the rights of the individual and increase tax receipts. The employer or the insurance carrier wants to minimize the cost of the case and close it successfully. The client's (claimant's) attorney believes it is best to maximize his client's disability rating. The counselor believes it is best to maximize the client's ability. The client is torn between getting all he or she can from the system and getting back to work to provide for the family. Obviously, all these pressures will be felt by the counselor. (p. 221)

The following vignette illustrates the complex demands that are faced by a rehabilitation counselor in the private, for-profit sector:

> Janet contracts with an insurance company to do return-to-work evaluations for clients it refers to her. She receives a phone call

from an attorney for the insurance company who pressures her to testify in a manner that will favor the insurance company's case. The attorney has sent her an independent medical report of a recent exam by an orthopedic specialist that shows that there is little or nothing physically wrong with the client. This goes against all the medical evidence for the past 3 years and against Janet's findings from her personal interview with the client. Janet feels that the client does have significant orthopedic problems. She is caught in a bind because her business is dependent upon referrals from this insurance company, and she does not want to jeopardize her business by being uncooperative. However, her ethical responsibility is first and foremost to be a client advocate.

As this second vignette demonstrates, private rehabilitation counselors may serve multiple constituencies, and these constituencies often have competing needs that force the counselor to make difficult choices. If Janet is guided by the CRC standards (ARCA, 1987), it is clear that her first loyalty should be unequivocally to her client. If she is a NARPPS member, however, she is instructed by the standards of that group to make the direction of her loyalty clear. NARPPS also recognizes that a rehabilitation practitioner has a responsibility to provide objective testimony in court. As a counselor, Janet must do what is right for her client and be prepared to deal with the consequences of decreased referrals if that is the result of her actions. To do otherwise would be a grave compromise of professional ethics. If she decides that her primary loyalty is to the company paying for her services, then she must terminate her counseling relationship with her client.

<hr/>

Gerald Corey's Commentary

I like Mary Ellen Young's point that rehabilitation counselors need to decide the philosophical model that will form the basis of their decisions. She shows that counselors who deal with persons with disabilities have the task of balancing the needs of their clients with the demands of institutions, even though doing so often presents dual relationship issues.

In my view, counselors owe it to their clients to identify and discuss with potential clients the values they hold that are likely to influence the outcomes of the counseling process. Rehabilitation counselors could inform their clients of the basic goals and expectations of the agency or a program. If there is a frank discussion about the degree of matching between the client's values and the counselor's values, there is less chance that the client will be exploited.

The focus of counseling needs to be established from the outset. Personally, I hope that the focus is much broader than the disability of a person and also includes a discussion of the meaning of a disability as well as educational and vocational options for the person. Humes et al. (1989) suggested that the environmental conditions that contribute to the individual impact of disability are often overlooked. They made some useful recommendations for assisting people with disabilities to function at a maximum level. These include (a) avoid using disabling language, (b) consider the effects of the environment and the individual's perceptions and expectations in the process of making educational and vocational plans, (c) emphasize abilities rather than limitations, and (d) recognize the complexity of disability and refer or consult when necessary.

I think that Humes et al. made a point that is consistent with the basic ideas developed by Young. In spite of certain legislative and social changes, people with disabilities still encounter numerous barriers to full participation in society. It is the challenge of rehabilitation counselors to facilitate a fuller participation of persons with disabilities in education and employment.

Barbara Herlihy's Commentary

As a practitioner who has limited familiarity with the work world of the rehabilitation counselor, I was intrigued by Mary Ellen Young's contribution. It is apparent to me that in considering role conflicts inherent in rehabilitation counseling, the issue is not one of dual relationships but one of multiple relationships. Maintaining ethical practice in a complex set of roles that might include counselor, gatekeeper to services, evaluator, and expert witness seems to be an extraordinarily demanding task. In addition, multiple obligations—to the client, to one's employer, to the customer (one who pays the bill), and to society—make it especially important that rehabilitation counselors be clear at all times about their primary loyalties.

Young raises a particularly interesting point about the paternalistic attitude that can exist in rehabilitation services provision. In a sense, the counselor who adopts such an attitude is creating another type of dual relationship, as "surrogate parent" who functions as a decision maker for the client. It seems to me that this issue is relevant to counselors who work in some other settings as well as in rehabilitation counseling. School counselors and others who work with *minor clients, and counselors who work with involuntary clients in such settings as hospitals or prisons, also must deal with an assumption imbedded in the system that their clients have limited autonomy. In these situations, it can be all to easy to slip into a parental, caretaker role, to the detriment of the client.*

Finally, it looks to me as if the rehabilitation counselor's own autonomy is often at risk. Conflicting demands make it difficult for rehabilitation counselors to serve as client advocates, yet this role is at the heart of their ethical standards.

If you were Deborah, the counselor in the first vignette presented by Young, how would you feel about the outcome of your interactions with Jeremy? How do you think you might balance the competing demands that have been placed on you? If you were Janet, the private sector counselor in the second vignette, how would you resolve your dilemma? Is Janet's dilemma a fairly typical one for other counselors who are in private practice, regardless of the nature of their clientele?

How well prepared are rehabilitation counselors to deal with complex ethical dilemmas like those faced by Deborah and Janet? Hosie, Patterson, and Hollingsworth (1989) reported that almost 80% of rehabilitation educators surveyed believed that the number of ethical dilemmas facing rehabilitation counselors is increasing, but only about 20% of training programs required a separate course in ethics. Within the realm of ethical dilemmas, those involving dual relationships may be among the most difficult to resolve. Dual relationship issues arise for public sector counselors because they manage case loads with case service budgets. Counselors must make decisions about allocation of resources for medical services, training and education, and equipment. Thus, they serve not only as gatekeepers to services and products but also as counselors. A complicating factor is that they are also evaluated on the number of successful closures, i.e., job placements, so that they have a great deal at stake in the outcomes of their services. Private sector counselors face an additional complication in balancing the competing interests of their employers, insurance companies who may be paying for counseling services, and requirements imposed by litigation.

It becomes clear that although all interested parties share the same goal—that of maximizing the disabled individual's independence and productivity—they may differ in how they believe the goal should be achieved. Further, rehabilitation counselors rarely function exclusively as counselors. They also screen to determine eligibility for services, evaluate disability and return-to-work potential, manage cases and coordinate services, and sometimes testify in court. Again, the goals of counseling may run counter to the services dictated by other roles.

Counselors, public and private, who provide expert witness testimony regarding a client's return to work potential may also have conflicts of interest depending on who is paying for their services. Clients who are being evaluated or tested should know how results are going to be used and give informed consent to that use. This is a problem when the evaluation is done at the request of the insurance company.

Finally, the power differential applies in some specific and unique ways in rehabilitation counseling. Stadler, in her contribution to chapter 3, suggested that a student who enters into a counseling relationship with a professor would be prudent to withhold any personal information that could lead to a negative evaluation by that professor. A parallel situation can arise in rehabilitation counseling. For instance, an injured worker might be circumspect in revealing to his counselor the extent of his recovery when the counselor holds the key to continuing availability of insurance benefits. In such a case, the trust and openness of the counseling relationship are compromised.

SUMMARY AND CONCLUSIONS

The work of the rehabilitation counselor is fraught with potential role conflicts that are inherent in the context in which the counselor practices. In both the public and private sectors, there are parties besides the client who have a vested interest in the outcome of counseling, and these interests are often contradictory. Because rehabilitation counselors play multiple roles, it may be nearly impossible for them to obey the admonition to avoid dual relationships that is contained in their ethical codes. What they can—and must—do, in these circumstances, is to work diligently to avoid causing harm to the client. In particular, their challenge is to preserve client autonomy and protect the client's best interests in a system that does not always support the client's independent decision making.

CHAPTER 10
GROUP COUNSELING

In chapter 4, we discussed dual relationship issues that arise in the academic environment when counselor educators work to prepare group counselors. Although this chapter is also about group counseling, the focus is different. Here, we focus not on preparation but on practice and examine dual relationship issues in conducting group work. Some of the questions we explore include these:

- What do codes of ethics say about dual relationships in group counseling?
- How can group leaders distinguish between appropriate and inappropriate personal and social relationships with group members?
- Are role conflicts inherent in serving as both the client's individual counselor and group counselor?
- Are there potential conflicts in admitting a former client into a counseling group? A friend or acquaintance?
- In working with involuntary groups, how can group leaders reconcile demands for confidentiality with demands for recording or reporting?
- In a productive group, when leadership and membership roles may become blurred, what role conflicts might emerge?
- What are the limits of leader self-disclosure? How could overextending the boundaries create a dual relationship?

Later in the chapter, George M. Gazda contributes his thoughts on one of these questions: the problems that might arise when a counselor serves as both individual therapist and group counselor for the same client.

ETHICAL STANDARDS

Like other AACD divisional codes that have been revised rather recently, the *Ethical Guidelines for Group Counselors* (ASGW, 1989) give extensive coverage to dual relationships. In the Dual Relationships section, guidelines include the following:

- Group counselors avoid dual relationships with group members that might impair their objectivity and professional judgment, as well as those which are likely to compromise a group member's ability to participate fully in the group.
  - —Group members do not misuse their professional role and power as group leader to advance personal or social contacts with members throughout the duration of the group.
  - —Group counselors do not use their professional relationship with group members to further their own interest either during the group or after the termination of the group.
  - —Sexual intimacies between group counselors and members are unethical.
  - —Group counselors do not barter (exchange) professional services with group members for services.
  - —Group counselors do not admit their own family members, relatives, employees, or personal friends as members to their groups.
  - —Group counselors discuss with group members the potential detrimental effects of group members engaging in intimate intermember relationships outside of the group.
  - —It is inappropriate to solicit members from a class (or institutional affiliation) for one's private counseling or therapeutic groups.

These guidelines are quite explicit with respect to some dual relationship issues. For instance, bartering for services is clearly prohibited. Few other ethical codes explicitly prohibit bartering: In fact, to our knowledge, the American Psychological Association is the only other professional association that has taken this stand. As we discussed earlier in chapter 6, Private Practice, bartering is an accepted practice in some cultures and communities. Although bartering can present some potential dual role problems, there may be instances when it works for all concerned. Some group counselors might argue that this is an example of how codes can overlook needed exceptions.

If you are a counselor for whom group counseling is a regular part of your practice, what are your reactions to the ASGW guidelines? Are there any standards with which you disagree or which you find difficult to follow in your actual practice?

PERSONAL VERSUS PROFESSIONAL RELATIONSHIPS

How can group leaders distinguish between appropriate and inappropriate personal and social relationships with group members? We think it is inappropriate for us to use our professional role to make personal and social contacts, and that it is certainly questionable to develop such relationships with current group members. In fact, we urge group counselors who look to their therapeutic groups as a source of friendships, or as a way to enrich their social lives, to examine their own personal needs and motivations. Group members should not be expected to perform the function of filling gaps in the professional's personal and social life.

Establishing friendships with current group members can put a strain on the therapeutic relationship and can cause problems for both the group leader and the members involved. The group member might well be inhibited from participating fully in the group for fear of jeopardizing the friendship. In addition, singling out an individual as a friend is bound to affect the dynamics of the group. Those members who are not chosen as friends are likely to feel rejection or resentment. It is the responsibility of group leaders to set appropriate boundaries around their professional as well as personal and social relationships with the members.

It is more difficult to handle the dual relationship issues that arise when personal and social relationships develop among group members. Pregroup screening can help to identify preexisting relationships among potential members that could be problematic. However, it is also probable that as the group progresses, certain members will feel drawn to each other and may want to form personal relationships outside the group. This has its advantages and its disadvantages. When members socialize outside group sessions, group cohesion might actually be increased. Yet such a practice can also destroy the cohesion of a group. If members have personal and social relationships outside the group, if they become a subgroup that discusses group matters, and if they refuse to bring this into the group itself, the progress of the group is inevitably impeded. Other signs that indicate counterproductive socializing include the forming of cliques and excluding of certain members from social gatherings, the forming of romantic involvements without a willingness to acknowledge these involvements in the group, a refusal to challenge one another in the group for fear of jeopardizing friendships, and an exclusive reliance on the group as a source of social life (Corey & Corey, 1992).

Some group leaders set ground rules at the outset that attempt to prohibit or discourage members from socializing outside of group time, and when the rationale is discussed and understood, this can be a useful approach. Yet friendships cannot be prevented from developing, and if this occurs and affects the group's functioning it is probably best to have an open discussion in group so that other members can share how they are being affected by these friendships. It is important to keep in mind that the primary purpose of a group experience is not for members to acquire friendships within the group (although this happens at times) but rather to teach participants attitudes and skills that they can use to form friendships in their everyday lives.

CONCURRENT INDIVIDUAL AND GROUP COUNSELING

Are role conflicts inherent in serving as both the client's individual counselor and group counselor? If a group counselor also sees a member of a group on an individual basis, does this necessarily present a role conflict?

In the position statement that follows, George M. Gazda identifies some potential ethical problems that can arise when a therapist provides both individual and group therapy for the same client.

Dual Role Relationships in Group Counseling

George M. Gazda

Ethical difficulties are faced by practitioners who establish groups from their individual practice and, conversely, suggest to

group members that they enter individual therapy with them. They could, for instance, be increasing both their practices and income through this practice.

In the *Ethical Guidelines for Group Counselors* (ASGW, 1989) the appropriateness of both individual and group therapy for the same client by one therapist is only obliquely addressed. For instance, under Orientation and Providing Information, such a decision is left up to the counselor: "Group counselors clearly inform group members about the policies pertaining to the group counselor's willingness to consult with them between group sessions."

The authors of the *Ethical Guidelines* conceive of concurrent individual and group therapy for the same individual by one therapist as a potential dual relationship. Under Dual Relationships, the entry that resembles the situation described earlier says "Group counselors do not use their professional relationship with group members to further their own interest either during the group or after the termination of the group."

Therapists, then, who include their clients in both individual therapy and as group members are participating in questionable dual relationships if those therapists are "furthering their own interest."

Elsewhere (Taylor & Gazda, 1991), I have specified some ethical issues called into question by this practice: (a) confidentiality and informed consent regarding material obtained in one setting and used in another, (b) transference and countertransference in concurrent therapy, (c) the potential for fostering an undue amount of dependency in group/individual clients, and (d) the increase in power that the therapist engaged in such dual relationships acquires.

Confidentiality. The most obvious problem concerning confidentiality is one in which the therapist may not be able to distinguish between information shared in the client's individual and group sessions. If given individually, that confidence is not subject to group disclosure by the therapist. This situation is made even more precarious if all group members are also in individual therapy with the same therapist.

Transference/countertransference. Psychodynamic therapists often point to problems with dilution of the transference in combined/concurrent group and individual therapy. In addition, the result of a client's having to share the therapist with others in a group adds the complication of sibling rivalry. The issues of the transference are quite sensitive, and the resolution of these issues is often crucial to the successful outcome of therapy. When the processes of concurrent therapy are compounded with the complex workings of the transference, the result is one that is often confusing.

Dependency. Related to the transference/countertransference issue is the issue of dependency. There is the potential that combined individual and group therapy will maximize client dependency on the therapist.

While seeing the therapist on an individual basis, the client will normally look to the therapist alone for help. The therapist is often seen as the parent and sometimes takes on this role. It is the task of the therapist to help the client to help himself or herself and gradually shift the relationship away from parent/child to that of helper/helpee. Some therapists work very hard at not allowing the parent/child relationship to form in the first place, but others encourage its development so that a transference takes place and a therapeutic bond can be more firmly established. Regardless of the therapist's predilections, concurrent therapy is going to increase both the advantages and disadvantages of dependency.

Power. There is a potentially unhealthy amount of power that can be attributed to the therapist by the client. In a sense, it is a countertransference problem that originates from client dependency. In the same manner as with dependency, concurrent therapy will compound power issues. The therapist with a fragile sense of moral responsibility can use this false omnipotence to further his or her own interests.

Gerald Corey's Commentary

George Gazda mentions that ethical difficulties are faced by practitioners who establish groups formed from their clients in individual therapy. If practitioners are increasing their income through this practice, then I think that what they are doing is certainly ethically questionable. The motivation of the therapist is at the heart of this matter. Some practitioners form groups based upon former individual clients, but once they are in a group they discontinue individual sessions.

I have no trouble with therapists who meet their own needs through their work, except when they place their own needs above the needs of the clients or meet their needs by exploiting their clients. Yalom's (1985) clinical experience has led him to the conclusion that concurrent individual and group therapy is neither necessary nor helpful, except in certain situations. My position is that concurrent individual and group therapy may not be needed by many clients, yet it can be beneficial for some clients at certain times in their therapy. For matters of practicality and cost effectiveness, concurrent therapy does have its limitations.

Gazda points to problems such as divulging confidentiality, the misuse of transference and countertransference, the creation of dependency, and the increase in power of the therapist. I agree with his analysis that these are all potential problems that can arise. I also think it is possible to deal effectively with these potential problems. Confidentiality does not have to be problematic because the client can be given the responsibility for deciding what issues to bring up in group. I do not see it as my function as a group leader to decide what problems a member will explore in a group. Thus, if I see a member for a private session, I do not feel the need to mention in the group what we discussed. However, if the member wants to use a private session to talk about trust issues pertaining to the group, or any other matter that is best expressed and dealt with in the group setting, then it is counterproductive to explore these topics privately.

Transference and countertransference issues will likely arise from concurrent therapy when the same therapist sees a client individually and in a group. However, this does not necessarily have to be problematic. In fact, transference and countertransference reactions are typically manifested in most group situations and need to be addressed. With some highly dependent clients the concurrent format might muddy the waters and could increase dependency. I question Gazda's assumption that concurrent therapy is likely to compound power issues. He asserts that "the therapist with a fragile sense of moral responsibility can use this false omnipotence to further his or her own interests." Yet is this not a problem for any practitioner with a "fragile sense of moral responsibility," regardless of the form of therapy practiced? Gazda's statement is more of a commentary about the character of the therapist as a person than a commentary on the therapeutic format used.

I believe that the same therapist could beneficially work with the same client individually and in group. For example, I know of a clinical social worker in a community agency who works in individual therapy with women with a history of incest and also offers a short-

term support group for incest survivors. She screens members carefully and determines which clients could benefit from concurrent private therapy and participation in a support group. In their individual therapy, they can explore in more depth certain personal issues that they may not have the time to explore in the group. The point is that concurrent therapy can work well if the therapist has a clear rationale for this form of treatment and if the therapist discusses both the possible benefits and risks of this treatment approach.

Barbara Herlihy's Commentary

I agree with George Gazda that, generally, counselors are wise to avoid serving as both individual and group counselor for the same client, when this situation can be avoided. However, my rationale for avoiding this type of dual relationship differs somewhat from that of Gazda. I am not psychodynamically oriented, so that while I am aware of transference/countertransference issues they do not guide my thinking on this question. I am also one of those therapists whom Gazda describes as working "very hard at not allowing a parent/child relationship to form in the first place," so that increased dependency is not a major issue for me.

My primary concerns are for confidentiality and the group dynamics. Gazda notes quite correctly that confidences given in individual sessions are not subject to group disclosure by the therapist, and I can foresee the damaging effects that such a disclosure—even an inadvertent one—could have on the client's trust and openness in the individual therapy. If we believe that clients must be in charge of their own self-disclosures, then therapists have no right to make disclosures for them in the group context. If I am conducting a group whose membership includes some of my individual clients, I do not want to find myself in a position of having to stop and consider before speaking, asking myself whether I had obtained certain information from a client in an individual session or whether it had been revealed in group. This impedes my ability to flow with the group process, and if I erred I might well damage the client's trust. It is a risk I prefer to avoid.

Additionally, as a private practitioner, I see something that smacks of greed in routinely recommending that clients see me for both individual and group therapy. This is not to suggest that I see anything wrong with concurrent individual and group counseling for a client, when the services are provided by different therapists or when concurrent therapy by the same therapist is clinically justified. Several clients who see me for individual counseling are also concurrently *attending aftercare groups at various hospitals. And for certain clients, I sometimes recommend that they join specific groups in addition to their continuing work with me. I think that a combination of individual and group therapy is particularly helpful to some clients (e.g., as Corey mentioned, adult survivors of childhood incest). When individual and group therapy are concurrent and provided by different therapists, I think the important factor is for the two therapists to work cooperatively, with the client's permission to communicate with each other, so that the goals of individual and group therapy are clearly understood by all three parties.*

In some instances, I think clients can benefit from joining a group after their individual therapy is completed. The continuing support they receive can be helpful in maintaining treatment gains and is usually quite affordable for them. For me, sequential individual and group therapy do not create the same ethical binds as do concurrent individual and group therapy.

Some situations do occur, however, in which individual and group therapy are provided by the same therapist. Treatment plans in inpatient settings routinely include individual and group therapy, and sometimes both modalities are provided by the same therapist. The key here, I believe, is that the ground rules surrounding disclosure are clearly understood by the patient. Thus, I see the issue of concurrent individual and group therapy as being multifaceted: Decisions are influenced by the setting in which the therapies occur, by the client's needs, and by the theoretical orientation of the practitioner.

> The viewpoints of three different writers have been presented here. On what dimensions do you find yourself in agreement with these views? Where do you disagree? What is your own stance toward the issue of concurrent individual and group therapy?

GROUP COUNSELING FOR FORMER CLIENTS

Herlihy, in the preceding commentary, touched on the issue of sequential individual and group therapy. Here we further explore the question of potential role conflicts that may be involved in admitting a former client into a counseling group. We also look at the question of admitting a friend or acquaintance into a counseling group.

We know of some counselors who form their groups largely from former clients in individual therapy. In fact, one colleague sees it as a useful progression to suggest a group experience after a certain number of individual sessions. Such a practice can be useful for a client's growth, and if routinely done in this manner seems more concerned with maximizing client benefit and minimizing client expenses than with lining the counselor's pocket.

One potential problem that we see, however, is possible jealousy on the part of some clients. When they were seen individually, they had the counselor to themselves for the hour. Now, as group members, they must share their counselor with perhaps eight other members. This can be therapeutically useful, but it is essential for the client to discuss his or her reactions in the group setting. Further, other group members may be jealous of the person who has had private therapy with the group leader, and these reactions need to be expressed and dealt with in the group.

Admitting a friend or acquaintance is a very different matter than admitting a former client to a group. In the latter case, a professional relationship is already established. In the former case, we have the shifting of roles from a personal relationship to a professional relationship, which we think could create many difficulties for the therapist, the friend or acquaintance who becomes a group member, and possibly for others in the group. Again, the bottom line seems to be the importance of predicting potential problems when dual role relationships are being considered and discussing them fully. When there is a shifting of roles, and when this is not explored openly, problems can arise in group settings. Hidden agendas will block the flow of group process.

INVOLUNTARY GROUPS

In working with involuntary groups, how can group leaders reconcile demands for confidentiality and for recording and reporting? It seems to us that it is absolutely essential that group counselors are "up front" with the members of an involuntary group. We think that it is possible to be therapeutic and at the same time carry out record-keeping and reporting functions. However, members have a right to know what records the counselor will be keeping, what will be reported, who will have access to the information shared in the group, and how this material will be used. Leaders also have a responsibility to inform members of involuntary groups if their participation—or lack of participation—will affect their length of stay in a hospital or prison setting.

Aubrey and Dougher (1990), in addressing ethical issues in outpatient therapy with sex offenders, maintain that nonvoluntary clients are particularly disadvantaged when it comes to resisting pressure from a group leader. Offenders who are referred by the court may behave in overtly seductive ways in an attempt to win the favor of the therapist. These authors caution therapists to be particularly aware of the potential pitfalls of dual relationships with such clients.

Group leaders may be tested by some members of an involuntary group. For instance, a group counselor may tell the participants of a group in a juvenile correctional institution that whatever is discussed will remain in the group. The youths may not believe this and may in many subtle ways test the leader to discover whether in fact he or she will keep this promise. For this reason, it is essential that group leaders not promise to keep within the group material that they may be required to disclose. Counselors owe it to their clients to specify at the outset the limits on confidentiality, and in mandatory groups they should inform members of any reporting procedures required of them as leaders (ASGW, 1989).

One of us (Herlihy) recently saw what can happen when members of an involuntary group test the leader. She was observing an adolescent inpatient group. The group met on a Saturday, and the leader was a contract therapist who was not on the regular hospital staff. The adolescents, aware that this leader did not already know them, decided to amuse themselves by switching identities. As the leader made rounds to check in with each member, one of the other members spoke up and assumed that member's identity. Eventually, the scheme broke down in confusion, and the leader discovered what was happening. At this point, the group took a break. When the group reconvened, the leader told the group that she had reported the ruse although she had not recommended consequences for their behavior. She did talk about her feelings, letting them know that she was frustrated because the group had wasted half of its time together. However, the fact that she had reported without first discussing her action with the members created a nontherapeutic atmosphere. The adolescents' sense of justice was offended. One of them stated, "It's okay that you don't see the humor in what we did, and we're willing to take responsibility for the consequences, but you shouldn't have let it go onto our charts without telling us first."

Inpatient groups in hospitals are only one of many settings in which involuntary groups may take place and in which group leaders may face difficult confidentiality issues. For instance, a leader of a group of parolees may be expected to reveal to the members' parole officer any information he or she acquires in the group concerning certain criminal offenses. It is a good policy for leaders to let members know that they may be required to testify against them in court. The clients of most licensed psychologists, psychiatrists, and licensed clinical social workers, and some licensed professional counselors are legally entitled to privileged communication. This means that these professionals cannot break the confidence of clients unless (1) in their judgment clients are likely to do serious harm to themselves or to others, (2) clients are gravely disabled, (3) child or elderly abuse is suspected, (4) disclosure is ordered by a court, (5) clients give specific written permission, or (6) the privilege is otherwise limited by statute.

Group leaders have some general guidelines for what disclosures they should and should not make about what occurs in group sessions. The AACD *Ethical Standards* (1988) caution group counselors that they must set a norm of confidentiality regarding all group participants' disclosures. However, they do specify exceptions: "When the client's condition indicates that there is clear and imminent danger to the client or others, the counselor must take reasonable personal action or inform responsible authorities. Consultation with other professionals must be used where possible." Honesty with the clients goes a long way toward building trust. Even though dual relationships may be discouraged by professional organizations, the reality is that they inevitably occur in many treatment facilities. If such relationships cannot be eliminated, at least professionals can be aware of potential problems and take steps to lessen the possible damaging effects of functioning in multiple roles.

LIMITS OF SELF-DISCLOSURE

In earlier chapters, we have discussed how overextending the boundaries of self-disclosure can create dual relationship conflicts. Here, we want to acknowledge that in a group self-disclosure brings up special problems. If we use the groups we lead for obtaining our own therapy, we will create confusing relationships. Are we the leader of the group, or merely another member? As leaders, we need to monitor our self-disclosure so that we are aware of what we are sharing and why we are sharing certain personal information. We need to develop our own guidelines that will help us determine what kinds of disclosure are helpful and what kinds of disclosure bog down the group. The following vignette reveals Glen's philosophy and practices of self-disclosure:

> Glen makes it a practice to be very self-disclosing in the men's groups that he facilitates in a community agency setting. He believes that one of the best ways to facilitate openness on the part of the other men is for him to model disclosure of his past and current difficulties as a man. He is also willing to take time for exploring a present concern if it is getting in the way of his being present as a group leader. Although he is a skilled group leader with considerable training, he firmly believes that his own realness is what helps to create a trusting and cohesive group.

What are your thoughts about Glen's willingness to be personal in these groups? Do you see any potential ethical or clinical problems in Glen's self-disclosures of his past and present difficulties as a man? What dual relationship concerns, if any, do you have in this case?

It is not the leader's role to use group time to work through his or her personal problems; however, leaders can engage in a wide range of other self-disclosing behaviors. With few words, they can let members know that they are personally affected by the members' sharing of problems. Members can benefit from knowing that the group leader can identify with their struggles. Leaders can express their persistent reactions to members and can offer feedback. They can model appropriate and timely self-disclosure by expressing how they are affected in the here-and-now context of the group.

In a productive group, leadership and membership roles can become blurred. However, a problem occurs when as group leaders we forget our primary role and purpose for being in the group. Our main purpose is to facilitate the process of growth of others, not to work through our own personal problems. If we become aware of pressing personal issues, we should consider joining a group where we do not have leadership responsibilities.

SUMMARY

In this chapter, we have highlighted some of the dual relationship issues that occur in group counseling. We think that the ASGW's revised *Ethical Guidelines* (1989) are clearly written and that they have addressed most of the dual relationship issues that commonly arise. However, like any ethical code, they cannot cover every possible contingency that a counselor might face. Sound professional judgment is called for when counselors determine whether and how to recommend concurrent individual and group therapy for a client, or to recommend group therapy subsequent to individual therapy. Special considerations also arise when working with involuntary client groups.

CHAPTER 11
CONSULTATION

Consultation is a complex, tripartite process that involves at least three parties: a consultant, a consultee, and a client system. The client system can consist of an individual, a group, an organization, or a community. Consultation has been defined as "a process in which a human services professional assists a consultee with a work-related problem with a client system, with the goal of helping both the consultee and the client system in some specified way" (Dougherty, 1990, p. 8).

Although counselors are often the service providers for consultation, consultation is not the same as counseling. In fact, Dougherty stated that consultation "deals exclusively with the consultee's work-related . . . problems. Consultation, by definition, never deals with the personal concerns of the consultee" (1990, p. 9). Nonetheless, it can be difficult, in actual practice, to determine where to draw the line between consultation and counseling. When this line is crossed, a dual role relationship is created. Dual role conflicts can also occur when a consultant functions as a supervisor to a consultee. Some of the questions that consultants encounter in their work, and that we explore in this chapter, are as follows:

- What guidance do codes of ethics provide to consultants regarding dual relationships?
- What conflicts occur when a consultant maintains two professional roles in the consultation relationship, such as counselor/consultant or supervisor/consultant?
- How can a consultant set clear boundaries to distinguish between work-related and personal concerns of the consultee?
- Is the consultant's ultimate obligation to the consultee or to the consultee's client? How can potential role conflicts be avoided?

ETHICAL STANDARDS

There is no generally accepted code of ethics specifically for consultants (Gallessich, 1982; Lowman, 1985), although the AACD and APA codes do offer some guidelines. The AACD *Ethical Standards* (1988) devote an entire section to consulting, and the APA *Ethical Principles of Psychologists* (1989) contain several statements that are equally applicable to both counseling and consulting functions.

Consultants must consider both the needs of the immediate client and of others who might be affected by the consultation services. Brown, Pryzwansky, and Schulte (1987) asserted that ethical guidelines "place tremendous burdens upon consultants to pay particular attention not only to their own behavior and the impact that it might make upon the welfare of the consumer, but also to the actions of the institutions that employ them" (p. 288). This seems to us to speak strongly to the need for consultants to monitor carefully their own behavior, which would include avoidance of dual relationships that could cause problems for the consultant, consultee, and entire system involved in the consultation process.

Consultants must be aware of their own personal needs and work to ensure that these needs do not replace the needs of the consultee (Robinson & Gross, 1985). Kelman (1989) suggested that consultants can avoid meeting their own needs by (1) being aware of the potential for manipulation, (2) using the values of the consultee (not of the consultant) as the basis for developing goals and strategies for change, and (3) keeping foremost the goal of enhancing the consultee's functioning.

The power differential, a major factor in creating a potential for harm in dual relationships, is a complex consideration in consultation. Although the consultant and consultee have equal status as peers in the relationship, their status is also unequal because the consultee is in need due to a work-related problem (Dougherty, 1990). Yet dependency relationships are to be avoided, as this AACD standard states:

- The consulting relationship must be one in which client adaptability and growth toward self-direction are encouraged and cultivated. The member must maintain this role consistently and not become a decision maker for the client or create a future dependency on the consultant. (AACD, 1988)

The position of the consultant with respect to ethical codes is summarized nicely by Dougherty (1990). He stated that consultants can refer to ethical codes for general guidance, but the bottom line remains that they must make informed, sound, and reasonable judgments on each issue they encounter.

> If you function as a consultant, to what ethical codes do you look for guidance when you encounter dual relationship dilemmas? Might you like to see a code of ethics developed specifically for consultants? If so, what might you want it to say about dual relationships?

ROLE CONFLICTS

Role conflicts often occur when a consultant blurs the boundaries between the professional and personal concerns of the consultee. The following example illustrates how this can occur:

> Wilma contracts with a community mental health agency to provide consultation for volunteers who work with people who are dying and their family members. Wilma has been hired as a consultant by the agency director to teach people basic helping skills (listening, attending, and some crisis intervention strategies). Because Wilma is working with these volunteers as a group, many of the participants express a need to talk about how they are affected personally by working with those who are dying. For many of the volunteers, the work is opening up feelings of helplessness, fears of dying, and unfinished business with grieving their own losses. Wilma decides that it seems more important to attend to the needs being expressed by the volunteers than to focus on teaching them helping skills. Her interactions with the volunteers focus more and more on helping them explore their personal issues, and only secondarily on teaching skills.

> - To what extent do you think that Wilma's shift in focus can be supported? On what basis?
> - What potential dual relationship issues do you see in this situation?

Conflicts can occur when a consultant maintains two professional roles in the consultation relationship, such as counselor/
consultant or supervisor/consultant. In the following position
paper, A. Michael Dougherty presents a rationale for avoiding these
types of dual relationships.

Consultation Issues

A. Michael Dougherty

Do the conflicts that might occur when a consultant maintains
two professional roles in the consultation relationship (such as
consultant/counselor or consultant/supervisor) outweigh the benefits that serving in the two roles may create?

I believe that counselors should be extremely cautious before
they engage in two professional roles in the consultation relationship. As a rule of thumb, counselors should take a conservative
stance and avoid maintaining two professional roles with their
consultees. My rationale for this stance includes seven
considerations.

First, the complexity of the consultation process has contributed to disagreement among authorities in the field as to the
boundaries of the consultant's role. This disagreement makes it
difficult to ascertain what is ethical or unethical in many situations surrounding consultation, including professional dual role
relationships. Counselors typically realize the complexity of the
counselor-client relationships. Because of its tripartite nature
(consultant/consultee/client system), the consultation relationship is much more complex than the counseling relationship. An
additional professional role only increases the complexity of an
already intricate and vague process and relationship. For example,
when does the feedback of consultation become the evaluation of
supervision? When does acknowledgement of the negative emotions of a consultee become counseling concerning those
emotions?

Second, there is disagreement in the field concerning the definition of consultation. The difficulty in defining consultation
makes it equally difficult to define the appropriate roles the consultant can assume during the consultation relationship. An additional professional role only complicates the difficulties
involved in determining appropriate roles during consultation. For
example, how does a consultant differentiate a work-related from

a personal concern of a consultee and then go about contracting to consult regarding the work-related concern and counsel regarding a personal concern? Because work-related and personal concerns are typically intricately intertwined and consultation is so very difficult to define, it is best to limit contact with the consultee to one professional role.

Third, counselors, when they consult, should be wary of multiple roles in relationships that might create conflicts of interest that could affect the efficacy of the consultant's role. Consultants should not allow themselves to be drawn into any roles that are incompatible with their stated purposes and contract. Consultants should decline to take on additional roles when the role created by the relationship reduces freedom of expression or objectivity, or limits the consultant's commitment to the consultee organization. By engaging in dual role relationships when consulting, counselors may easily jeopardize their commitment to the consultee organization. For example, when a consultant takes on the additional role of supervisor, the consultant may be placed in the conflict of being expected to share information with parties-at-interest about a supervisee and yet maintain the confidentiality of the consulting relationship because the supervisee is also a consultee. Consider the following situation:

> As a consultant, you agree to supervise a person who is also your consultee. In a meeting, the consultee/supervisee's immediate superior asks you for some information to be used in the consultee/supervisee's annual evaluation. As both a consultant and supervisor you have noticed some professional skill deficits in the consultee/supervisee and have been working with him to upgrade his skills.

What kind of information could you share as a supervisor without breaking your obligation to maintain the confidentiality of the consulting relationship? The level of difficulty in answering this question suggests that professional dual role relationships involve a great amount of risk in terms of conflicts of interest.

Fourth, counselors, when they consult, need to guard against putting the consultee in interrole conflict in which two roles cause contradictory expectations about a given behavior. For example, consultation focuses on work-related concerns and counseling focuses on personal concerns. Because it is difficult to differentiate these two foci, it is best to keep the expectations as simple as possible so that the consultee will not confuse the two relationships and inadvertently bring up personal issues during consultation and work-related ones during counseling.

Fifth, the training of counselors conditions them to almost unconsciously move toward affective concerns and personal problems in their counseling practice. It is hard to turn off this tendency in other types of relationships such as consultation. This tendency can be particularly dangerous if the counselor, when consulting, determines that the locus of the work-related concern lies more in the personal issues of the consultee than in the client system itself. Further, it is easy to move toward counseling consultees when they talk about the anxiety they are having about a work-related problem. Counselors might, therefore, have a tendency to want to offer counseling services to a consultee based on the perception that the consultee will benefit both personally and professionally from such an additional relationship. Focusing on the emotional needs and concerns of consultees, however, breaks the peer relationship inherent to consultation and should therefore be avoided. Consultants should remember that referring the consultee for counseling is typically an option.

Sixth, the consultee may have an obligation to his or her organization not to use consultation for personal purposes (such as counseling) because the organization has consultation occurring for professional not personal growth. Further, if the consultant agrees to counseling and this is kept private, the consultee might wonder later what other kinds of "cheating" the consultant might do (e.g., breaking confidentiality). So dual role relationships, if not approved by the consultee organization, may well raise some issues regarding the professional behavior of the consultant and consultee alike.

Seventh, confidentiality in consultation refers to the consultant and not to the consultee. Therefore, word may get out that the consultant is "such a great counselor." Many prospective consultees who have work-related concerns may avoid seeking consultation because they are concerned that the consultant will bring up and "try to fix" their personal concerns. Professional dual role relationships may be "bad business" for consultants and could reduce the number of consultees who seek consultation.

In summary, professional dual role relationships are best avoided whenever possible when consulting. They simply make a very complex process and relationship even more complex. The additional weight of another relationship makes it more difficult

for the consultant and consultee alike to go about the business
of assisting the client system in being more effective.

Gerald Corey's Commentary

*One of Michael Dougherty's main points is that the consultation
process is complex because of the tripartite nature of the consultation
relationship (consultant/consultee/client system). In general, I agree
with his stance of being cautious before engaging in more than one
role. Typically, the dual roles that might take place are those of
consultant/counselor or consultant/supervisor.*

*The best way to avoid dual relationships is to be clear about the
contract at the outset of the consultation process. Dougherty indicates
that consulting has the purpose of helping consultees with their work-
related concerns (as opposed to their personal concerns, or as opposed to providing supervision). If consultants do take on multiple
roles, the chances for conflicts of interest also increase. What might
a consultant do in cases where it becomes evident in the course of
dealing with work-related concerns that a consultee's ability to work
effectively is hampered by his or her personal problems? It is not the
job of the consultant to shift roles and assume the function of a
personal counselor. The consultant can be therapeutic by listening
to some extent, and then encouraging the consultee to accept a referral for the specific professional help he or she might need. Consultants cannot be all things to all people, and if they attempt this
unrealistic goal, they dilute their capacity to implement the contract
that should guide the consultation process. Dougherty's concluding
point is indeed one worth pondering: "Professional dual role relationships are best avoided whenever possible when consulting. They
simply make a very complex process and relationship even more
complex."*

Barbara Herlihy's Commentary

*In reading Michael Dougherty's statement, it struck me that there
are many parallels between consultation and supervision when one
considers dual relationship issues. Both consultation and supervision involve tripartite relationships—consultant/consultee/client
system in the one case and supervisor/supervisee/client in the other.
Both avoid focusing on personal concerns: Consultation focuses on*

work-related problems and supervision focuses on professional development. Professionals who serve as consultants and as supervisors are cautioned against entering into counseling relationships with those individuals with whom they have contracted professionally. They are advised, instead, to refer.

Yet it can be difficult to distinguish where the appropriate boundaries lie between consultation and counseling or between supervision and counseling. Both consultants and supervisors are typically trained as counselors and have a natural tendency to focus on affective and personal issues when they listen to the concerns of others. It seems to me that the complexity and special tripartite nature of both the consultation and supervision relationships place an extra burden on professionals to be clear about the boundaries of their relationships, and to be particularly sensitive to the problems that dual relationships can create.

Dougherty has shed some light on the nature of conflicts that occur when a consultant attempts to function in the dual role of consultant/counselor or consultant/supervisor. He makes an excellent point, with which we both agree, in cautioning consultants to avoid becoming entangled in dual relationships. The dual role of consultant/supervisor should be avoided because supervision involves evaluation, and therefore power of the supervisor over the supervisee, and thus violates the peer nature of the consultation relationship. Elsewhere, Dougherty (1990) noted that supervision "allows the consultant to build an illegitimate power base, creates the potential for conflicts of interest, and violates the original consultation contract" (p. 145).

The dual role of counselor/consultant is also to be avoided. Yet in practice, it can be difficult to distinguish between work-related and personal concerns of the consultee. The AACD *Ethical Standards* (1988) state that the focus of the consultation relationship should be on work-related problems rather than on the personal concerns of the consultee. The consultation relationship is ideally based on a contractual agreement that is clearly understood by consultees. Consultants have obligations to consultees that are similar to those of therapists. Yet "counseling contaminates the consultation relationship" (Dougherty, 1990, p. 145). Again, when the consultant determines that the problem resides more in the consultee's personal concerns than in the client or client system, the consultant should refer the consultee.

THE CONSULTANT'S ULTIMATE OBLIGATION

Is the consultant's ultimate obligation to the consultee or to the consultee's client? Consultants have an obligation to both the consultee and to the consultee's clients (indirectly). Because consultants provide indirect services to clients, they have responsibilities to these clients as well as to the consultees. There is controversy with regard to the consultee's ultimate obligation. Again, the best way to avoid potential role conflicts is to develop a clear contract at the very beginning of the consulting relationship. Informed consent is extremely important in specifying the rights of the consultees. Consultees have a right to be fully informed about the nature of consultation, the goals and procedures of the consultation process, issues of confidentiality, and potential areas of risk. By having a full and clear discussion early on, a relationship of trust is established and potential conflicts are avoided.

> If you do consulting work, what criteria do you use to determine when to refer a consultee for personal counseling? What elements do you believe a consulting contract needs to contain in order to prevent later misunderstandings?

SUMMARY

Although many professionals who do consulting work are also counselors, consultation is clearly not the same as counseling. It can be difficult to "switch hats," yet blending the counselor and consultant roles can lead to complex dual relationship conflicts and can have negative consequences for all parties involved. Consultants must also avoid the dual role of supervisor/consultant. Several factors complicate the work of the consultant. These include the lack of general agreement on the definition of consultation; controversy regarding whether the consultant's ultimate obligation is to the consultee or to the client system; the need to avoid focusing on the consultee's personal concerns despite a natural inclination to do so; and the complex, tripartite nature of the consultation relationship.

PART IV:
CONCLUDING COMMENTS

CHAPTER 12
KEY THEMES, QUESTIONS, AND DECISION MAKING

In this concluding chapter, we highlight some key concepts or themes that have emerged throughout the book and present questions for reflection and integration. Finally, we outline a model of a decision-making process that we see as useful when confronted with dual relationship issues.

KEY DUAL RELATIONSHIP CONCEPTS

Twelve themes—or concepts—have been woven throughout the tapestry of this work:

1. Dual relationship issues affect virtually all counselors and human development specialists, regardless of their work setting or clientele. No helping professional remains untouched by potential dual role conflicts and dilemmas. We have examined how dual relationship issues affect professionals in counselor education programs, private practice, college and university counseling centers and other areas of college personnel work, schools, and rehabilitation counseling facilities. We explored these issues as they apply to working with individual clients, couples or families, and educational and therapeutic groups. We also looked at the complex nature of dual relationship dilemmas when relationships are tripartite, such as those involving supervisor/supervisee/client and consultant/consultee/client systems.

Although we have attempted to cover a broad range of issues, we realize that there are a number of special areas of concern that we have not addressed. For instance, some counselors conduct phenomenological research, including qualitative research and case studies. Although researchers are ethically prohibited from establishing therapy relationships with research participants, they may face dual relationship dilemmas in attempting to balance research needs with client needs for intervention or services. Members of the clergy often function in multiple roles and may face conflicts when they serve as counselors, spiritual leaders, and even fund raisers with parishioners and their families. Working with involuntary clients (a client population we have only briefly discussed) can present special dual relationship dilemmas for counselors who work in the criminal justice system.

Despite the fact that we have not been able to discuss dual relationships in all counseling specializations, we feel confident in concluding that dual relationship issues are indeed pervasive in our profession.

2. Nearly all codes of ethics caution against dual relationships. In recent years, revisions of various codes have given more extensive coverage to dual relationship issues. Yet attempts to codify problematic dual relationships have often generated more debate. This has been particularly clear with respect to the revised codes of the American Association for Marriage and Family Therapy, the Association for Specialists in Group Work, the American Psychological Association, and the proposed regulations for psychologists in California.

It seems clear to us that we cannot look to codes of ethics to provide all the answers to the dual relationship questions we face, although the codes do provide some guidance. From an ethical (and legal) perspective, if we go against a standard in our professional code of ethics, it is incumbent on us to provide a rationale for doing so. Further, as practitioners, it is our ethical responsibility to devise safeguards to prevent harm to clients who may be involved in dual relationships with us. We must openly discuss the possible risks and benefits of any dual relationship we consider entering. Learning to deal with dual roles can help us to appreciate complexity in human relationships. In the last analysis, there is no substitute for our professional judgment, integrity, and good will.

3. Not all dual relationships can be avoided, nor are they necessarily always harmful. Dual relationships are fraught with complexities and ambiguities. They are unavoidable in some situations, and they sometimes contain potential both for risk and for benefit to clients. Throughout the book, we have given examples and brief vignettes of various dual relationships. In some cases the harm to the client was severe, as in instances of a sexual intimacy with a client or sexual harassment of a student. However, we also saw some situations in which there were benefits to the blending of roles. Examples are mentoring relationships between professor and student or between supervisor and supervisee. Counselor educators who teach group counseling courses often do so by combining didactic and experiential learning and by playing multiple roles, and this can enrich the students' learning experience.

4. With the exception of clear agreement that sexual dual relationships with current clients are unethical, there is little consensus about most dual relationship issues. Dual relationships—especially nonsexual dual relationships—have been getting increased attention lately. This attention has served to highlight the fact that counseling, as a profession, has more questions than answers about the issues involved. Many issues continue to be debated. In fact, in no setting or format is there complete agreement on the issues involved.

5. Dual role relationships challenge us to monitor ourselves and to examine our motivations for our practices. As practitioners, we need to engage in an ongoing process of self-reflection. It is all too easy to deceive ourselves into thinking that we have the best interests of our clients in mind. For example, we may encourage our clients who are in individual therapy with us to join a therapy group that we are forming. This may not be what our clients need, and if we are not honest with ourselves, we run the risk of exploiting the clients. It is essential that we ask ourselves, whenever a dual relationship issue arises, whose needs are being met—the client's or our own?

6. When we are considering becoming involved in a dual relationship, it would be wise to seek consultation from trusted colleagues or a supervisor. Willingness to seek consultation is a sign of professionalism. We may also save ourselves a costly and painful malpractice judgment if we are able to demonstrate that we acted in good faith and sought consultation. As mentioned in chapter 1, a trend seems to be emerging for practitioners to "reasonably know" that a dual relationship is developing and to consult to see whether it can be prevented. If it cannot be prevented, then we are expected to terminate the relationship or, at the least, to identify safeguards to minimize potential risks of harm. Colleagues can help us to gain another perspective on potential problem areas in dual role relationships that we might have overlooked. Working with supervisors or colleagues can be instrumental in helping us maintain our objectivity and can enhance our ability to appraise situations honestly.

7. There are few absolute answers that can neatly resolve dual relationship dilemmas. Because of the multidimensional nature of many dual relationships, professionals must ultimately distinguish between those nonsexual dual relationships that are harmful and those that are benign. Although we can find some general guidance in the ethical standards, when it comes to making decisions in specific cases, we often must deal with many gray areas. As we pointed out in the first chapter, conscientious professionals looking for guidance regarding dual relationships will find that experts provide conflicting interpretations of ethical codes. Ethical codes are guidelines for practice rather than absolute prescriptions—thus stressing the importance of the professional's informed judgment. However, there is a delicate balance in this judgment: Chaos would result if professionals were allowed to interpret ethical codes in any way they saw fit.

Rather than thinking in terms of the "best answer," it may be better to consider more than one acceptable way to respond to ethical dilemmas in dual relationships. Answers that may be appropriate for us may not be appropriate for you in your situation. Simply because we have differing views about a specific dual relationship issue does not mean that one of us is right and the other is wrong. For instance, you may be able to counsel separate individuals within a family in private counseling and also work with the entire family. You may have the capacity to retain your objectivity, to avoid taking sides, and to shift roles quite effectively for the benefit of all the family members. Others may have trouble in shifting gears and keeping separate who has said what, and thus might decide that this practice will not work for their clients or for them as practitioners. The therapeutic styles and preferences of individual practitioners must be taken into account, as must the unique needs of each client. Thus, we need to be able to tolerate ambiguity, and we will not find security in the absolute answers that others may be quick to offer us.

8. The cautions for entering into dual relationships should be for the benefit of our clients, rather than to protect ourselves

from censure. With the emerging trends it may well be the case that dual relationships will be legislated and will thus leave little room for individual variation. Rules and regulations developed by professional associations and governing boards may be a trend in the 1990s. At a recent state convention, one of us (Corey) heard a presenter predict that by 1992 or 1993 most forms of dual relationships will be illegal. His advice to the audience was to avoid *any* form of dual relationships in order to reduce the chances of a malpractice suit. It is to be hoped that we will not be so driven by legal mandates that we fail to consider what our clients need and the role of our professional judgment.

9. In determining whether to proceed with a dual relationship, consider whether the potential benefit of the relationship outweighs the potential for harm. Some writers have concluded that dual relationships should be entered into only when the risks of harm are small or when there are strong, offsetting, ethical and clinical benefits for the consumer. In assessing the impact of dual relationships, it is prudent to consider risks to both the client and the professional. We also need to reflect on the possible effects on other consumers, other professionals, the profession itself, and society. Although we may identify some benefits to certain dual relationships, we must be cautious in proceeding with these relationships.

10. Whenever we are operating in more than one role and when there is potential for negative consequences, it is our responsibility to develop safeguards and measures to reduce the potential for harm. Some of these safeguards include securing informed consent, engaging in ongoing reflection and discussion of conflicts that arise, seeking supervision and consultation with other professionals, and documenting our rationale for entering into a dual relationship. We should also record any procedures we have taken to maximize the potential benefit and to minimize the potential risks.

11. It is the responsibility of counselor preparation programs to introduce issues pertaining to dual relationships and to teach students ways of thinking about alternative courses of action. We suspect that some students who are preparing to be counselors have given little thought to the complexities involved in dual relationships. We hope that the subjects that we have raised will be discussed extensively in ethics courses and in courses such as group supervision, practicum, and internship. When students are involved in supervised field placements, they are bound to encounter some dilemmas related to the dual relationship controversy. As counselor educators and supervisors, we should encourage students to bring their concerns about these dilemmas into our classes for discussion and debate. We can also introduce issues through case vignettes and role-playing exercises. We hope that we will do more than provide students with a list of do's and don'ts and will challenge students to think through their own positions on issues.

12. Counselor education programs have a responsibility to develop their own guidelines, policies, and procedures for dealing with dual relationships within the program. Some studies show that sexual intimacies are not uncommon between counselor educators and students, and between supervisors and supervisees. Other studies reveal that supervisors blend the roles of supervisor and therapist. Yet other studies show that counselor educators sometimes attempt to fulfill the dual role of counselor and educator to the same individual. Counselor educators need to be clear about the primary role they play in their relationships with students. We think that the faculty in every program should be engaged in a continuing discussion about ways to prevent harmful dual relationships within the program. As educators and supervisors, if we cannot deal with dual relationships effectively, what chance will we have to teach students how to deal with these issues? If we are not modeling effective ways of thinking about and dealing with all forms of dual relationships, how can we expect our students to grapple constructively with them? At the very least, we recommend that faculty meetings be devoted to a discussion of ways to address dual relationship issues and that programs develop some general policies about the management of dual relationship concerns. Ideally, faculty groups, with student representation, can develop some practical guidelines and procedures for preventing harmful dual relationships. It is time that we proactively address these issues. If we do not create our own meaningful guidelines, we fear that legislative bodies and governing boards will create them for us.

QUESTIONS FOR REFLECTION
AND INTEGRATION

Throughout the book, in each chapter, we have tried to involve you, our readers. We have asked questions that we hope have encouraged you to think about the issues we have raised. Here in the last chapter of the book, we include a summary list of some of the questions that have recurred in various forms. As you review this list, we want you to consider: What is your own stance toward these issues? In what ways do they affect your work as a professional?

- Are **sexual relationships with former clients** (or students or supervisees) ever ethically acceptable? If so, how much time needs to pass between terminating the professional relationship and beginning the personal one? What about **social relationships with former clients**? Collegial or peer relationships with former students or supervisees?

- How should our profession deal with the issue of **sexual attraction** between counselors and clients? How can counselor education programs prepare prospective counselors so that they are able to draw clear distinctions between feeling a sexual attraction and acting on that attraction?

- What steps can the profession take to **prevent sexual improprieties** with clients, students, or supervisees? What is your own role in prevention?

- Do the **codes of ethics** that govern your professional identity, work setting, and clientele address dual relationships in a way that is helpful to you? If you want to see changes made in your codes, how do you want them to read?

- If you are a **graduate student**, what kinds of training do you want to receive in order to feel prepared to cope with dual relationship issues? What kinds

(continued on next page)

of relationships do you want—and not want—to have with your professors?

- What are the appropriate boundaries of a **supervisor's role**? Can supervision address personal concerns of the supervisee without creating a dual role conflict? Where should boundaries be drawn and maintained between counseling and supervision?

- Is **bartering** with clients for goods or services or **accepting a gift** from a client ever ethical? Under what circumstances might you find either of these practices acceptable?

- What are the limits to **social relationships** with current clients, students, or supervisees? In your work, what distinctions do you draw among counseling relationships, social relationships, and friendships?

- What do you see as the proper limits of **counselor self-disclosure**? What dual relationship problems could be created if you were to overextend these limits?

- What special dual role conflicts do you encounter when you function in a **tripartite relationship** as a supervisor or consultant? To whom do you owe your strongest ethical obligation—to your supervisee or consultee, or to the client who is ultimately served? What role conflicts do you encounter in attempting to balance these obligations?

- If, in your work, you function in **multiple roles**—which might include any combination of counselor, supervisor, administrator, course instructor, case manager, colleague, and group leader—what role conflicts do you most frequently encounter? How do you resolve them?

A DECISION-MAKING MODEL FOR
DUAL RELATIONSHIP ISSUES

One picture that has emerged for us, as a result of examining and pondering these questions, is a model of a decision-making process that can be useful when confronted with dual relationship issues:

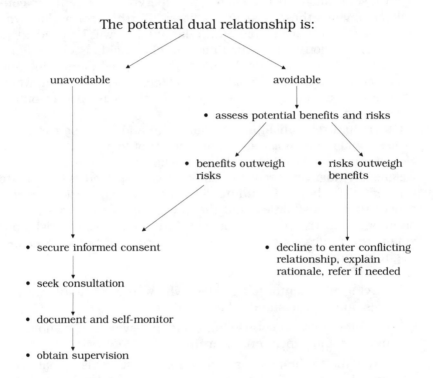

The potential dual relationship is:

unavoidable   avoidable

- assess potential benefits and risks

- benefits outweigh risks   • risks outweigh benefits

- secure informed consent   • decline to enter conflicting relationship, explain rationale, refer if needed
- seek consultation
- document and self-monitor
- obtain supervision

It seems clear to us that some dual relationships, built into the counselor's job description or work environment, are indeed unavoidable. Examples include

- the rehabilitation counselor who must manage the case budget or testify in court regarding a client's return-to-work potential
- the counselor in a rural, isolated community whose clients are also her banker, pharmacist, and beautician

- the school counselor who must report child abuse and then continue to function as the child's counselor, liaison with child protective services, and witness in court.

In these instances, the professional's obligation is to take all possible steps to minimize the risks of harm. The client's informed consent is an ethically important first step that entails a full and open discussion with the client (or supervisee, student, or consultee) in which these risks are explored. Further, counselors who are engaged in unavoidable dual relationships will be prudent to seek consultation both at the time the relationship is entered and periodically throughout its duration. Ongoing self-monitoring and documentation are additional prudent measures. When unavoidable dual relationships become problematic, it is wise to obtain supervision.

Other dual relationships are avoidable, and in these cases the professional has a choice as to whether or not to proceed into them. Here it is essential that potential and risks and benefits be carefully weighed. A judgment needs to be made regarding factors that create a potential for harm, including differences in expectations, divergences in responsibilities, and the power differential. In some instances, when the potential benefits are great and the risks are small, the professional may decide to proceed. Some examples might include

- serving as a mentor to a student who wants to pursue learnings outside the standard curriculum
- teaching a group counseling class in a way that combines didactic and experiential learnings
- attending to the personal concerns of a supervisee that are impeding his or her performance as a counselor (but not to the extent of converting the supervisory relationship into a counseling relationship).

In yet other cases, a careful consideration of potential risks will lead the professional to conclude that it is best not to enter into a dual relationship. Although the temptation to do so might be well motivated, the risk of harm is strong. Examples that we would include here are

- entering into a sexual or romantic relationship with a client, student, or supervisee

- becoming the personal counselor of a current student or employee
- entering into a business relationship with a client.

When a potential dual relationship can and should be avoided, professionals need to take steps to ensure that clients understand the rationale for not proceeding with the problematic relationship. For instance, in the first example given here this might involve acknowledging a sexual attraction, discussing the risks of harm in acting on the attraction, and referring the client or supervisee.

Although the decision-making model helps to clarify our thinking, each of us will continue to encounter situations in our work that raise difficult questions for which the answers remain elusive. Our expectation is that we have stimulated thinking and self-examination. We certainly hope that we have not contributed to the current confusion—and in some cases, panicky practices—by publishing this book. Our participation at professional conferences continues to reveal a strong interest in a host of dual relationship controversies. What troubles us is the dogmatic approach captured by such statements as "You are unethical if you engage in any kind of dual relationships. Either dual relationships are ethical or they are unethical. You can't have it both ways." "The ethical codes prohibit dual relationships, so there is no room for discussion."

At the other extreme, we have heard professionals make comments like these: "Dual relationships are unavoidable. Because ethical standards pertaining to them are unenforceable, they should just be ignored." "I have no problems with dual relationship issues. As a trained and experienced professional, I can rely on my own judgment. All these cautions about the need for consultation and supervision are just overreactions."

In our view, neither of these extremes represents the best of our profession's ability to reason through the difficult issues involved in dual relationships. As is the case with learning to make ethical decisions in other areas of professional practice, many situations involving dual relationships defy easy answers. To some degree, the personal style of each counselor needs to be taken into consideration in resolving dual relationship dilemmas. Some practitioners may be comfortable practicing in the context of multiple roles and multiple responsibilities, whereas others may need more clear-cut boundaries.

Closing Thoughts

Coauthoring this book has been a learning experience for each of us. When we first agreed to undertake this project, we each thought that we had some very definite opinions regarding certain dual relationship issues. Then, as work progressed and the various guest contributors raised points we hadn't considered and presented new slants on points we *had* considered, we found ourselves rethinking our previous positions. We each can say that we have ended this project by being less certain and more informed.

Indeed, certainties are rare in the counseling profession. We make no claim to having discovered answers to complex and difficult questions. Rather, we hope to have raised some important issues, to have explored a range of viewpoints, and to have discussed our own positions. We hope that the various chapters have provided material for thoughtful reflection and a springboard for ongoing discussion. We invite you to make use of the tear-out evaluation sheet at the end of this book and send it to us with your reactions to the issues and the positions that we developed.

We expect that ethically conscientious professionals will continue to struggle with the dual relationship dilemmas that they face in their work. In the absence of certainties, we must rely on our informed, reasoned professional judgment and consultation with colleagues—which are, in themselves, hallmarks of ethical behavior.

REFERENCES AND SUGGESTED READINGS

Akamatsu, T.J. (1988). Intimate relationships with former clients: National survey of attitudes and behavior among practitioners. *Professional Psychology: Research and Practice, 19*(4), 454–458.

Alonso, A. (1983). A developmental theory of psychodynamic supervision. *The Clinical Supervisor, 1*(3), 23–36.

American Association for Counseling and Development. (1988). *Ethical standards.* Alexandria, VA: Author.

American Association for Marriage and Family Therapy. (1991). *AAMFT code of ethics.* Washington, DC: Author.

American College Personnel Association. (1989). *Statement of ethical principles and standards.* Alexandria, VA: Author.

American Mental Health Counselors Association. (1987). *Code of ethics.* Alexandria, VA: Author.

American Psychiatric Association. (1989). *The principles of medical ethics, with annotations especially applicable to psychiatry.* Washington, DC: Author.

American Psychoanalytic Association. (1983). *Code of ethics.* New York: Author.

American Psychological Association. (1987). *Casebook on ethical principles of psychologists.* Washington, DC: Author.

American Psychological Association. (1989). *Ethical principles of psychologists.* Washington, DC: Author.

American Psychological Association. (1990). Ethical principles revised. *The APA Monitor, 21*(6), 28–32.

American Psychological Association Ethics Committee. (1987). Report of the ethics committee: 1986. *American Psychologist, 42*, 730–734.

American Psychological Association Ethics Committee. (1988). Trends in ethics cases, common pitfalls, and published resources. *American Psychologist, 43*, 564–572.

American Rehabilitation Counseling Association. (1987). *Code of professional ethics for rehabilitation counselors.* Alexandria, VA: Author.

American School Counselor Association. (1984). *Ethical standards for school counselors.* Falls Church, VA: Author.

American School Counselor Association. (1983). *Position statements.* Falls Church, VA: Author.

Anonymous. (1991). Sexual harassment: A female counseling student's experience. *Journal of Counseling and Development, 69,* 502–506.

Association for Counselor Education and Supervision, Supervision Interest Network. (1990). Standards for counseling supervisors. *Journal of Counseling and Development, 69,* 30–32.

Association for Specialists in Group Work. (1989). *Ethical guidelines for group counselors.* Alexandria, VA: Author.

Association for Specialists in Group Work. (1991). *Professional standards for the training of group workers.* Alexandria, VA: Author.

Aubrey, M., & Dougher, M.J. (1990). Ethical issues in outpatient group therapy with sex offenders. *Journal of Specialists in Group Work, 15,* 75–82.

Austin, K.M., Moline, M.E., & Williams, G.T. (1990). *Confronting malpractice: Legal and ethical dilemmas in psychotherapy.* Newbury Park, CA: Sage.

Bajt, T.R., & Pope, K.S. (1989). Therapist-patient sexual intimacy involving children and adolescents. *American Psychologist, 44,* 455.

Bartell, P.A., & Rubin, L.J. (1990). Dangerous liaisons: Sexual intimacies in supervision. *Professional Psychology: Research and Practice, 21*(6), 442–450.

Bates, C.M., & Brodsky, A.M. (1989). *Sex in the therapy hour: A case of professional incest.* New York: Guilford Press.

Beauchamp, T.L., & Childress, J.F. (1989). *Principles of biomedical ethics* (3rd ed.). New York: Oxford University Press.

Bennett, B.E., Bryant, B.K., VandenBos, G.R., & Greenwood, A. (1990). *Professional liability and risk management.* Washington, DC: American Psychological Association.

Bernard, J.M. (1979). Supervisor training: A discrimination model. *Counselor Education and Supervision, 19,* 60–68.

Bernard, J.M. (1987). Ethical and legal considerations for supervisors. In L.D. Borders & G.R. Leddick (Eds.), *Handbook of counseling supervision* (pp. 52–57). Alexandria, VA: Association for Counselor Education and Supervision.

Bernard, J.M., & Goodyear, R.K. (1991). *Fundamentals of clinical supervision.* Needham Heights, MA: Allyn & Bacon.

Board of Behavioral Science Examiners. (1989, November/December). Sex should never be a part of therapy. *The California Therapist,* pp. 21–28.

Bok, S. (1979). *Lying: Moral choice in public and private life.* New York: Vintage Books.

Borders, L.D. (1991). A systematic approach to peer group supervision. *Journal of Counseling and Development, 69,* 248–252.

Borders, L.D., Bernard, J.M., Dye, H.A., Fong, M.L., Henderson, P., & Nance, D.W. (In press). Curriculum guide for training counseling supervisors: Rationale, development, and implementation. *Counselor Education and Supervision.*

Borders, L.D., & Leddick, G.R. (1987). *Handbook of counseling supervision.* Alexandria, VA: Association for Counselor Education and Supervision.

Borys, D.S. (1988). *Dual relationships between therapist and client: A national survey of clinicians' attitudes and practices.* Unpublished doctoral dissertation, University of California, Los Angeles.

Borys, D.S., & Pope, K.S. (1989). Dual relationships between therapist and client: A national study of psychologists, psychiatrists, and social workers. *Professional Psychology: Research and Practice, 20*(5), 283–293.

Bouhoutsos, J., Holroyd, J., Lerman, H., Forer, B.R., & Greenberg, M. (1983). Sexual intimacy between psychotherapists and patients. *Professional Psychology: Research and Practice, 14,* 185–196.

Bradley, L. (1989). *Counselor supervision: Principles, process, and practice* (2nd ed.). Muncie, IN: Accelerated Development.

Brown, D., Pryzwansky, W.B., & Schulte, A.C. (1987). *Psychological consultation.* Boston: Allyn & Bacon.

Caplan, A.L. (1988). Informed consent and provider-patient relationships in rehabilitation medicine. *Archives of Physical Medicine and Rehabilitation, 69,* 2–7.

Caplan, G. (1970). *The theory and practice of mental health consultation.* New York: Basic Books.

Certified Insurance Rehabilitation Specialists. (1986). *Code of professional ethics.* Rolling Meadows, IL: Author.

Committee on Women in Psychology, American Psychological Association (1989). If sex enters into the psychotherapy relationship. *Professional Psychology: Research and Practice, 20*(2), 112–115.

Corey, G. (1981). Description of a practicum course in group leadership. *Journal of Specialists in Group Work, 6,* 100–107.

Corey, G. (1990). *Instructor's resource manual for theory and practice of group counseling* (3rd ed.). Pacific Grove, CA: Brooks/Cole.

Corey, G., & Corey, M.S. (1991, January 17). Learning to wrestle with ethical dilemmas [Focus on Graduate Students]. *Guidepost,* p. 25.

Corey, G., & Corey, M.S. (1992). *Groups: Process and practice* (4th ed.). Pacific Grove, CA: Brooks/Cole.

Corey, G., Corey, M.S., & Callanan, P. (1988). *Issues and ethics in the helping professions* (3rd ed.). Pacific Grove, CA: Brooks/Cole.

Corey, G., Corey, M., Callanan, P., & Russell, J.M. (1980). A residential workshop for personal growth. *Journal of Specialists in Group Work, 5,* 205–215.

Corey, M.S., & Corey, G. (1986). Experiential/didactic training and supervision workshop for group leaders. *Journal of Counseling and Human Service Professions, 1,* 18–26.

Cormier, L.S., & Bernard, J.M. (1982). Ethical and legal responsibilities of clinical supervisors. *Personnel and Guidance Journal, 60,* 486–491.

Council for Accreditation of Counseling and Related Educational Programs. (1988). *Accreditation procedures manual and application.* Washington, DC: Author.

DeLucia, J.L. (1991). An interview with H. Allan Dye: Perspectives on the field of group work. *Journal of Specialists in Group Work, 16,* 67–73.

Department of Consumer Affairs. (1990). *Professional therapy never includes sex.* Sacramento, CA: Author.

Doehrman, M.J. (1976). Parallel processes in supervision and psychotherapy. *Bulletin of the Menninger Clinic, 40,* 1–104.

Donigian, J. (1991, Winter). Dual relationships: An ethical issue. *Together, 19*(2), 6–7.

Dougherty, A.M. (1990). *Consultation: Practice and perspective.* Pacific Grove, CA: Brooks/Cole.

Dougherty, A.M. (In press). Ethical issues in consultation. *Elementary School Guidance and Counseling.*

Dougherty, A.M., Dougherty, L.P., & Purcell, D. (1991). The sources and management of resistance to consultation. *The School Counselor, 38,* 178–186.

Dougherty, C.J. (1991). Values in rehabilitation: Happiness, freedom, and fairness. *Journal of Rehabilitation, 57*(1), 7–12.

Draft of APA ethics code published. (1991, June). *APA Monitor, 22*(6), 30–35.

Dye, H.A., & Borders, L.D. (1990). Counseling supervisors: Standards for preparation and practice. *Journal of Counseling and Development, 69,* 27–32.

Egan, G. (1990). *The skilled helper: A systematic approach to effective helping* (4th ed.). Pacific Grove, CA: Brooks/Cole.

Engels, D., Wilborn, B., & Schneider, L. (1990). Ethics curricula for counselor preparation programs. In B. Herlihy & L. Golden, *Ethical Standards Casebook* (4th ed.). Alexandria, VA: American Association for Counseling and Development.

Ethics update. (1988, December). *APA Monitor, 19,* 36.

Fagan, T.K., & Jenkins, W.M. (1989). People with disabilities: An update. *Journal of Counseling and Development, 68,* 140–144.

Ferris, P.A., & Linville, M.E. (1985). The child's rights: Whose responsibility? *Elementary School Guidance & Counseling, 19,* 172–180.

Forester-Miller, H., & Duncan, J.A. (1990). The ethics of dual relationships in the training of group counselors. *Journal of Specialists in Group Work, 15,* 88–93.

Gabbard, G., & Pope, K. (1988). Sexual intimacies after termination: Clinical, ethical, and legal aspects. *The Independent Practitioner, 8*(2), 21–26.

Gallessich, J. (1982). *The profession and practice of consultation.* San Francisco: Jossey-Bass.

Geller, J.D., Cooley, R.S., & Hartley, D. (1981–1982). Images of the psychotherapist: A theoretical and methodological perspective. *Imagination, Cognition, and Personality, 1,* 123–146.

Gartrell, N., Herman, J., Olarte, S., Feldstein, M., & Localio, R. (1987). Reporting practices of psychologists who knew of sexual misconduct by colleagues. *American Journal of Orthopsychiatry, 57*(2), 287–295.

Glaser, R.D., & Thorpe, J.S. (1986). Unethical intimacy: A survey of sexual contact and advances between psychology educators and female graduate students. *American Psychologist, 41*(1), 42–51.

Gorlin, R.A. (1990). *Codes of professional responsibility* (2nd ed.). Washington, DC: BNA.

Gottlieb, M.C. (1990). Accusations of sexual misconduct: Assisting in the complaint process. *Professional Psychology: Research and Practice, 21*(6), 455–461.

Gottlieb, M.C., Sell, J.M., & Schoenfeld, L.S. (1988). Social/romantic relationships with present and former clients: State licensing board actions. *Professional Psychology: Research and Practice, 19*(4), 459–462.

Greenburg, S.L., Lewis, G.J., & Johnson, M. (1985). Peer consultation groups for private practitioners. *Professional Psychology: Research and Practice, 16*, 437–447.

Group for the Advancement of Psychiatry Committee on Medical Education. (1990). *A casebook in psychiatric ethics.* New York: Brunner/Mazel.

Gumaer, J., & Martin, D. (1990). Group ethics: A multicultural model for training knowledge and skill competencies. *Journal of Specialists in Group Work, 15*, 94–103.

Haas, L.J., & Malouf, J.L. (1989). *Keeping up the good work: A practitioner's guide to mental health ethics.* Sarasota, FL: Professional Resource Exchange.

Harrar, W.R., VandeCreek, L., & Knapp, S. (1990). Ethical and legal aspects of clinical supervision. *Professional Psychology: Research and Practice, 21*(1), 37–41.

Hayman, P.M., & Covert, J.A. (1986). Ethical dilemmas in college counseling centers. *Journal of Counseling and Development, 64*, 318–320.

Heppner, P.P., & Roehlke, H.J. (1984). Difference among supervisees at different levels of training: Implications for a developmental model of supervision. *Journal of Counseling Psychology, 31*, 76–90.

Herlihy, B., & Golden, L. (1990). *Ethical standards casebook* (4th ed.). Alexandria, VA: American Association for Counseling and Development.

Herlihy, B., Healy, M., Cook, E.P., & Hudson, P. (1987). Ethical practices of licensed professional counselors: A survey of state licensing boards. *Counselor Education and Supervision, 27*, 69–76.

Holroyd, J.C., & Bouhoutsos, J.C. (1985). Biased reporting of therapist-patient sexual intimacy. *Professional Psychology, 16*(5), 701–709.

Holroyd, J.C., & Brodsky, A.M. (1977). Psychologists' attitudes and practices regarding erotic and nonerotic physical contact with patients. *American Psychologist, 32*, 843–849.

Holroyd, J.C., & Brodsky, A.M. (1980). Does touching patients lead to sexual intercourse. *Professional Psychology, 11*(5), 807–811.

Holub, E.A., & Lee, S.S. (1990). Therapists' use of nonerotic physical contact: Ethical concerns. *Professional Psychology: Research and Practice, 21*(2), 115–117.

Hosie, T.W., Patterson, J.B., & Hollingsworth, D.K. (1989). School and rehabilitation counselor preparation: Meeting the needs of individuals with disabilities. *Journal of Counseling and Development, 68*, 171–176.

Hotelling, K. (1988). Ethical, legal, and administrative options to address sexual relationships between counselor and client. *Journal of Counseling and Development, 67*, 233–237.

Hotelling, K. (1991). Sexual harassment: A problem shielded by silence. *Journal of Counseling and Development, 69*, 497–501.

Howard, S. (1991). Organizational resources for addressing sexual harassment. *Journal of Counseling and Development, 69*, 507–511.

Huey, W.C. (1986). Ethical concerns in school counseling. *Journal of Counseling and Development, 64*, 321–322.

Huey, W.C., & Remley, T.P. (1988). *Ethical and legal issues in school counseling.* Alexandria, VA: American Association for Counseling and Development.

Humes, C.W., Szymanski, E.M., & Hohenshil, T.H. (1989). Roles of counseling in enabling persons with disabilities. *Journal of Counseling and Development, 68*, 145–150.

Keane, J. (1990, March). Ethical considerations in small counseling centers. *Commissioned VII Counseling and Psychological Services Newsletter* (American College Personnel Association), p. 3.

Keith-Spiegel, P., & Koocher, G.P. (1985). *Ethics in psychology: Professional standards and cases.* New York: Random House.

Kelman, H.C. (1989). Manipulation of human behavior: An ethical dilemma for the social scientist. In W.G. Bennis, K.D. Benne, & R. Chin (Eds.), *The planning of change* (2nd ed.). New York: Holt, Rinehart & Winston.

Kitchener, K.S. (1984). Intuition, critical evaluation, and ethical principles: The foundation for ethical decisions in counseling psychology. *The Counseling Psychologist, 12*, 43–55.

Kitchener, K.S. (1988). Dual role relationships: What makes them so problematic? *Journal of Counseling and Development, 67*, 217–221.

Kitchener, K.S., & Harding, S.S. (1990). Dual role relationships. In B. Herlihy & L. Golden, *Ethical standards casebook* (4th ed., pp. 146–154). Alexandria, VA: American Association for Counseling and Development.

Leslie, R. (1989, September/October). Dual relationships: The legal view. *The California Therapist*, pp. 9–13.

Leslie, R. (1991, January/February). Dual relationships hearings held. *The California Therapist*, pp. 18–19.

Levenson, J.L. (1986). When a colleague practices unethically: Guidelines for intervention. *Journal of Counseling and Development, 64*, 315–317.

Lewis, G.J., Greenburg, S.L., & Hatch, D.B. (1988). Peer consultation groups for psychologists in private practice: A national survey. *Professional Psychology: Research and Practice, 19*, 81–86.

Lloyd, A.P. (1990). Dual relationships in group activities: A counselor education accreditation dilemma. *Journal of Specialists in Group Work, 15*, 83–87.

Lombana, J.H. (1989). Counseling persons with disabilities: Summary and projections. *Journal of Counseling and Development, 68*, 177–179.

Lowman, R.L. (1985). The ethical practice of psychological consultation: Not an impossible dream. *The Counseling Psychologist, 13*, 466–472.

Mabe, A., & Rollin, S. (1986). The role of a code of ethical standards in counseling. *Journal of Counseling and Development, 64,* 294–297.

Margolin, G. (1982). Ethical and legal considerations in marital and family therapy. *American Psychologist, 37*(7), 788–801.

Martin, J.S., Goodyear, R.K., & Newton, F.B. (1987). Clinical supervision: An intensive case study. *Professional Psychology, 18,* 225–235.

Mitchell, M.E., & Sink, J.M. (1983). *Process, issues, and needs in private-for-profit rehabilitation* (Rehabilitation Research Review Monograph No. 4). Washington, DC: National Rehabilitation Information Center.

National Association of Rehabilitation Professionals in the Private Sector. (1981). *Standards and ethics.* Twin Peaks, CA: Author.

National Association of Social Workers. (1990). *Code of ethics.* Silver Spring, MD: Author.

National Board for Certified Counselors. (1989). *Code of ethics.* Alexandria, VA: American Association for Counseling and Development.

National Education Association. (1975). *Code of Ethics of the Education Profession.* Washington, DC: Author.

National Federation of Societies for Clinical Social Work. (1985). *Code of ethics.* Silver Spring, MD: Author.

Nelson, M.L., & Holloway, E.L. (1990). Relation of gender to power and involvement in supervision. *Journal of Counseling Psychology, 37,* 473–481.

Newman, A.S. (1981). Ethical issues in the supervision of psychotherapy. *Professional Psychology, 12,* 690–695.

Parr, G.D. (1991). Dilemmas in the workplace of elementary school counselors: Coping strategies. *Elementary School Guidance & Counseling, 25,* 220–226.

Patrick, K.D. (1989). Unique ethical dilemmas in counselor training. *Counselor Education and Supervision, 28,* 337–341.

Pellegrino, E. (1983). What is a profession? *Journal of Allied Health Professions, 12*(3), 168–170.

Pellegrino, E. (1984a). The family of medicine, broken or extended? The need for moral cement. *Journal of Family Practice, 19*(3), 287–290.

Pellegrino, E. (1984b). Conscience, virtue, integrity, and medical ethics [Editorial]. *Journal of Medical Ethics, 10*(4), 171–172.

Pellegrino, E. (1985). Professions as the conscience of society. *Journal of Medical Ethics, 11*(3), 117–122.

Pierce, K.A., & Baldwin, C. (1990). Participation versus privacy in the training of group counselors. *Journal of Specialists in Group Work, 15,* 149–158.

Pope, K.S. (1985). Dual relationships: A violation of ethical, legal, and clinical standards. *California State Psychologist, 20*(3), 4–6.

Pope, K.S. (1986). New trends in malpractice cases and changes in APA's liability insurance. *Independent Practice, 6*(4), 23–26.

Pope, K.S. (1988). How clients are harmed by sexual contact with mental health professionals: The syndrome and its prevalence. *Journal of Counseling and Development, 67,* 222–226.

Pope, K.S. (1990). Therapist-patient sex as sex abuse: Six scientific, professional, and practical dilemmas in addressing victimization and rehabilitation. *Professional Psychology: Research and Practice, 21*(4), 227–239.

Pope, K.S., & Bouhoutsos, J.C. (1986). *Sexual intimacy between therapists and patients.* New York: Praeger Press.

Pope, K.S., Keith-Spiegel, P., & Tabachnick, B.G. (1986). Sexual attraction to clients: The human therapist and the (sometimes) inhuman training system. *American Psychologist, 41*(2), 147–158.

Pope, K.S., Schover, L.R., & Levenson, H. (1980). Sexual behavior between clinical supervisors and trainees: Implications for professional standards. *Professional Psychology: Research and Practice, 11*, 157–162.

Pope, K.S., Tabachnick, B.G., & Keith-Spiegel, P. (1987). Ethics of practice: The beliefs and behaviors of psychologists as therapists. *American Psychologist, 42*, 993–1006.

Pope, K.S., & Vasquez, M.J.T. (1991). *Ethics in psychotherapy and counseling: A practical guide for psychologists.* San Francisco: Jossey-Bass.

Rabinowitz, F.E., Heppner, P.P., & Roehlke, H.J. (1986). Descriptive study of process and outcome variables of supervision over time. *Journal of Counseling Psychology, 32*, 292–300.

Reyes, D.M. (1991, Winter). Dual relationships: A student's view. *Together, 19*(2), 6.

Richards, D. (1990). *Building and managing your private practice.* Alexandria, VA: American Association for Counseling and Development.

Riger, S. (1991). Gender dilemmas in sexual harassment policies and procedures. *American Psychologist, 46*(5), 497–505.

Roberts, G.T., Murrell, P.H., Thomas, R.E., & Claxton, C.S. (1982). Ethical concerns for counselor educators. *Counselor Education and Supervision, 22*, 8–14.

Robiner, W.N. (1982). Role diffusion in the supervisory relationship. *Professional Psychology, 13*, 258–267.

Robinson, S.E., & Gross, D.R. (1985). Ethics of consultation: The Canterville ghost. *The Counseling Psychologist, 13*, 444–465.

Rodolfa, E.R., Kitzrow, M., Vohra, S., & Wilson, B. (1990). Training interns to respond to sexual dilemmas. *Professional Psychology: Research and Practice, 21*(4), 313–315.

Rubin, S.E., & Millard, R.P. (1991). Ethical principles and American public policy on disability. *Journal of Rehabilitation, 57*(1), 13–16.

Rubin, S.E., & Roessler, R.T. (1987). *Foundations of the vocational rehabilitation process* (3rd ed.). Austin, TX: Pro-Ed.

Rutter, P. (1989). *Sex in the forbidden zone.* Los Angeles: Jeremy Tarcher.

Ryder, R., & Hepworth, J. (1990). AAMFT ethical code: Dual relationships. *Journal of Marital and Family Therapy, 16*(2), 127–132.

Schafer, C. (1990, March 1). Ethics: Dual relationships come under scrutiny. *Guidepost*, pp. 1, 3, 16.

Schoener, G.R., & Gonsiorek, J. (1988). Assessment and development of rehabilitation plans for counselors who have sexually exploited their clients. *Journal of Counseling and Development, 67,* 227–232.

Sell, J.M., Gottlieb, M.C., & Schoenfield, L. (1986). Ethical considerations of social/romantic relationships with present and former clients. *Professional Psychology: Research and Practice, 17,* 504–508.

Slovenko, R. (1980). Legal issues in psychotherapy supervision. In A.K. Hess (Ed.), *Psychotherapy supervision: Theory, research and practice* (pp. 448–469). New York: Wiley.

Stadler, H. (1986). Preface to special issue. *Journal of Counseling and Development, 64,* 291–292.

Stadler, H.A. (1986). To counsel or not to counsel: The ethical dilemma of dual relationships. *Journal of Counseling and Human Services Professionals, 1,* 134–140.

Stadler, H.A. (1990). Counselor impairment. In B. Herlihy & L. Golden (Eds.), *Ethical standards casebook,* (4th ed., pp. 177–187). Alexandria, VA: American Association for Counseling and Development.

Stadler, H., & Paul, R.D. (1986). Counselor educators' preparation in ethics. *Journal of Counseling and Development, 64,* 328–330.

Steere, J. (1984). *Ethics in clinical psychology.* Cape Town: Oxford University Press.

Stoltenberg, C.D., & Delworth, U. (1987). *Supervising counselors and therapists: A developmental approach.* San Francisco: Jossey-Bass.

Tabachnick, B.G., Keith-Spiegel, P., & Pope, K.S. (1991). Ethics of teaching: Beliefs and behaviors of psychologists as educators. *American Psychologist, 46*(5), 506–515.

Taylor, L.J. (1985). Being an ethical professional in private sector rehabilitation. In L.J. Taylor, M. Golter, G. Golter, & T.E. Becker (Eds.), *Handbook of private sector rehabilitation* (pp. 212–230). New York: Springer.

Taylor, R.E., & Gazda, G.M. (1991). Concurrent individual and group therapy: The ethical issues. *Journal of Group Psychotherapy, Psychodrama, and Sociometry, 44*(2), 51–59.

Texas State Board of Examiners of Professional Counselors. (1990). *Standards of professional and ethical conduct* (rev.). Austin, TX: Author.

Upchurch, D.W. (1985). Ethical standards and the supervisory process. *Counselor Education and Supervision, 25,* 90–98.

Vasquez, M.J.T. (1988). Counselor-client sexual contact: Implications for ethics training. *Journal of Counseling and Development, 67,* 238–241.

Vasquez, M.J.T. (1991). Sexual intimacies with clients after termination: Should a prohibition be explicit? *Ethics and Behavior, 1*(1), 45–61.

Vasquez, M.J.T., & Kitchener, K.S. (1988). Introduction to special feature. *Journal of Counseling and Development, 67,* 214–216.

Vinson, J. (1989, September/October). Reflections on dual relationships: Therapist beware. *The California Therapist,* pp. 15–17.

Wagner, C.A. (1981). Confidentiality and the school counselor. *Personnel and Guidance Journal, 59,* 305–310.

Whiston, S.C., & Emerson, S. (1989). Ethical implications for supervisors in counseling of trainees. *Counselor Education and Supervision, 28,* 318–325.

Williams, G.T. (1990). Ethical dilemmas in teaching a group leadership course. *Journal of Specialists in Group Work, 15,* 104–113.

Wise, P.S., Lowery, S., & Silverglade, D. (1989). Personal counseling for counselors in training: Guidelines for supervisors. *Counselor Education and Supervision, 28,* 326–336.

Woody, R.H. (1988). *Protecting your mental health practice: How to minimize legal and financial risk.* San Francisco: Jossey-Bass.

Yalom, I.D. (1985). *The theory and practice of group psychotherapy* (3rd ed.). New York: Basic Books.

BOOK EVALUATION—TEAR OUT SHEET

To the owner of this book:

Writing *Dual Relationships in Counseling* has been a challenge and a learning experience for both of us. Our hope is that as you read and thought about some of the issues, you were able to gain clarity on your own positions on these issues. We would appreciate your comments so that we can assess the impact of this book and so that we can make improvements in future editions.

School: _____ Instructor's Name: _____

City: _____ State: _____ ZIP: _____

1. In what class did you use this book? _____

2. What, if any, other texts were used? _____
   _____

3. What did you like **most** about this book? _____
   _____
   _____

4. What did you like **least** about this book? _____
   _____
   _____

5. What was the most important learning from reading this book? ____
   _____
   _____
   _____

6. After reading this book, what are some key questions you still hope to ponder? _____
   _____
   _____

7. How useful were the articles (position statements) by various guest contributors? _____
   _____

8. How valuable were Herlihy's and Corey's commentaries? _____
   _____

9. What issues that we raised were most relevant and most important to you? _____

    _____

10. What are some topics or issues that you would like to see expanded or added to a future edition? _____

    _____

11. What are your suggestions for improving this book? _____

    _____

12. In the space below or in a separate letter, please write any other comments about the book or about your experience in thinking about the issues we raised. Thank you for taking the time to write to us.

— — — — — — **FOLD HERE** — — — — — —

— — — — — — **FOLD HERE** — — — — — —